Jennie Bond has been the BBC's royal correspondent since 1989. She has also presented most of the BBC's news and current affairs programmes on both television and radio. After graduating from Warwick University in 1972, she began her career in journalism on local newspapers in Surrey before joining the BBC in 1977. Her reporting career has taken her around the world several times and has made her one of the most familiar faces on television news. She is married to a former journalist, Jim Keltz, who is now a househusband looking after their twelve-year-old daughter, Emma. She also has two step-children, Stephen and Danielle. She lives with her husband and daughter in London and Devon.

Reporting

ROYALTY

Behind the Scenes with the BBC's Royal Correspondent

Jennie Bond

headline

First published in 2001
by HEADLINE BOOK PUBLISHING

First published in paperback in 2002
by HEADLINE BOOK PUBLISHING

Jennie Bond would be happy to hear from readers with their comments
on the book at the following e-mail address: jennie.bond@bbc.co.uk

10 9

ISBN 0 7472 4024 8

Typeset by Palimpsest Book Production Limited,
Polmont, Stirlingshire
Designed by Jane Coney
Printed and bound in Great Britain by
Clays Ltd, St Ives plc

HEADLINE BOOK PUBLISHING
A division of Hodder Headline
338 Euston Road
London NW1 3BH

www.headline.co.uk
www.hodderheadline.com

To Jim and Emma for putting up with me, my pager and all my broken promises, and to my parents for their unfailing support, encouragement and love

CONTENTS

CHAPTER ONE – *'It's a bit of a graveyard'*   1

CHAPTER TWO – *'Great news, bad timing'*   21

CHAPTER THREE – *Now we are three
(in more ways than one)*   45

CHAPTER FOUR – *Annus horribilis:
part one*   65

CHAPTER FIVE – *Annus horribilis:
it's not over yet*   85

CHAPTER SIX – *Annus horribilis:
the final episode*   101

CHAPTER SEVEN – *In search of
calmer waters*   125

CHAPTER EIGHT – *Pot shots at the Prince*   153

CHAPTER NINE – *Getting to know Diana*   183

CHAPTER TEN – *A year of travels and trauma*   201

CHAPTER ELEVEN – *Divorce*   225

CHAPTER TWELVE – *We meet again*   253

CHAPTER THIRTEEN – *On a mission*   265

CHAPTER FOURTEEN – *The death of Diana*   287

CHAPTER FIFTEEN – *Picking up the pieces*   297

CHAPTER SIXTEEN – *Stepping off the
                  roller-coaster*   313

CHAPTER SEVENTEEN – *Checkmate?*   333

CHAPTER EIGHTEEN – *What next?*   355

INDEX   363

ACKNOWLEDGEMENTS

My heartfelt thanks go to all the team at Headline Publishing who offered me encouragement, friendship and professional advice throughout the writing of this book. In particular: Heather Holden-Brown, Celia Kent, Amanda Ridout, Sarah Thomson, Louise Weir, Lucy Ramsey, Kerr MacRae, Bob McDevitt, Louise Rothwell and Justinia Baird-Murray; also to photographer Robin Marshall and copy editor Hugh Morgan. Thanks, too, to John Pawsey for suggesting the whole idea in the first place.

CHAPTER ONE

'It's a bit
of a graveyard'

I was on my hands and knees scrubbing the kitchen floor
when the phone rang. Cursing the inconvenience, I struggled up, tiptoed across the wet tiles and grabbed the
receiver, hands dripping.

'Hello,' said a refined voice on the other end. 'I just wanted
to pass on a message from the Princess.'

I realised at once that it was one of the band of young women
who were now running the Princess of Wales's office. It was
1996, and her latest press secretary had recently parted company
with Diana.

'The Princess wants me to tell you to carry on wearing red on
television. She says it suits you.'

'Oh, right,' I mumbled, unsure quite what to say next. 'Tell
her, thanks very much.'

'Goodbye, then,' came the response. And she was gone.

I chuckled to myself, thinking what a strange world I was
living in where Kensington Palace could intrude so suddenly

on my occasional bouts of domesticity. Then I picked up my bucket – and got back down to finish the floor.

It was a small incident in the often bizarre story that it's been my job to tell over the past twelve years or so. It said something about the Princess's sense of humour – and her sometimes curious priorities. Why, with all that was going on in her life, should she have cared about or even noticed what a television presenter was wearing? Perhaps the message was her way of showing friendship. It was an amusing and harmless gesture. But to me it was also another example of how – whatever I'm doing or wherever I am – the royal story can still get its talons into me. For twelve years, I have lived my life on the correspondent's equivalent of a choke chain. My pager and my mobile phone are my masters. I may think I have my day planned, but all too often the Royal Family prove my undoing. The shrill bleep of my pager ends all delusions of a family outing and I'm yanked back to work. Before I know it, I'm racing to the office, phoning the Palace for more information as I drive and fending off incoming calls from the news desk while I try to write a script in my head. It's a strange way to live, and if I have learned anything at all, it is never to make a promise to my family. I am simply not reliable.

Four years earlier, another phone call had shattered the peace of a welcome day off work. My daughter, Emma, ran out to the kitchen – her tiny feet pattering across the floor. It was as far as she could stretch to reach the phone on the white worktop. But even at two years old her willpower was strong enough to overcome most obstacles. 'Hello,' she said, 'has Mummy got to go to work?'

Through all the years that have followed, those words have stayed with me, causing mild pangs of guilt as I remember how, at such a young age, my child had become accustomed to my erratic, unpredictable lifestyle.

As any kind of correspondent, you are at the beck and call of your bosses and at the mercy of world events. But for a general reporter, when a story is over, it's over. As a specialist, you can never leave your work entirely behind. The end of a shift doesn't mean the end of your day's work. When your brief is running hot, perhaps for months, you have to run with it – no matter what your personal commitments. And, especially in those early years of my time as royal correspondent for the BBC, my story wasn't just hot – it was boiling. Inside that cauldron was a Royal Family containing all the ingredients for a television drama that commanded top ratings: marital strife, reports of attempted suicide, public confessions of adultery and, ultimately, tragedy.

It is a job that has made the Royal Family a very large part of my life, while, for them, I am a necessary inconvenience. It has taken me inside the Palace gates and ways of thinking – but only as far as they have deemed unavoidable. It has catapulted me around the world several times and involved me in all sorts of adventures and dramas. And it has given me a front-row seat for a tumultuous decade in the life of the Royal Family.

It wasn't a post I'd ever sought or even considered. Back in 1989 I was enjoying life as a general reporter at the BBC when one of my bosses asked me to pop into his office. I wondered if I'd done something wrong. But he was smiling.

'I've got a proposition for you,' he said. 'How do you fancy being court reporter?'

My initial reaction was relief: clearly, this was not going to be some kind of dressing-down. But my next thought was one of horror. Every self-respecting journalist in those days could take a good shorthand note, but somehow this skill had passed me by. I'd muddled through with my own improvised form of note-taking, but how, I wondered silently, would I possibly be able to keep up with a judge at the Old Bailey?

'We were pretty impressed with the way you covered Prince Charles's fortieth birthday a couple of months ago. So how about taking it on full-time?'

His voice cut through my panic as I suddenly realised that we were talking about the royal job.

My predecessor, Michael Cole, had left in something of a blaze of publicity after advance details of the Queen's Christmas message had appeared in some of the newspapers. Reporters like myself had been filling in on the royal stories since his departure. Now the time had come for a new royal specialist.

'It's a bit of a graveyard,' continued my boss. 'But I'm sure you'll make a go of it.'

His words did not instil either confidence or enthusiasm in me. 'Well,' I said, 'I'm really not convinced that this is what I want to do. But if you think it's a good idea, I'll give it a try – as long as you can guarantee that fifty per cent of my work will still be as a general reporter.'

'Fine,' he said. 'I don't imagine this brief will keep you too busy.'

If only he could have foreseen what the next few years were to bring.

Television was still a relatively new world to me. My training had been first in newspapers and then – for eleven years – with BBC Radio. Though I had always imagined myself as a broadcaster, I'd somehow got caught up behind the scenes. The newsroom at Broadcasting House, then the home of BBC Radio, had been a male-dominated arena, and there was an onus on the few women who worked there to prove their ability.

I began as a sub-editor, writing – if I was lucky – perhaps the last fifteen seconds of Radio 4's *Six o'Clock News*. In those early days I'd listen, heart pounding, as the newsreader broadcast my carefully crafted words to the waiting world.

'And now the weather outlook. It will be cloudy in the north at first, but sunny spells should spread to all parts of the country by the afternoon.'

A triumph indeed!

But writing was a very laborious process in that pre-computer era. Instead of word processors, the newsroom was furnished with a splendid team of typists who would take dictation from the journalists. There was no room for shyness; you had to stand and spout forth the latest gems of news, in proper BBC style, as the ladies tapped away on their typewriters. They ruled the newsroom comprehensively – terrifying even the most senior editor as they sat, fingers poised over the keyboard, waiting for pearls of wisdom to drop. If you hesitated, unsure perhaps about how to phrase the newest nuances of the Middle East peace process, their impatience would silently permeate your whole being. For years afterwards I had nightmares about standing there in the newsroom with thirty seconds until we were on air and the typist tut-tutting as I remained utterly tongue-tied. If, however, you showed you could hack it as a female journalist, there was an eagerness to promote you and, as new jobs and challenges came along, I found that the years flew by. But I was still *behind* the news, not on it.

So I applied for a job as a radio reporter. I loved the freedom of getting out of the office. I relished the challenge of learning to broadcast – accurately and with as much authority as I could muster – on any subject that came up. It was exciting to travel everywhere with my passport in my bag and a suitcase in the car. Suddenly my life was unpredictable again, as it had been to a lesser extent as a local newspaper reporter. This, though, was a far more prominent platform and the possibilities seemed endless.

One December evening in 1988, the phone interrupted my quiet Friday dinner with my husband. Jim answered. It was the office, wanting to talk to me. 'Do you want to go to Australia,' said my boss, 'to cover Prince Charles and Diana? They're going for the bicentennial celebrations.'

It was a dream of an assignment to be offered. Three weeks in the sun in the depths of the British winter, covering a pretty straightforward, innocuous story on the other side of the world. Any one of my colleagues on the general reporting team would have jumped at the chance. How could I even pause for thought? But I did. I'd never been away from home on business for any length of time. I didn't know what my husband would think of it.

'Could I ring you back tomorrow and let you know?' I asked my boss. I could sense his incredulity that I needed time to think about his offer. But he agreed.

I discussed it with Jim. He said I should go if I wanted to, but he didn't look too pleased. I suggested he should come out to join me after the tour for a holiday in Australia. He said I must be mad: Australia was the last place on earth that he, an American, wanted to visit. I looked on the map and discovered that a name which conjured up romance in my mind was more or less on the way home.

'OK,' I said. 'I'll go to Australia, and you can meet me on the beach in Penang in February.'

He demurred for a moment or two, and then said: 'It's a deal.'

I rang the office first thing the following morning and told them to get me accredited for what would turn out to be the first of many royal tours.

I had no understanding then of what complex creatures royal tours are. Although many of my colleagues would argue that we royal correspondents are pampered by the Palace – with transport and hotels either laid on or recommended for us – a tour by any member of the Royal Family is akin to a travelling circus. As well as the Royal Household (ladies-in-waiting, equerries, private secretaries, press secretaries, dressers, valets, hairdressers and cooks) there may be up to fifty or so press, carrying tons of equipment. All of us have to make our way around the designated country or countries, attending perhaps half a dozen engagements in different venues each day. This first trip to the Antipodes was to prove a sharp learning curve for me.

Nothing, though, could detract from the sheer exhilaration of jetting off to the other side of the world. My first sight of Australia, as we flew over the northern town of Broom, was of scorched red earth below. And then a sense of wonder as we travelled on, it seemed forever, over this vast continent until, a full four hours later, we finally saw Sydney sprawled below us. It was hard to believe that my night was now Jim's day, my summer his winter. I collected my luggage, found a taxi and drank in the freshness of everything around me as we headed for my hotel.

The next day I began to get to know some of the tightly knit band of Fleet Street's royal reporters. They seemed a bullish crowd, suspicious of this female interloper who knew nothing about the subject. But they were also full of fun, very witty and, beneath their initial scepticism, perfectly friendly. I also met up with my colleagues from BBC Television and immediately realised what a lonely furrow the radio reporter ploughs. I was on my own, with just my tape recorder and some equipment for transmitting my reports that I had no idea how to use. Reporting for television, meanwhile, were two senior correspondents, two producers, two crews, two picture editors and various support staff. This was seen as a major tour, and my sense of inadequacy was growing by the minute.

My first sight of the Prince and Princess of Wales was two distant figures on the steps of the Opera House as the extraordinary celebrations of Australia's bicentenary got under way in Sydney Harbour. I was far too concerned with the events going on around me to worry about the state of their marriage – though, as we now know, it was already over in all but name. I quickly discovered that there was little opportunity to view the couple at close quarters, and certainly no chance to talk to them. I had much to learn about every aspect of royal reporting.

Many events on a royal tour are covered by the press on a 'pool' basis. In other words, the Palace decrees that there is room for only a limited number of cameras and reporters, and we are told to divide up the available passes among us. It's frequently the cause of much squabbling and complaint. But on that first tour I was determined to hold my own, and argued for a pool position when the Princess went to a gala at the Opera House. She was astonishingly elegant and clearly relished being the centre of attention. I stood and watched, rather enjoying myself and scribbling down the odd note or two about the proceedings; I knew I wouldn't need too much detail for a brief radio report.

When I got back to the hotel, I was astonished to find a gang of my Fleet Street colleagues waiting, pens poised. They descended on me like a gaggle of geese, jostling for prime position. Horrified, I quickly realised that I was expected to give them a 'pool briefing' about all I had seen and heard. They fired questions at me so fast I could hardly think straight. 'Who had designed the Princess's dress?' 'Which earrings had she been wearing?' 'Was her necklace the one given her by the Sultan of Brunei?'

To none of these questions did I have an answer. In truth, I hadn't even noticed whether she'd been wearing a necklace and earrings at all. As for her dress, well, it was gorgeous and very elegant . . . but who'd designed it? No idea! It was a severe test of my embryonic relationship with my newspaper colleagues. But I'm glad to say that, despite my early failings, it is a relationship that has survived.

I had other lessons to learn on that first tour. One was that briefings from the royal entourage can happen anywhere at any time. I quickly sensed that I had to keep a sharp eye out for a huddle of reporters gathered under a tree, or in some other shady spot, during a lull in engagements. This often signalled that one of the Prince's staff was gently guiding the press on how things were going as we made our way around Australia. Painfully aware that I was no expert on royal matters, I kept up as best I could.

And that's pretty much what I did on the technical side, too. Indeed, my predominant memories of that tour are of the horror of trying to master the mystery of sending radio reports back to London. I'd been given various bits of equipment, bristling with wires, sockets and switches which, I'd been assured, would prove a doddle to use. I should have cottoned on that this wasn't necessarily true when they also counselled me to take a selection of screwdrivers and a torch. The tape recorder wasn't a problem:

I was used to that and reasonably confident. The rest of the equipment so thoughtfully packed for me in a large black bag looked like bomb-making paraphernalia. Clearly, I would have to try to come to grips with it. So when I should have been taking in the fantastic sights and sounds of Sydney, I spent long hours on my hotel-room floor, unscrewing the socket on the wall to reveal a terrifying spaghetti junction of wires on to which I was expected to clip various bits of technology. All this in an effort to send 'quality' voice reports back to the news desk from any port of call in Australia. Well, either the equipment was faulty or I simply never got the hang of it. I endured fruitless, frustrating hours crawling hot and tired around various hotel bedrooms, brandishing my screwdriver. Wires spewed from sockets in every major city as I dismantled them one by one. My phone bills soared as I sought advice from the technical support teams in London, who did their best to talk me through the problems. More often than not I ended up filing my reports on an ordinary phone line – which, to me, at least had the distinct advantage of sounding as if I was indeed on the other side of the world.

By the time we got to Adelaide, I'd more or less given up trying to make my arsenal of equipment work. The Prince and Princess looked as if *they'd* had enough as well, when they arrived at an open-air welcoming ceremony in temperatures well over forty degrees Celsius. The crowds had been waiting for several hours, and quite a number of people had fainted. As the obligatory speeches began, I was distracted by the sight of a huge paddle steamer making its way up the river. Suddenly, it seemed as if we were in New Orleans rather than South Australia. It really was too hot to concentrate, but eventually I wrote my report and, back at the hotel, took a cursory crawl around the floor in pursuit of the enemy socket. This time, though, the mere sight of it – as neat and impenetrable as a vestal virgin – was enough to persuade me to abandon all pretensions of trying to file 'in quality'. I picked up the phone.

Half an hour later, downstairs in the hotel bar, I met up with some of my colleagues. One thing I learned quickly about travelling with a gang of journalists is that there's never any danger of a quiet night. You can guarantee that one or other of us will have done some pretty extensive research into the best restaurants or clubs. Whether we get there is quite a different matter because, with the multiplicity of deadlines and demands from our various news desks, the cacophony of pagers and mobile phones frequently demolishes plans for eating out. In Adelaide, though, my male companions were looking unusually determined to get their act together. The reason, I soon discovered, was that someone had told them about a seafood restaurant a few miles from the hotel, where the waitresses wore nothing but cling-film! The idea was as absurd as it was intriguing. I told them I was game for a laugh, but it turned out to be one of those moments when they were all talk and no trousers. No one had established whether the restaurant existed, and in the end we all trooped into a quaint and highly respectable hostelry in the centre of town where the waiters and waitresses were fully clothed. I shall always wonder, though, whether there really was a cling-film restaurant in Adelaide – or was someone having a joke at our expense?

The last stop took us to the tropical heat of Darwin, in Australia's Northern Territory. It was like stepping into an oven but, being an avowed sun-worshipper, I basked in the searing heat and thoroughly enjoyed the royal visit to a crocodile farm while my fellow reporters, gently dripping, sought any available shade.

Darwin is very proud of its crocodiles. Its inhabitants like to tell you that the saltwater crocs that live in the bay are partial to the odd walkabout. They swear that from time to time a twelve-footer can be spied ambling up the high street – sending shoppers into a spin. I'm sure it's a myth, but I couldn't help taking a sneaky glance over my shoulder every now and then.

It was a fabulous end to my first experience of royal travel. I loved the pioneering feel of Darwin – a relatively new city on the edge of so much hostile wilderness. I adored the fact that when I went outside late at night to record some atmospheric sound for my radio reports, my glasses steamed over as if I had walked into a sauna.

'Yes!' I shouted, running into the heat, arms outspread, to capture the full blast. And I did my best to transport my listeners over to Australia with me by relaying some of those exotic night-time sounds of the tropics.

It was a long and exhausting tour, but I was savouring the camaraderie of working with a band of specialist reporters who guided me through some of the protocol of royal coverage. After waving goodbye to Charles and Diana, I left Australia thinking it wasn't a half bad job to have. But I was heading back to my life as a general reporter.

First, though, it was time to make my way to Penang for that long-awaited rendezvous with my husband. I flew into the tiny airport earlier than expected, hired a car and drove to the hotel. After a slight altercation with the receptionist, during which I had to convince her that I *was* married to one of her guests, I was shown up to Jim's room. I crept in, hoping to find him still asleep. Annoyingly, my surprise was ruined. The room was empty. I enquired if anyone had seen him.

'Oh yes,' the receptionist volunteered, 'he left for a walk along the beach half an hour ago.'

I wondered why she hadn't informed me of this *before* having a row about taking me up to the room. But as I headed off along the most wonderful stretch of white sand I'd ever seen, there seemed little point in being cross. Suddenly, in the distance, I saw a familiar figure ambling along looking out to sea. I ran up to him, delighted that our meeting was happening just as I'd originally planned: on the beach in Penang. We spent that day lazing by the swimming pool, swapping stories about our three weeks apart. The following day we set off to drive all over this new country. Malaysia worked its magic on us; we wallowed in the lush beauty of Southeast Asia, and work seemed a world away.

All too soon we were back in the UK and, with itchy feet, I began agitating for a spell as a TV reporter. Radio reporters were entitled to spend a couple of months at BBC Television, and I was keen to have a go before I was too old. At thirty-seven I was already way past the age that most people break into TV work, and I didn't rate my chances very highly. Perhaps that's why my bosses reacted swiftly, and moved me to television within just a few weeks of my request.

The morning of my first day's work at TV Centre brought with it a whole new anxiety. What to wear? Clothes hadn't mattered much in radio, but now, faced with the prospect of standing in front of a camera, I realised how bare my wardrobe was. The best I could do was a black and green summer dress. Well, at least it showed off my tan!

The TV newsroom seemed huge and alien, but it was exciting to be working at the Centre. Like anyone else on their first visit, I was tickled to see faces that were so familiar on the screen become flesh-and-blood reality. And they all looked so petite. For as I was soon to learn, television is an unforgiving medium and adds at least ten pounds to your finely honed figure. There were other lessons to learn, too. Reporting for television is a very different discipline from radio reporting. My training had been to tell the story as an eyewitness; to paint a picture in words. Now, as I quickly realised, many of those words would be redundant; there were pictures to explain the story, and my job was to complement them with extra information.

And then there is the 'piece to camera'. That's the twenty seconds or so when you see the reporter talking directly to camera, hopefully with some pertinent words or analysis. Even after years of television experience, I still find this procedure a bit of an ordeal. The real challenge is not so much in remembering the words; it's trying to look relaxed and reasonably friendly at the same time. I seem to have the sort of face that looks rather severe when it's not smiling. Some might say that in repose it's almost glum. It's the sort of face that leads bystanders occasionally to shout at me as I wander along the street – perfectly happy but deep in thought – 'Oi, love, cheer up! It might never happen!'

But it is rare, indeed, for there to be much to smile about in a news story, and the circumstances in which you are doing your piece to camera are not often conducive to making you look relaxed. The usual scenario is that as soon as a story breaks you are besieged with calls from the news desk. The first and most obvious duty is to check the facts you've been given – and find out more. That sounds simple enough, but it can take what seems to be an agonising amount of time. With the advent of twenty-four-hour news, the deadline is always *now*, and even while you are making a call to establish what has happened, a producer will be tugging on your sleeve to escort you to the on-air studio. The only way to tackle this first interview on a breaking story is to stick to the basic rule: say what you know to be true and, if you don't know the answer, admit it. Of course, I don't always succeed and, like others, find myself drifting off into the realms of speculation, but I try to avoid that as much as possible.

Once the first details of the story have been broadcast, we have to get on with the far more complicated job of putting together a full report. For that, we need relevant pictures. If it's about Prince Charles, for example, my producer and I have to find out where he is and try to get a camera crew to the scene. It has to be done fast and, infuriatingly, the demand for crews often outstrips the supply. Then we find ourselves begging the news desk to assign a crew to our story at the expense of someone else's. Other images will be needed, too: will I be talking about the Palace, about other members of the Royal Family, or about newspaper reports? If so, we need the pictures to cover my words. Some can be ordered from the BBC's vast library, but clearly the preference is for newly shot pictures. The next frantic search will be for someone authoritative to interview – someone close to the Royal Family or a relevant commentator. This is where a specialist's contacts come into play. Who's best for this particular story? Where are they? Will they talk? Can we get a camera crew and a reporter to them in time? Do we need a dispatch rider to whisk the interview back to TV Centre to save crucial minutes? And then, of course, it's down to the correspondent to write a clear and concise script. Every word must count because, generally, your report will be allocated only about one and three-quarter minutes in the news bulletin. By this time, that bulletin is probably frighteningly close.

With the script half-written if you're lucky, you shut yourself in an edit suite with a picture editor and start the process of putting words and pictures together. It's generally at about this point that I realise I'm now desperately short of time to get down to Buckingham Palace to do my piece to camera. So, leaving the report half-finished and hoping the editor can continue in my absence, I fly out of the door, jump in the car and race down to the Mall. On the way, I compose the words in my head or, if I've managed to write them out already, I balance the script on my steering wheel and try to read it as I drive. Either way it's essential that I've learned the words by the time I get to the Palace. Traffic lights are invaluable as make-up stops – offering just enough time to check my mascara and lipstick and to plaster some powder on my nose. I scream to a halt near the Palace, praying that I won't get a parking ticket, and race down the road, hairspray at the ready, for my rendezvous with the cameraman. A quick check in the lens to see if I look vaguely presentable, a squirt of the spray and – more in hope than expectation – I launch into my first attempt at the piece to camera. All too often, crowds gather around, staring at me and chatting as if I was still behind the TV screen unable to hear them.

'Oh, look,' they say, 'there's that woman from the telly. What's her name, now? It's Judy someone, isn't it? No, no – maybe it's Jennie. Oh! Doesn't she look different?'

I try to ignore them, to concentrate on the job and get back to the edit suite – the seconds are ticking away and it's going to be touch and go as to whether we get this report finished on time.

'I like her outfit, though, don't you? That colour really suits her.' The voices pierce my concentration. I falter, grimace and grind to a halt. The cameraman sighs. 'Oh, look!' I hear them say. 'Now she's gone and forgotten her words!'

I wonder if it would be acceptable behaviour to whack them with my handbag. I decide against it – and try again. Other hazards intervene: joggers, oblivious to the camera, run directly in front while I'm in mid-flow; a police car flashes by, siren screaming, drowning out my words. Often, the wind contrives to turn my hairdo into a version of Arthur Scargill's – neatly swept over to one side; it's time for another dose of hairspray. Eventually, though, I get it right: the piece to camera is done. With luck, there's a motorbike rider waiting to fire it back to TV Centre. I run to the car and drive hell for leather, phoning the edit suite as I go to check on how they are doing with my report. My head aches; I feel a wreck. And people wonder why I don't always look relaxed in those pieces to camera!

Back in the early days, though, no one recognised me, and I had only myself to blame when things went wrong. It was in November 1988 that I was asked to cover the story that indirectly led me to become a royal correspondent. Prince Charles was about to celebrate his fortieth birthday. On paper it didn't look too exciting: he was going to visit a few places in Birmingham, ending up in a disused tramshed, where the Prince's Trust was throwing a party. I drove north and soon found myself comprehensively lost in the middle of the city. I felt mild panic as I went round in circles, but eventually I found my camera crew already filming the Prince glad-handing shoppers in a mall. In all honesty, there wasn't much to say about this, but the newsroom wanted a piece, so I cobbled together some words and made a beeline for the edit van. When we are on the road, the van – in other words a portable studio manned by a picture editor – travels with us, offering a haven from the outside world and a comforting space where the desperate business of compiling a report can happen. My lunchtime effort that day was eminently forgettable, but at least it made it to air – which always placates the editor.

Thanks to the Prince, things looked up significantly after lunch, in television terms at least. By mid-afternoon, other duties completed, he'd arrived at the tramshed. Pop music was blaring and the shed was crammed with partygoers determined to make the fuddy-duddy Prince defy his approaching middle age. They fêted him, joked with him and finally persuaded him to dance. In the first of many such speeches I have heard him make over the years, Charles responded to the atmosphere with a witty performance – mercilessly poking fun at himself.

'Only the other day,' he told the hundreds of partygoers, 'I was enquiring of an entire bed of old-fashioned roses who were forced to listen to my demented ramblings on the meaning of the universe as I sat, cross-legged in the lotus position, on the gravel path in front of them . . . I was enquiring what would happen on my birthday in a tramshed in Birmingham.'

The Prince's self-mockery about his habit of talking to plants won over his audience instantly and provided me with a very amusing piece of television. I sometimes think back and wonder whether it was far more the Prince's *bons mots*, rather than my alleged skills as a reporter, that impressed my bosses into offering me the royal job.

But I *did* feel that I was beginning to get the hang of it. Royal stories, I realised, often had very little real substance. They were just series of interesting pictures which essentially spoke for themselves. The script required a deft touch – just enough to help the story along without duplicating the pictures. Above all I was determined not to deliver a flowery script. Gushing was *not* my style.

It wasn't long before my bosses felt I'd got the hang of it, too, and that sudden offer of becoming royal reporter came along and flummoxed me. It was a little daunting to take over from someone who had lost his job for trusting his colleagues too much. I'd always been far too frank and open myself, quite apart from the fact that I'd consistently said I didn't want to become a specialist. But there was a fascination about the royal brief that was hard to ignore, and I was flattered to be asked to do it. So it was that, after years of general news, I found myself suddenly and unexpectedly appointed the BBC's royal reporter. Soon, my first visit to Buckingham Palace would beckon.

CHAPTER TWO

'Great news, bad timing'

There was a time when the appointment of the BBC's court correspondent was approved not only by the management but also by royalty itself. Another of my predecessors, the late Godfrey Talbot, told of how he was summoned to Buckingham Palace and ushered in for an audience with King George VI and Queen Elizabeth before the final seal was put on his job. I'm glad to say that things had changed a great deal by the time I came on the scene. Indeed, I muddled along for a fair while without coming face to face with anyone from the Palace. Eventually, though, I fixed a meeting with the Queen's press secretary, Robin Janvrin.

So it was that, one Tuesday at 12 o'clock, I found myself driving my rather scruffy car through the Palace gates. It cannot be denied that there is a certain thrill about being allowed past the throngs of tourists and onlookers. They crane their necks, curious about who could possibly be inside this unpretentious car with its muddy wheels and dirty windows. The police on duty at the gates wondered the same thing, but their list of expected guests confirmed that I was, indeed, a genuine visitor.

Once inside, I parked the car on the forecourt and locked it. 'You needn't really bother with that here,' said one of the policemen, grinning. I laughed, thinking how right he was; with all the security at the Palace the chances of someone breaking into my car were remote.

My high heels crunched across the gravel as I headed towards the Privy Purse door, where I'd been told I would find the press office. The crowds poked their cameras through the railings and took my photo on the off chance that I might turn out to be someone important. Feeling increasingly self-conscious, I walked up the red-carpeted steps, and was just wondering where I would find the doorbell when as if by magic a footman in scarlet livery appeared. The door swung open, revealing a large, but very ordinary, hall.

'Good morning, Miss Bond,' he said, waving me in. Hopelessly impressed that he knew my name, I stepped inside the Palace.

I was directed into a small waiting room to the right. It's a cosy room, with a few chairs, some impressive paintings and a side-table on which copies of the *Telegraph* and *The Times* were laid. A bottle of mineral water stood unopened, and I was considering helping myself to a drink when two enormous guardsmen came in, their bearskin hats under their arms like cuddly pets. Sweat was pouring down their faces. They clicked their heels and bowed to me as if, for a moment, I was royalty myself. Then they set about the purpose of their visit, and reached for the bottle. The mineral water, it seemed, was there to revive senior officers after the exertions of the Changing of the Guard – which I had just missed.

I sat for a few minutes, nervously glancing at the newspapers, half-expecting the Queen to pop her head round the door at any moment. Would *she* say, 'Good morning, Miss Bond,' just as the footman had? Clearly, I had yet to appreciate the size of Buckingham Palace. It is, of course, far more than the Queen's official residence. It's a vast office block where hundreds of people work, and many live. Visitors come and go all the time but, in twelve years of dropping by there, I've yet to catch sight of the Queen.

'Jennie, how nice to see you!' The quiet, cultured voice broke into my reverie. It was Robin Janvrin, hand outstretched, inviting me out of the waiting room and into his office, just a few feet away. This time the room was large, the high ceiling accentuating the sense of space. But it was still not grand by any means. A bookcase ran the length of one wall, full of worthy tomes. A solid-looking desk, laden with paperwork, dominated one corner of the room, and there was a good-sized television set. Robin and I sat at a round table and, after a few minutes, a footman arrived bearing a silver tray with coffee and biscuits. Well, this is pleasantly hospitable, I thought, as Robin got down to the business of explaining how the Palace machinery worked.

Everything, it seemed, revolved around the Wednesday List – so called because it's updated every Wednesday. It lists all the forthcoming engagements of the senior members of the Royal Family, and would become my bible for knowing who was up to what and when. The first thing that strikes you about the Wednesday List is how busy most of the family are. The Princess Royal, in particular, carries out a staggering number of engagements, frequently travelling the length of the United Kingdom in a day to get from one appointment to the next. But, of course, as I was to learn, it was not the planned and organised events that would be taking up so much of my time in the coming years – it was the unexpected.

Robin showed me around the rest of the press office: a surprisingly small set-up with a few ramshackle offices ranged along a corridor. They were functional and rather cluttered, but everyone was extremely welcoming and polite. Little did they know then how many battles we were to have in the decade to follow and how they would come to regard me – more often than they would care to admit – as a pushy bitch. I left the Palace after half an hour or so, feeling better equipped to handle the brief, with at least some idea of how things worked and knowing the faces that went with the voices.

One of the first occasions that I had to seek guidance from them as a fully fledged royal reporter was when I found myself standing outside a building where I've since spent many a freezing hour: the King Edward VII Hospital for Officers in London. For it was there, in March 1989, that we discovered that the Princess of Wales was having four wisdom teeth removed. To be frank, this was another of those occasions when once the basic facts had been established there wasn't much more to be said. Those facts were duly given to me by the Palace 'voices'. They weren't much to build a report on, but they were all we were going to get. And what were we to do for pictures? There was obviously no sign of the Princess – she was tucked up somewhere inside the hospital, recovering from the surgery. There were no visitors and no doctors to interview. In fact, there was very little information of any kind to be had. Nevertheless, there we stood outside the hospital, a bunch of cold reporters and their disgruntled cameramen keeping vigil. We took shots of flowers arriving, hopefully for the Princess; we took shots of the plaque on the wall, of the windows where we thought her room might be. We filmed anything that moved – and quite a lot that didn't.

It was, though, an excellent opportunity to get to know some of my fellow 'ratpackers' better. I hadn't seen most of Fleet Street's specialist royal reporters since our trip to Australia a year earlier. Then I had been a mere interloper on the royal scene. Now I was one of them; but I was acutely aware that I still had a lot to learn. One of those things was how to do the dreaded piece to camera in front of a crowd of your colleagues. By now I was reasonably comfortable about performing under the scrutiny of a sole cameraman, but to try to remember my words as I stood just a few yards from all those hardened hacks was daunting, to say the least. They laughed at me as I dabbed powder on my nose and brushed my hair but, when I opened my mouth to address the waiting camera, all their banter died away – and there was a hushed silence. It was infinitely worse than all their babble. I dried up instantly, too embarrassed to go on. It took half a dozen attempts to produce a rather uninspired piece of work. Things, I thought, could only get better.

Even in the midst of getting to grips with a new job, my thoughts were drifting towards the idea of another holiday. Our trip to Penang and the rest of Malaysia a year earlier had done wonders for my husband's rather subdued desire to travel. So, taking a break from matters royal or otherwise, we set off for Southeast Asia once again. We couldn't resist the urge to revisit one or two favourite stops: 'The Beach of Passionate Love' on the east coast of Malaysia was one of them. It's a long expanse of ever-warm sand, fringed with palm trees and very little else. It's worth the trip just to say you've been there. Though I was in my late thirties and Jim was nearly fifty, we pretended we were kids again, travelling around on buses with our possessions crammed into backpacks. It was steamy hot and fabulous fun.

We spent a night in a tree house in the middle of the jungle watching wildlife at the water-hole below and listening to the fantastic sounds outside, while rats scurried around inside our makeshift shelter. We took a tiny boat out to a Muslim village built on stilts in the middle of the ocean. There we ate supper with the villagers, sat gossiping by candlelight with other visitors and slept on a wooden floor, with the sea rolling around beneath us. The next morning some of the local folk were selling their craftwork as souvenirs: beads and bracelets laid out on simple tables alongside beautifully sculpted pieces of driftwood. One unusually shaped piece of wood caught my eye, and I decided to bargain for it. The woman selling it asked a ridiculous price; ridiculous because it was so low, no more than a couple of pence in sterling. I couldn't have lived with myself if I'd accepted, so I offered twice as much. She looked confused, and then outraged. Angrily, she demanded even less than her first price. Not to be outdone, I took four times as much out of my purse. It was the strangest reverse auction I have ever attended, but in the end we reached a compromise whereby neither of us appeared to feel the other was being ripped off. The driftwood sculpture was mine, but not before she'd thoughtfully wrapped it in a sheet of rather damp newspaper. To this day, my treasured work of art from that Muslim village is scarred by the newsprint that neatly transferred itself on to the porous wood.

From Malaysia, we ventured up into Thailand and felt the calm of that country's Buddhist philosophy sweep over us. As far as I was concerned, the BBC might have been a whole universe away, for this was before we were all issued with the pagers, mobile phones, laptops and e-mail addresses that now keep us in contact day and night, wherever we are in the world. It was bliss.

I was hardly back home from that holiday when it was announced that the Princess Royal was to visit Ethiopia with the charity Save the Children. The office decided I should go, too, a prospect that delighted me. It would be a worthwhile story, and Ethiopia was reputed to be a beautiful land. I began researching the history and politics of the country and had just arranged to have a terrifying number of inoculations when there was a coup in Addis Ababa. The visit was cancelled, and so were my jabs. I was disappointed that the chance to see such an ancient corner of Africa had vanished but not unhappy to avoid the inoculations. As things turned out it was just as well. I'd been wondering why I'd been feeling so unbelievably tired, despite my holiday. I was about to discover the answer.

'The test was positive,' said the nurse at the family planning clinic. My knees buckled. I felt weak with joy and stunned with sheer shock. 'There's no doubt about it – you're pregnant,' she continued. 'Is that good news for you or . . .' Her voice trailed off.

'Yes, yes – it's fantastic,' I said quietly. 'I'm not sure what my husband will think about it but yes, it's amazing . . . unbelievable. Thank you so much.'

I drove home very slowly, knowing that one thing was certain. Nothing would ever be the same. The life Jim and I had shared for the past seventeen years was about to change radically. He had two wonderful children from his first marriage and I felt very close to them. But what would he think about starting over again with nappies and bottles at almost fifty? He had a successful radio career: his voice was well known in London, and he liked to be free to roar off on his motorbike or read a book whenever he fancied. How would he take to the restrictions new parenthood would impose?

He was pottering about in the garden when I got home. I looked through the French windows, enjoying those few last quiet moments when life seemed unchanged. He walked towards the patio.

'Well?' he asked. I burst into tears.

And the rest, as they say, is history. Jim decided it must have been 'Buddha's will' – after that holiday in Thailand – and I spent the next few months floating on cloud nine.

It was not, though, a convenient time to get pregnant. For eleven years in radio my life had been completely predictable. My working hours hadn't varied, there'd been no travel and the shift system had given me a lot of time at home. Now, with a new job in which I was permanently on call and faced with the prospect of jetting around the world, I was about to embark on the most demanding job of all – motherhood. I made an appointment to see my boss.

'What's up?' he asked as I sat down in his office. 'Fed up with those royals already?'

'Well, not exactly,' I said. 'But I'm afraid I've made a really bad career move.'

He stopped smiling and looked concerned.

'I'm really sorry,' I went on. 'I know I haven't had the job long, but I'm pregnant.'

Poor chap. He'd no doubt thought he was pretty safe from having to deal with all the complications of maternity leave when he appointed me. After all, I was thirty-eight. But he was delightful.

'Ah! Is that all?' he laughed. 'Well, that's great news! I

thought we were in *real* trouble for a moment and you'd gone off the job.'

So all was well with my world. We celebrated Jim's fiftieth birthday – and my pregnancy – with a big family party in the garden of our London home. I showed off my slightly swollen stomach with pride, still astonished to find myself in this incredibly happy state. At work, my colleagues shared my joy and, strangely, at least two of them shared my condition. There seemed to be an outbreak of unexpected pregnancies at the BBC among women on the threshold of forty.

'Which loo are you all using?' asked a happily childless newsreading friend, who was also thirty-eight. 'Because I'm going to make sure I use another one!'

I was fortunate that pregnancy suited me from the start: I felt brilliant throughout, and worked until the last few weeks. In August my small bulge and I found ourselves outside Clarence House, reporting for the first time on the Queen Mother's birthday. She was eighty-nine, and this was my first brush with the army of fans who will forever be associated with the carnival atmosphere of 4 August.

There was already a set pattern to the order of events around Clarence House but, unfortunately, back then I wasn't aware of it. I certainly wasn't prepared for the stampede of cameramen who thundered through the gates the instant they were opened. One moment I was standing chatting quite happily with my crew in the early morning sunshine; the next, amid a crazy clattering of cameras, tripods, ladders and all manner of photographic equipment, we were being propelled towards the press pen, everyone fighting to get there first. You learn to do a lot with elbows in this business. I have worked with photographers from the national papers for many a long year and they're a great bunch of people. But when push comes to shove we're all intent on getting the best possible shot from the prime position – and all too frequently, it has to be said, push *does* come to shove! My particular speciality is 'being a tripod'. When my cameraman is busy, I try to look ahead to where we'll need to be next, and bag the best spot by standing in it, legs apart, resolutely fighting off attempts by the rest of the press or overeager members of the public to crowd in on the space our tripod will need. You work very much as a team with your cameraman, acting as his eyes when he's filming, doing everything to help him get the right shots. I often think that a journalist's work is easy by comparison. If we miss a fact or two, we can generally pick it up afterwards with a quick phone call. The cameraman's task is far less forgiving. The shot presents itself only once: a birthday wave from the Queen Mother, a gunman lurching towards Prince Charles, a tear from the Queen as she says farewell to *Britannia*. These are moments that cannot be re-created and, if missed, they are gone.

I suppose I had hopes that, once inside the gates of Clarence House and carefully positioned, we might find ourselves close enough to exchange a word or two with the Queen Mother. But I would hope in vain. Our job was to stand and wait, watching for any twitch of the curtains in Clarence House and poised for the first appearance of this grand old lady. She's a consummate performer, always aware of the cameras and willing to linger long enough for everyone to get a decent shot. But that's absolutely as far as it goes: a word or two on camera is not part of the equation.

Although she clearly knows who I am and the job I do, I've spoken to the Queen Mother at any length on only one occasion: when the Queen threw a fiftieth birthday party for Prince

Charles at Buckingham Palace. It was a cold November evening and I'd been working all day putting together reports about the Prince's earlier celebrations in Sheffield. I still had the *Nine o'Clock News* to do, but along with other royal correspondents I'd been invited to look around the Palace and observe the party for fifteen minutes or so. It was fraught; I really had no time to spare, but felt I should at least get a first-hand feel of the party. The Palace was floodlit outside and a seething mass of royalty, celebrity, music and entertainment inside. Every room and every gallery had a different entertainer – from rock bands to opera and from clowns to magicians.

Wondering where I'd find the Queen Mother, I took a guess that she'd be in the room with the rock music. I was right. There she stood, looking even tinier and more vulnerable without her customary hat, chatting animatedly with some of the guests. I watched from a distance, keen simply to study her and improve my background knowledge. Suddenly, a brusque command pierced my thoughts: 'Jennie, you mustn't stand there eavesdropping.'

I looked round to find one of the Palace press secretaries looking at me in a distinctly displeased fashion. 'You obviously missed the press briefing,' she hissed. 'But you are not meant to linger, or listen or try to talk to a member of the Royal Family.'

'Oh, terrific!' I moaned. 'I thought perhaps, just for once, I might have said hello to the Queen Mother. But never mind. I'll go and stand in a corner.'

So I skulked off to another room, where I found an old friend – Nick Owen, then the royal correspondent for ITN. Always delighted to see one another and share a bit of gossip, we kidnapped a couple of glasses of champagne from a passing footman and propped ourselves against a wall for a good natter.

We were so absorbed that we hardly noticed the two small figures, each with her handbag on her arm, coming towards us. I looked up just in time to see the Queen pointing at us and, leaning forward, saying to her mother: 'Oh, look, Mummy. There are *those* two. They're *always* on television. Let's go and say hello.'

Over they came, smiling broadly and as friendly as could be. The four of us spent perhaps five minutes together, chatting about all that was going on at the Palace that night. It was my only real conversation with the Queen Mother, and it seemed abundant proof to me that sometimes it's the courtiers and advisers who keep the press at bay more often than some of the Royal Family themselves might deem necessary.

Back in 1989, however, I was just one of a mass of faces peering out from the crowded press pen as the Queen Mother passed by. She gave a wave and a smile to the cameras before applying herself to the far more important business of meeting the people: something which she's always made appear a pleasure rather than a duty. It was the first of many birthday walkabouts that I was to witness at Clarence House.

My own birthday, a couple of weeks later, was memorable for a far more tragic reason. I'd spent the day at the office covering general stories and had got home late, after the main evening news. I was three months pregnant and feeling a little weary. I'd had perhaps a couple of hours sleep when, at about 1 a.m., the phone woke me. I stumbled across the room to answer it.

'Jennie, we need you to get down to the Thames right now. A pleasure boat has gone down – no details yet of casualties, but it looks bad.'

Another disaster on my birthday! I couldn't believe it. On the same day two years earlier I'd had a similar call, this time after working a night shift, to go to Hungerford. A twenty-seven-year-old man called Michael Ryan had gone berserk and shot dead sixteen people – including his mother – before turning the gun on himself. Now, it seemed, there was another tragedy in the making. I got dressed quickly, trying not to wake Jim, and jumped in the car.

The sight of the Thames that night will stay with me for ever. Searchlights were beamed on to the murky water, ambulances and police cars were all around. Despite the throng of people there was an eerie silence. And of the pleasure boat, the *Marchioness*, there was no sign at all. I discovered that many of the survivors had already been taken to hospitals nearby. The race was on to find the forty or fifty people who were still thought to be missing. As a reporter on the scene of a disaster, you feel helpless.

It was like that at Lockerbie when, after driving through the night from London, we abruptly came across the disjointed cone of the wrecked plane lying silently in a pitch-black field. As dawn broke, we saw the debris from the cabin, strewn across the town: aircraft seats, bits of suitcases, shoes, handbags and books. And, of course, the bodies – some of them grotesquely stranded on the rooftops. It was the same when the ferry, the *Herald of Free Enterprise*, went down at Zeebrugge. As the shocking death toll slowly unfolded I remember hopelessly, helplessly, trying to offer some comfort to waiting relatives.

But the job of a reporter is not to dispense words of comfort; it is to absorb the mood, gather the facts and relay an accurate account of what is happening. That was my role by the Thames as the search for survivors from the *Marchioness* continued, despite fast-fading hopes. We went on air with a special bulletin early in the morning. By now we had at least two camera crews, a couple of producers and extra reporters on the scene. I'd been up for twenty-four hours, apart from my brief flirtation with bed, but was keen to stick with the story I'd been watching develop all night. Government ministers began to arrive. We saw Michael Portillo, then Transport Minister, making his way to the riverside and grabbed him for an interview. He made all the appropriate noises and comments but, in reality, there was little anyone could do or say that would help. Everyone realised that by now the rescue work was no more than a salvage operation.

Eventually, that operation had to reap its grim harvest. We watched in silence as the first of fifty-one bodies was brought slowly and gently to the surface. The appalling loss of the *Marchioness* and so many of her partygoing passengers will always be etched on my mind. But I remember that day for other reasons, too. It was the day that the gremlins that periodically afflict our efforts to broadcast almost stopped me from getting anything about the disaster on the evening news.

As usual when we're on location, an edit van had been dispatched along with a satellite truck to bounce our reports back to the Centre. I always enjoy the moment when I finally get into the van and sit down away from the hurly-burly to start editing. For an hour or so, you become immersed in a concentrated piece of teamwork between yourself and the picture editor. You've gathered as many facts and shots as you can; now it's the moment of truth when you find out whether it all hangs together and you can write a decent script. It's always a race against the clock – and often a pretty desperate one.

'We'd better crack on,' said my producer that day. 'There are loads of tapes to look at, and they want a four-minute piece plus a live spot from you.'

My picture editor and I began to sort out the best shots and decide how we'd tell the story of the dreadful night and day gone by. By about 4.30 p.m. we were making good progress when suddenly the producer hurled open the van door and screamed: 'Quick, get down there – the Prime Minister's on her way.'

This was not what I'd wanted to happen so late in the day. But, of course, there was no choice and we rushed down to record Mrs Thatcher's words of solace.

Half an hour later we were back in the van, a little breathless but well on track when, with an awful spluttering and coughing, the generator that powered all the equipment abruptly stopped. Horrified, I looked at the picture editor.

'No worries,' he said confidently. 'I'll just top it up with diesel and it'll be fine.'

I carried on putting the finishing touches to the script. The minutes ticked by. Too many of them for my liking. I got out to ask what was happening. The answer was only too obvious. This was not a mere fuel problem; something had gone catastrophically wrong with the generator.

'It's no use,' said the picture editor. 'I've tried everything.'

I felt ill. I'd been up for nearly thirty-six hours at a very vulnerable stage of my pregnancy, we had twenty minutes to go until we were on air – and I was about to screw up one of the biggest television news stories I'd ever handled.

'There must be something we can do,' I groaned. 'Let's just send what we've done so far, and they can stitch it together back at TV Centre. They've still got a bit of time.'

He looked at me as if I was a sandwich short of a picnic.

'How can we send it?' he shouted. 'The tapes are stuck

tight in the machines, and the machines don't have any power!'

Forlornly, I realised that things were even worse than I'd thought. Everything we'd edited, including the Prime Minister's contribution, was encased in the innards of the machines – and we had no way of getting it out. We attacked the machines with screwdrivers, trying to prise open the stubborn shutters. But the tapes refused to budge.

Close to tears, I rang the news desk. There was sheer panic in the voices at the other end.

'The only thing to do is to send the best pictures you've got from the rushes, and rerecord your track in the satellite truck,' they ordered. 'We'll do all we can to make something of it here.'

Trembling with tension, I helped the engineers find the important shots on the rushes – the original tapes we'd filmed before beginning our edit – and send them through the air to TV Centre. It was alarmingly close to our deadline but, with a rather unsteady voice, I rerecorded my script and prayed that some brilliant editor would manage to make sense of it all. I didn't have a chance to wait and see. I had to jump over a wall and race back to the riverside to appear live after my report . . . if there *was* a report. All fingers and thumbs because of my nerves, I plugged in my earpiece, clipped on a microphone and faced the camera.

Miraculously, I heard my report being broadcast to the nation. It wasn't the polished piece of work I'd intended, but the basic facts and pictures were there, thanks to some wizard in TV Centre. As it ended, the presenter came to me for my live update. I hoped that none of the panic of the past half-hour would show on my face, but I'm sure it did. I left the scene of so much unhappiness at about 7 p.m. and got home shattered, both physically and emotionally. It had been a truly awful day.

My husband looked concerned. He made me some supper and said: 'You should remember that you're thirty-nine now [Oh yes, I thought, it was my birthday yesterday!] and you're pregnant. You can't go on like this – or you'll lose that baby.'

I knew he was right. I wanted this baby more than anything else in the world, and I shouldn't be taking risks. At the same instant I remembered that I had to get up at 3.30 the next morning to present the *Today* programme.

'You're crazy,' said Jim despairingly. 'And stupid.'

The often daunting assignment of presenting a major current affairs programme like *Today* was made much easier that morning because I'd been an eyewitness to the story that was still dominating the news. I'd been a reserve presenter on the show for about a year, loving and loathing it in almost equal measure. On the night before a programme, I would surf all the news bulletins, wondering who'd be lined up for me to interview in the morning. It could be the Chancellor or the Foreign Secretary; it could be an expert on the Middle East or a City analyst; or, even trickier, it could be a 'funny' story – with a tongue-tied interviewee who'd never been on the radio before and was certain to forget all the witty lines that had seduced our researchers into booking him. The night would pass fitfully, my subconscious worrying that the alarm wouldn't go off or that there'd be a power cut and the clock would stop.

At 3.30 without fail, the shock of the radio coming on would propel me – in a single terrified move – out of bed and into my clothes. One joy of working on radio, especially first thing in the morning, is that you can't be seen. Though I always did my best to look reasonable, there was no need to fuss, which left the mind concentrated on the job in hand. The measure of that job would become apparent as soon as I arrived in the *Today* office. Usually, I was there some time before my fellow presenter: a barometer of my relative lack of confidence. Diligent producers would have prepared briefing notes on the topics and interviewees to be tackled in the two and a half hours of broadcasting to come. But no matter how good the notes, ignorance is all too easily uncovered on live radio or television.

Then there is the inexplicable mental blackout. Even the most seasoned presenters admit that your mind can occasionally go completely blank in the middle of an interview, leaving you with no idea of what question to ask next. Indeed, it can get even worse. One household name told me how, at a key point in a complex discussion on live radio, she looked at her interviewee across the studio desk and thought: Who the hell is he?

On those early mornings in the *Today* office at Broadcasting House, I would scour the newspapers and cuttings for every detail about the stories that were due to crop up. I'd always work frantically right up to the last minute, thinking up questions, writing introductions and studying the running order so that I'd feel fully in control. John Humphrys, of course, would swan in a full hour and a half later than me and spend his time reading the papers, gossiping with the editor and eating a bowl of cereal. He'd take a fleeting look at the briefings prepared for him, but was rightly so supremely confident in his own ability and knowledge that he didn't need to swot up like me.

With five minutes to go, we'd walk down the corridor to the studio, put on the headphones and wait for that green light to come on.

'Good morning. This is *Today*, with Jennie Bond and John Humphrys. The headlines this morning . . .'

For the next couple of hours I'd be immersed – as if I'd been thrown into the deep end of a swimming pool and had no choice but to sink or swim. John, always immeasurably more relaxed than me, would like nothing better than a good chat while prerecorded features were being played. He'd want to know what I'd been up to, how my husband felt about the prospect of becoming a father again, or what was the latest gossip in the newsroom. He'd often carry on nattering right up to the last few seconds, nonchalantly ignoring the flashing green light which was warning us that the item was about to end and we would be live on air again. I did my best to join in but was rather poor company, with more than half my mind on the pressing problem of what was coming up next.

Today was one of the most challenging jobs in journalism I've ever done. But, without fail, when the programme was over I'd feel a sense of triumph that I'd been brave enough to do it – and couldn't wait to do it again!

Perhaps my main claim to fame on *Today* is that the wonderful Sue MacGregor and I were the first all-women duo to present the show. It seems extraordinary now that such a small detail should prove noteworthy. But on that morning in 1989 anyone would have thought a couple of apes had climbed down from the trees to make broadcasting history! A photographer from the *Daily Express* took our picture, and the next morning we were national news ourselves (albeit in a small way) for having performed a feat until then reserved for the male species only.

Despite my foolhardiness in putting in such long hours so early in my pregnancy, my unborn baby clung on. And, after the tragedy of the *Marchioness*, life returned to calmer climes.

For a few days at least. But the last day of August brought a new drama. The call from the news desk came in the early hours of the morning.

'It's all over the papers,' the voice shouted at me as I struggled to force myself out of a deep sleep. 'They say Princess Anne and Mark Phillips are splitting up. Can you get in as quickly as possible?'

This was not an easy story to confirm in the middle of the night, but it rang true: there'd been a good deal of speculation about the marriage after stolen love letters written to the Princess by the Queen's equerry, Commander Tim Laurence, had been sent to a newspaper.

I got dressed as quickly as possible, struggling by torchlight to find suitable clothes, and drove to TV Centre. The *Breakfast* office was a hive of activity. They were already busy tracking down people close to the Royal Family to interview as well as sending a correspondent up to Balmoral, where the Queen and the Duke were on holiday. They wanted me to put together a report about the rumours of the Princess's marriage difficulties and then get down to Buckingham Palace to go live into the programme at seven.

First, though, I had to establish whether the story was true. Disturbing a Palace press secretary in the middle of the night is never a good idea. But on occasions like this there's no choice. I didn't have to explain why I was ringing.

'Yes, yes, I know all about it,' came the voice at the other end. Mine was clearly not the first call to rupture his sleep. 'I'm afraid I can't help you, Jennie. I can't confirm or deny it.'

'But I've got to go live on television in a couple of hours from outside the Palace. What do you suggest I say?' I moaned.

'Well, that's entirely up to you. All I'm saying is that there's no comment from the Palace at the moment.'

'Ah – so there *will* be some comment later?' I said, grasping at straws.

'I didn't say that,' he replied dryly. 'But it's possible.'

The conversation went on for some time as I struggled to pick up enough signals to allow me to go on air confident that the story was true.

'So if I were to go and stand outside the Palace and say that there's *expected* to be an announcement that the Princess and Mark Phillips are separating, would I be making a real fool of myself?' I pleaded.

'Well, Jennie, only you can make that judgement.'

I could tell I wasn't going to get any further. But the Palace certainly wouldn't want me to go on air with a story like that if there was no truth in it. And they hadn't denied the newspaper reports. It was enough to go ahead. From then on, it was a mad dash between the edit suite, where we compiled a background report about the marriage, and Buckingham Palace, where I had to appear live on camera. Gradually, the guidance from inside the Palace became firmer. It was clear now that there would be an announcement, and it would come during the course of the morning.

The pattern of such events was to become depressingly familiar in the years that followed, as more royal marriages broke up. But on this first occasion it was both flattering and nerve-racking to be among the handful of accredited royal correspondents who were invited to the Palace for a special briefing.

Inside the press secretary's office we were given the facts in a short statement making clear that the Princess and her husband were splitting up amicably and, in those well-worn words, 'there were no plans for divorce' – words which have unfailingly, in the fullness of time, heralded a royal divorce.

Outside the Palace the cameras were ready to roll. There was no time to write a script: it was a question of getting the news on air as fast as possible. I ran out of the Palace gates clutching the piece of paper from the briefing, trying to memorise as much of it as possible as I scurried across the road to Canada Gate. Outside-broadcast trucks from all the main TV channels were lined up with satellite masts bristling and a mass of cables running to the cameras. The sound engineer pinned on my microphone while I rummaged through the disgrace that is laughingly known as my handbag in search of my earpiece. In a few seconds we were ready to go on air.

One of the best things about live news reports is that they tend to be short and sweet. As the countdown begins, your heart beats furiously, you worry that your mind will go blank or you'll say something absurd. On major occasions like this, I'm always conscious that just over my shoulder the Queen's staff – and very possibly the Queen herself – are watching and listening.

I once mentioned this to the Queen. It was during a visit to Hungary, and I thought the conversation could do with some light relief. She was surrounded by a group of extremely well-meaning local dignitaries who were gallantly doing their best to speak English, but with accents so thick it was almost impossible to decipher a single word. I launched myself in for the rescue.

'Do you know, Ma'am,' I blurted out rather too loudly, 'when I'm standing outside your home burbling on during the *Six o'Clock News* about something that's happened to you or your family, I often wonder whether you're sitting there inside thinking: What *is* that woman going on about now?'

She seemed to enjoy the thought and smiled broadly. She said she did, indeed, often watch the *Six o'Clock News*, but gave no inkling about whether she'd ever felt like coming across the road to set me right.

In any event, on the day of her daughter's separation, the Queen was not in residence at the Palace, and my reports passed without royal comment. The courtiers had handled a sticky situation with considerable skill. More than thirty years earlier, Princess Anne's aunt, Princess Margaret, had endured a cruelly rough ride when she had fallen in love with a divorced man. Forced in the end to choose between the man she loved and her royal status, she'd agreed to give him up. Now, though, times were changing and divorce had entered the inner sanctum of the Royal Family itself with surprisingly little adverse comment. Like it or not, there was a growing acknowledgement that royalty was not very different in its private affairs from the rest of society.

I got home, exhausted, at about 10 o'clock that evening: the end of another long stint. But I was feeling strong and well. Pregnancy seemed to me to be the most natural condition in the world – and I was loving it!

CHAPTER THREE

Now we are three (in more ways than one)

It was rather appropriate that one of the last big royal stories to catch me on the hop before I went off on maternity leave was the announcement of someone else's pregnancy. News came on 12 September 1989 that the Duchess of York was expecting her second child. Her baby was due just a couple of weeks before mine. The monarchy always bathes in the reflected glory – or otherwise – of the stories surrounding the various members of the Royal Family. This was a happy story to tell, and it went some way to obliterating the negative impressions created by the break-up of Princess Anne's marriage a few days earlier.

This was a happy time for me as well. After seventeen years of work, during which I had watched innumerable colleagues set off to have their babies, it was finally my turn to swan out of the office door on maternity leave. Six months of freedom beckoned, and I was determined to enjoy every minute. To be at home while my husband was working was a totally new experience for me.

To have time to clean those unseen corners around the house, to tidy my knickers drawer and cluttered wardrobes: all these mundane tasks seemed deeply satisfying. The days flew by in a haze of domestic bliss, and before I knew it the baby was due.

Jim was quite a radio star in London in those days. His morning appearances as an unconventional weatherman on the local commercial station, LBC, had drawn something of a cult following. His wry humour and husky American drawl certainly set him apart from the rest, and his fans were eager to share the joy of parenthood with him. Every morning they called the station to find out if I'd had any twinges. I'd sit in bed listening to the progress reports on my condition, and on the day the baby was due there was a positive outburst of curiosity.

'We want to send our very best wishes to Jim's wife, Jennie,' the LBC presenter's voice wafted across my bedroom. 'As you know by now, their baby is due today, and you've all been phoning in to wish Jennie good luck.'

It was strange to share this deeply personal experience with so many people, but I was touched by their good wishes. I prepared to give birth. Sadly, though, I turned out to be something of a disappointment on that day – and the next, and indeed for more than a week thereafter. So much so that, as the baby resolutely stayed put and the calls kept coming in, both to the radio station and occasionally to our home, I began to feel a bit of a failure.

Twelve days overdue and feeling like a small, grounded whale, I despaired of ever giving Jim's fans anything to cheer about. We went for a long, slow walk across Hampstead Heath. The baby clearly enjoyed its ride, tossing and turning all the way, and then went back to sleep. In the evening a builder came round to talk about an extension to the house and, in the midst of complex discussions about the best roofing material to use, I finally felt something a bit stronger than a twinge.

Twenty-four hours later, we were the exhausted, doting and hopelessly proud parents of a little girl who – to us – was the most perfect creature ever to grace this world. Her name had been chosen by her father long before she was born. Always an insatiable bookworm, he'd been reading *Madame Bovary* during the early weeks of my pregnancy and, enthralled, he had asked if we could call our baby Emma.

Cards and gifts came flooding in from his fans, and Emma was famous all over London on that first day of her life as news of her arrival dominated LBC's early morning show. We left hospital after forty-eight hours and were hardly through the front door before Jim sat down with Emma in his arms and began reading to her. He hasn't stopped since. As the weeks went by, I settled into motherhood as easily as I'd adapted to pregnancy – and found that I didn't miss work one jot.

When Emma was four months old, however, the bank balance decreed that I should return to gainful employment. If I'd thought life was complicated before, I quickly discovered that *this* was a whole new ball game. With Jim busy on his show and my unpredictable lifestyle, we needed some belt-and-braces childcare arrangements and I'd found an excellent child minder plus a couple of night nannies who could sleep over if a big news story broke. But nothing could prepare me for that first morning when I had to leave my tiny baby and head back to the world of television.

I soon remembered, though, that there was very little time to worry about home. I was still a general reporter, as well as royal correspondent, and there was plenty going on. In that first week I was sent to Liverpool to report on an outbreak of tuberculosis at Alder Hey Children's Hospital, to the Palace for the Queen's Birthday Honours and to a bomb explosion at the RAF base at Stanmore. Emma survived my absence; our childcare arrangements seemed watertight, and I set my mind to preparing for an important event that was looming on the horizon: the Queen Mother's ninetieth birthday.

Although I had by now got used to dealing with Buckingham Palace, the Queen Mother's establishment at Clarence House remained an unknown quantity to me. I knew that she liked to run her household in her own independent way and that many of her staff had been with her for decades. Then, as always, her life followed a rigid pattern which, paradoxically, provided her with both stability and variety. Her household – staff, dinner services, cutlery, clothes and all – would move between her various homes and royal palaces as tradition dictated. The Queen Mother, it was said, simply did not countenance the word 'change'. Nor did she like a fuss made about things. But even *she* conceded that her ninetieth birthday merited something out of the ordinary, and, indeed, the celebrations began in late June with a pageant on Horse Guards Parade in London. It was a wonderful extravaganza, rivalled only by the pageant held for her hundredth birthday. But, as always when you're the reporter, the magic of the moment is lost in a mire of trying to ensure that you've got the best camera shots *and* some sensible words to go with them.

The next day I was enjoying a quiet time in the office when my pager – by now permanently strapped to me – sounded its piercing bleep.

'Prince Charles fallen off horse,' the message read.

I called the news desk. The Prince, it seemed, had been playing polo when he'd taken a nasty tumble. He was in hospital in Cirencester – and that was where I was headed, too. I called home with the bad news, checked that Jim and Emma could manage without me and got in the car. These first two weeks back from maternity leave were proving something of a baptism of fire.

Luckily, I'd remembered to pack a suitcase of odds and ends to see me through a night or two. It's something that every general reporter learns to carry in the boot of their car. The only problem is that the clothes are, by definition, the sort that you really don't want to wear any more. That's why you can afford to leave them in the car for weeks on end. It's only when the dreadful moment comes to pull them out of the case and appear on camera that you remember why they were so very expendable. The crew and I got to Cirencester in time to file a report for the evening news. Prince Charles, it turned out, had broken his arm and would be staying in hospital for a few days. That would give me ample opportunity to show off my ghastly array of crumpled clothing. We booked into a hotel and I settled down to the novelty of an unbroken night's sleep.

Keeping watch outside the hospital was pretty boring, but that's not unusual. For all the glamour associated with a job in the media, a disproportionate amount of a reporter's life entails standing on various newsworthy street corners or doorsteps, often in the freezing cold or driving rain. At least this time it was June and the weather was fine. And on the second day the Princess of Wales came to visit her husband – which gave us all something to talk about. I was glad, though, when the news desk finally gave me the all clear to come home. We had used up our supply of emergency night nannies, and I was fretting about missing out on vital moments of my little girl's life.

Happily, the rest of the summer was taken up with a story

closer to home: the Queen Mother's birthday. Overshadowing that, though, were the storm clouds that were gathering in the Gulf. And in August Saddam Hussein's forces invaded Kuwait. Before long, like so many of my colleagues, I would be asked if I wanted to go to the Gulf to report on the crisis. It was an exciting prospect but, with a child so young, it seemed irresponsible to agree. I was grateful that the BBC had seen fit both to ask me and to accept, without prejudice, my decision to stay with my family.

If I couldn't go to the Gulf, there was another ambition that I still hankered to achieve: to present the news on television. I began to make moves to add a third string to my bow, alongside my roles as royal correspondent and general reporter. I made an appointment to see one of my bosses.

'I constantly see all sorts of people reading the news,' I told him, 'and I keep thinking: why isn't that me?'

'Yes, well, I've been thinking that, too,' he replied, taking the wind out of my sails. 'We were just considering that when you disappeared off on maternity leave.'

I could have kissed him! I knew this wasn't big time – we were talking about presenting only the daytime news summaries, but it was a start. I felt elated.

Newsreading is all too often an exercise in presenting a calm face to the watching public, even when all hell is going on behind the scenes. The skill is to prevent any of that panic showing, particularly in your eyes. Any sense of unease or embarrassment will leave the viewers feeling uncomfortable, when the whole idea is to make them completely relaxed about you popping into their living room every evening.

Another skill is to learn to keep talking coherently while the director is giving you instructions in your earpiece. You can hear not only the director but pretty well everything that's going on in the gallery, where the programme editor and all the technical staff sit. On busy days that can be quite a cacophony, with producers running in and out with last-minute updates or news of impending problems later in the bulletin.

'We haven't got the graphics yet,' you hear them moan. 'We'll never make our slot – you'll have to move us down the running order.'

'Well, what the hell do you expect me to run instead [this from the bulletin editor, sounding ready to commit murder]? Everything's late today – we've got virtually nothing ready to go to air.'

With all this going on in your ear, the newsreader's job is to stay composed, concentrate on the autocue – and trust that something will turn up soon that's ready for broadcast!

It was a day rather like that which produced one of my most embarrassing moments in live broadcasting. As I went into the studio to present a weekend bulletin, I knew it was touch and go whether the lead story would be ready. That in itself is not unusual. The difficulty on this occasion, though, was that nothing else was ready either. Inexorably, the seconds ticked away until we heard the continuity announcer's cheerful tones: 'This is BBC Television. It's 5 o'clock – time for the early evening news with Jennie Bond.'

The signature tune started . . . the countdown sounded in my ear: 'Ten, nine, eight . . .'

'Just read the headlines as slowly as you can.' The director was doing his best to stay calm.

I took a deep breath, allowed a brief thought to flicker across my mind that I could always fill the gaping hole that lay ahead with a royal story or two, and kicked off with the headlines.

'Slower, slower,' the instructions came in my ear. 'If you can stretch them out a bit, we'll be OK – the lead's on the way to TX [the transmission room].'

I could picture the scene down in the videotape area where we edit our reports – I'd been in that situation too many times myself. An ashen-faced correspondent would be slumped in the edit suite, drained of all emotion, as an assistant ran frantically towards TX, clutching the taped report that had been finished with a heart-stopping sense of desperation seconds earlier. The television would be on in the edit suite, but the correspondent wouldn't have the courage to watch – petrified that, after all that, the story hadn't made it the twenty yards to TX in time.

On that evening I couldn't go much slower, and there was only one headline left to read. After that, it was anyone's guess as to what we'd do next.

'We've got it!' the director shouted in my ear, the relief in his voice all too evident.

Struggling to keep first the terror and then the joy out of my eyes, I read the introduction to our lead story and, with the viewers blissfully unaware of the panic which had preceded it, the report went on air. I allowed myself to relax just a smidgen, though there was still frighteningly little ready in the rest of the bulletin.

It was then that two most unusual catastrophes occurred simultaneously. Suddenly, the plastic tubing that held my earpiece together snapped apart, leaving me with no contact with the director or the editor in the gallery. The studio is a curiously isolated place; the only other person there when you're reading the news is the floor manager, and I was about to explain what had happened when the second disaster hit me. The lead story, which was still on air, abruptly froze – and then the tape started crazily spinning backwards at breakneck speed. Before I'd had time to tell anyone about my earpiece problem, the camera cut back to me and I saw myself on the monitor just as the viewers would have seen me – looking horrified.

'I'm so sorry. We seem to have some technical difficulties with that report,' I heard myself say.

But, I thought, what the hell do I do next? I've no idea what's ready for broadcast and I can't hear anything the director's trying to tell me.

It's at times like this that the famous 'newsreader's paper shuffle' comes into play. The scripts are there for the very good reason that the autocue might break down and we need a backup. But they're also invaluable as props when something like this goes wrong. This is how it goes: you smile (to indicate that you're perfectly in control), look down purposefully, shuffle the pieces of paper around meaningfully – and hope to God that when you face the camera again there'll be something on the autocue that makes sense.

On the day in question, my paper shuffle seemed to go on for an eternity, but when I finally plucked up the courage to look up there was indeed a script on autocue, and I launched myself into it with immense gratitude. As I read it, I prayed silently that the report I was introducing had made it to TX and was in one piece. Thankfully it had, and it was. While that was on air, I had to explain to a bemused editor why I had apparently ignored all the instructions she had been relaying to me via the director. The earpiece was beyond repair, but somehow we struggled through the rest of the bulletin, with the floor manager valiantly improvising sign language to tell me what was next. I like to kid myself that the viewers hardly noticed that anything was wrong; but that bulletin did not go down as one of my finest moments in broadcasting.

Most of those finest moments – such as they are – probably go unnoticed, because they are occasions when, against all the odds, you have managed to fend off disaster. I remember one particularly fraught bulletin when the director shouted, 'Stop! Stop!' in my ear. I considered it rather a strange request, as I was in the middle of a sentence about the Middle East and, fortunately, decided to ignore him. It turned out that he was shouting at a producer. I'm sure, though, that a moment of confusion, if not panic, flashed across my eyes.

Back in 1990, when I started presenting, I had fondly imagined that I would be given an intensive training course. But, as with many things in life, I found myself simply thrown in at the deep end. There was just time for a couple of run-throughs on how to read the autocue before I was booked to do it for real.

My immediate reaction was to have a mammoth crisis about what to wear. I emptied my wardrobe, tried on everything – and left it all in a discarded heap on the floor. I rushed out to the shops and bought a blue and white striped jacket with a lace-collar blouse. I still had much to learn about dressing for the camera.

The next major problem was my hair. Unruly at the best of times, it was far too long and wild for studio work, as I was soon to discover. And then there was the question of jewellery. How much? How little? How big? I would soon find out – through the painful method of trial and error. Make-up was not so much of an issue. I knew there would be a team of artists to help me, and I was happy to put my trust in them.

I felt appallingly nervous as I dressed for work that day. I filled

Emma's bottles with milk, got her ready and dropped her off at the child minder's.

'Don't watch!' I shouted, as I waved them goodbye. 'I'll be far too embarrassed if I know you're looking.' Not that Emma, still only seven months old, had the least idea of what was going on.

I crept into the make-up room at Television Centre feeling very self-conscious. But I soon came to realise that one of the very best things about newsreading is the half-hour of pampering, excellent company and scintillating gossip on offer there. You arrive, frazzled after an early start sorting out the family, followed by a ghastly journey to work, and collapse into the comfortable high-backed make-up chair. A cup of coffee is waiting for you, and a genius of a make-up artist who will gently perform magic on your sallow complexion, baggy eyes and wrinkles. Over the years, I've shared much of my life – and quite a few of my secrets – with my friends in the make-up department. Most are working mothers, too, often with far more stressful lives than mine, and I like to think we've been a source of strength to one another. The make-up room is also a bit of a chat bar, with other presenters popping in for one reason or another. There are always jokes being fired around, and it is positively the place to find out who's doing what to whom, and what's going on in the Beeb as a whole.

I'm sure they saw me as quite a challenge on that first day, but they managed to calm my hair and to make me look fairly respectable for my debut. I emerged into the newsroom to take my place in the presenter's seat – wondering what on earth I had let myself in for. Looking back, the worst aspect of that day was the fact that the summaries were read from the middle of the newsroom. This meant that the editor and all my colleagues were sitting around me, two or three on each side of a semicircular desk. And, ironic as it seems, even though you know you are broadcasting to millions of people around the country, there is something excruciatingly embarrassing about performing in the clear sight and earshot of your peers.

Presenters are often asked what they do with all the hours in between news bulletins. Someone even once asked me if I 'retired' to my dressing room and sat, in a white towelling robe, waiting to be summoned back for the next 'performance'. Nothing could be further from the truth. The presenter is very much one of the working team of journalists. You spend the day in the clothes you arrived in, sitting at your computer, keeping an eye on the wires – news agency reports coming in from around the world – suggesting stories and rewriting the scripts provided by the producers. Lunch is almost invariably a sandwich eaten at the desk, and the only glamour is the occasional return visit to the make-up room for a freshen-up.

I've seen a tape of my first attempt at newsreading that day. I started on time, got to the end and didn't trip over any words. That's about the best you can say. I looked like a frightened rabbit caught in someone's headlights; my hair was still pretty wild and my striped jacket made you think I was about to go rowing on the Thames. (The next time I wore it, a viewer kindly wrote in and suggested I took the jacket back to the jumble sale whence, he presumed, I had acquired it.) After my three minutes of glory, as I finally reached the words 'And that's all for now; more news at eleven o'clock', I looked as if I was about to burst into tears with sheer relief.

The first is always the worst, I suppose. But in the years that I've presented the news, the number of unforeseen hazards that can cause havoc has never ceased to amaze me. Something I hadn't been prepared for was the added pressure of reading precisely to time.

'You gained about three seconds in each bulletin,' my editor complained. 'It makes my life hell when you do that.'

'Sorry,' I said, somewhat crestfallen. 'I'll try to get it right tomorrow.'

There's always a bit of a war between the newsroom and the department we call 'presentation', which supervises the smooth transition of the network from one programme to the next. Obviously, when a live transmission like the news overruns, it gives 'presentation' a headache about how to make the rest of the schedule fit together. So they bawl out the news editors, who get cross first with the correspondents who've stolen a few extra seconds for their reports, and then with the newsreader for not going fast enough. In those early days, I used to take the criticism very much to heart; but trying to speed up can be counterproductive. There's a real danger of stumbling over your words in the rush to get to the end exactly on time. And when you make one mistake, your concentration becomes focused on the effort not to make another – so much so that, almost inevitably, you trip over your tongue again. That's embarrassing for both you and the viewers. Eventually, with experience, I learned to go at a pace that was comfortable and to leave the timing problems to the editor.

Making a stuttering fool of yourself from time to time is something that comes with the territory of live broadcasting. Of course, you are never without support in the studio: you have the wonders of the autocue. You only have to watch the news in some of the countries where that doesn't exist to realise how amateur we would all look without it. But it remains both friend and foe. You grow to rely on the comforting thought that the words will just roll around, in the right order, even if you are totally confused. It can, however, be a false haven. The autocue operator is only human, working under the same pressures as everyone else, and the technical equipment can break down on a whim. At one moment you could be bowling along so smoothly that a small part of your mind might even wander off to consider what's for supper. The next instant the words you are so confidently reading can freeze, leaving you in mid-sentence and looking embarrassingly vacant. You search for the right place in the written script, vainly hoping that no one will notice your agitation. You stumble on, reading from the script and looking up at the camera whenever you dare, until – at last – the autocue lurches back into life. You feel you want to leap out from behind the desk to kiss it, but resisting the urge you continue with the bulletin with a look of love in your eyes.

And then there is the 'dreaded word' syndrome. That's when you know that a particularly nasty mouthful is going to roll up on that script, come hell or high water. It could be one of the many foreign names that crop up in world current affairs: Noboru Takeshita, for example, or Willy Wo-Lap Lam, or President Olusegun Obasanjo. It might be one of those potential tongue-twisters that could go gravely wrong: the Chief Constable of Kent is always a tricky one, and the seemingly innocent words 'City news' have more than once come out as 'Shitty news'. Or it could be an individual bugbear, a simple word that has given you personal grief over the years for no apparent reason. Faced with something like this, you conscientiously rehearse and perfect the problem in the privacy of the newsroom, or perhaps in the loo.

As you strut into the studio, you remain acutely aware that this 'dreaded word' is very shortly going to stand up and challenge you in front of several million viewers. You mutter it under your breath, feigning an air of insouciance as you joke and josh with the floor manager and the gallery. In the back of your mind the word looms like a giant, poised to make a very public fool of you. The countdown to the news begins; suddenly you are on air and, nine times out of ten, you pronounce the 'dreaded word' without even a hint of hesitation. The cruel irony is that you totally screw up another word that even a two-year-old could master.

One of my personal *bêtes noires* is a word which, on the face of it, should not give anyone even the merest pause for thought. It is 'apartheid'. For some reason I have a tendency to pronounce it as 'apart-ide', whereas the correct BBC pronunciation is 'apart-ade'. This always troubles me. It came to haunt me one Saturday afternoon when I was reading the news. The lead story was about the former South African Communist Party leader, Jo Slovo, who had died. The script followed this statement with the fact that he had 'spent his life fighting apartheid'. Nothing too difficult about that. But going through my head over and over again as I made my way to the studio was that word 'apartheid'. I was determined to get it right.

As the opening music played, I whispered, 'apart-ade, apart-ade,' to myself, and felt my chest tighten with tension.

'. . . Three, two, one, and cue Jennie.' The orders came into my ear from the director.

'Good evening,' I said. So far, so good. 'The former South African Communist Party leader, Jo Slovo, has died. [Apart-ade, apart-ade, I thought to myself.] He spent his life farting . . .'

The gales of laughter that howled into my earpiece from the gallery did nothing to ease my sense of humiliation. I struggled to continue.

'Er . . . fighting apartheid,' I quickly corrected myself (incidentally pronouncing apartheid in an impeccable BBC fashion).

But the damage had been done. I was the laughing stock of the newsroom for an hour or two – and my flatulent *faux pas* even fetched up in the *Guardian* a couple of days later.

After my first few weeks of reading the news, I realised that my rather meagre supply of smart clothes would soon need supplementing. People are always surprised that the BBC doesn't provide its presenters with a clothing allowance, but it's true. You can't even put in your dry-cleaning bills – which, with all the make-up rubbing off on collars and lapels, can be pretty steep. So I had to set about finding some reasonably priced jackets that would look good in the studio. You learn quickly that clothes that look fine on television when you are out on the road can be a disaster in the close-up environment of the studio. Anything too fussy is distracting; stripes or checks can strobe or shimmer on camera, and anything too shiny can make you look as if you've just come in from the rain. When I wore a black leather jacket one evening – an extremely classy little number, as it happens – I was besieged with letters from viewers.

'You looked like a biker on television the other night,' complained one lady.

'Your outfit was quite unsuitable for the news,' wrote another.

Mind you, I have to admit that I also got several letters from men who thought my change of image was altogether delicious.

These days I always look for a suit that's simply cut, with a clean, neat neckline, made from a fabric that sits well but is not elaborate in any way. Though I've worn plenty of outfits that come from the cheaper end of the market, I have to admit that, in recent years, I have indulged my liking for suits by my favourite designers: Louis Feraud, Gina Bacconi and Ade Bakari.

I learned hard lessons, too, about asserting myself when it

comes to make-up. When I started, there seemed to be a different make-up artist every day, and all too often I could be found in the loo changing their handiwork because I was too embarrassed to say I didn't like it. Sometimes I got it horribly wrong – as one rather vitriolic lady let me know.

'Dear Miss Bond,' she wrote. 'You wear far too much blusher. In fact, you look like an ageing Barbie doll. You look so ridiculous that whenever you come on television I have to reach for the remote control and turn you off immediately. Please try to do something about it. Yours sincerely . . .'

Stung by her words, I looked at myself in the mirror – and concluded that, perhaps, she was right. I've been more careful with the blusher ever since.

I still cringe when I think back on one occasion when I came in to read the early morning news; there wasn't much time to spare and I'd never met the make-up artist before. She was a woman of a certain age, who'd clearly plied her trade for many years. She sent out signals that made it very clear that she was not to be messed with. I sat in the chair obediently and submitted to her will. To be fair, she made quite a reasonable job of my face. Then she decided to tackle my hair.

'You need it all swept back off your face,' she barked. 'Viewers like to see who's talking to them.'

Whipping out a lethal-looking instrument of torture, she began to backcomb my hair with a vengeance. It expanded into a massive candyfloss of tight tangles, which she then smoothed over, scraping my hair back from my forehead. I looked like a cross between the late lamented Dusty Springfield and Barbara Cartland, but I was too timid to question her wisdom.

'Gosh,' I said lamely. 'That's certainly a new look for me. Thanks very much.'

'It looks perfect,' she purred – smiling at last, clearly pleased that she had triumphed.

When I went into the newsroom, no one said a word. Perhaps, I thought, it didn't look so weird after all. Anyway, there was no time to worry about it: I had to get on with the news.

I was hardly out of the studio after reading the bulletin when the phone rang.

'What the bloody hell have you done to your hair?' It was my brother-in-law, a forthright character at his meekest. 'You look like a hooker from the 1960s,' he guffawed. 'Why on earth did you let them do that to you?'

I did my best to explain and, after I'd put the phone down, some of my colleagues who'd clearly overheard the conversation gently added their thoughts. They were *not* complimentary. I rushed to the loo and furiously brushed out the beehive of hair that had been mine for a terrible half-hour or so. I vowed *never* to let anything like that happen again.

Having three jobs – royal correspondent, general reporter and presenter – certainly meant that my life was busier than ever. I had done it all backwards. Just when I needed a sensible, undemanding business life so that I could be with my little girl, I was letting myself be pulled in three directions at once. But, I have to admit, it was fun.

The royal story was fairly quiet in 1990, but I soon had plenty on my hands as the Gulf War began to dominate the headlines. I was given a challenging role in London, putting together hourly updates on what was a fast-moving crisis. It was a deadly serious and dramatic story, and even though I couldn't be part of the action itself it was exciting to have even a small part in the telling of it. It was also the first real test of our child minder's forbearance. I had to be at work by 7.30 each morning, and that meant an early start for Marie as well, as I dropped by at the crack of dawn to deliver Emma, still half-asleep, into her arms.

In the middle of the crisis, Emma had her first birthday and took her first steps. I was there for the birthday – but missed the other landmark. That, though, is the cross that working mothers – and fathers, too – have to bear. As my workload increased, Jim was taking on more and more childcare duties. He loved being with Emma and seemed to want to share every moment with her. Of course, I loved to be with her just as much, but my job was very demanding and Jim was coming towards the end of his.

Even though I'd had only a desk job during the Gulf War, it had been an exceptionally busy few weeks and, when it was over, the prospect of a spot of early summer sunshine was enticing. We decided to try our luck in Cyprus. The night before our flight, I put Emma in the bath and noticed some strange red spots on her body. She seemed perfectly well, and there was no sign of a temperature, but the spots were quite distinct – and appeared to be multiplying. I called a friend over. She took one look and, with the confidence of a consultant, declared: 'It's chickenpox.'

My heart sank. Surely, now, we would have to cancel the holiday?

'I shouldn't worry about it,' my friend went on. 'Most kids hardly notice they've got it. Just cover her face up a bit so people on the plane can't see her spots – it's pretty contagious.'

I'm ashamed to admit that's exactly what we did. Emma ran around the plane and arrived, unperturbed by her first flight, to spend two weeks in Cyprus seemingly oblivious to her rash. We had a grand holiday and were delighted we hadn't turned back at the last moment. But I *do* have to apologise to anyone who was with us on that flight and subsequently came down with chickenpox.

I returned to work, ready for the fray. It was just a few months later, when Emma was eighteen months, that we came to a crossroads in our life. Jim's contract with LBC came to an end. We had to decide whether he should look for another job or take the radical step of becoming a househusband. I say 'radical' because that was how many people saw it then. It took us very little time to decide that it was the best and obvious course of action. He wanted to be with Emma; we both agreed that having one parent at home was the ideal option for her. And we seized it with both hands.

It meant halving our income in one fell swoop, and immediately I felt the added pressure of being the only breadwinner. But it was a decision that seemed right from the very start – and one that none of us, Emma included, has ever regretted.

Besides, though we didn't know it yet, we were on the brink of the busiest year of my entire working life: the Queen's infamous 'annus horribilis'.

CHAPTER FOUR

Annus horribilis:
part one

G iven the disaster that 1992 turned out to be for
the Queen and the Royal Family, the year began
surprisingly well. In an effort to get the public to
understand more about the work of the monarchy, a BBC
documentary team had been allowed unprecedented access to
the Queen over a twelve-month period. In February 1992 the
finished product, *Elizabeth R*, was screened.

Along with other royal correspondents, I was invited to a
preview. Like most of them, I was fascinated by the insight
the film gave us into what went on behind Palace doors.
Though I'd had the job for a couple of years, I hadn't yet
met the Queen, and this frank portrait – observing her daily
life at close quarters – was like a treasure-trove. Here was
a woman who would always, and inevitably, be far removed
from the reality that most of us share. Nevertheless, this was
not the cold and rather distant monarch whom her public image
generally suggested. Eddie Mirzoeff's film showed a Queen who

was totally dedicated to her duty, but who liked nothing better than to go to the races.

'Look,' we saw her saying as she peered down from the royal box at Epsom on to the crowds below, 'there's my friend. He kissed my hand the other day!'

We saw her as a daughter who could affectionately chastise her mother. 'No, Mummy,' she argued, wiping her eye after watching the horses through binoculars. She was having nothing of the Queen Mother's suggestion that her eyes were watering because of the emotion of the race. 'If you look into the wind like that, your eyes are bound to water,' she insisted.

And we saw her childlike pleasure when she won the royal box sweepstake, pocketing £16 with a little swagger.

This was a portrait of a grandmother taking her grandchildren for a pony ride and of a monarch, in statutory ceremonial robes, posing patiently for an official portrait. As she stared out of the Palace window, she whiled away the time by making wry comments to the artist about the goings-on in the Mall. 'I think there are a few more tourists out there today . . . Look at all those balloons stuck in the trees. They're rather nice – better than a lot of crows.'

This, I realised, was a woman with a delightfully dry sense of humour. The film was given a prime-time slot and won great acclaim. But later that year a documentary about Prince Charles's life would cause a less welcome stir.

A few days after reporting on *Elizabeth R*, I packed my bags for my debut royal tour for television news. It was an important one: the Prince and Princess of Wales were off to India – and I was going with them.

The BBC was then in the throes of a major shake-up in the way it required us all to work – the painful transition to the buzzword of the moment: multi-skilling. All of a sudden, cameramen were meant to be able to edit, editors to do the camerawork, and dispatch riders doubled up as sound engineers. Nowadays it's the norm for one person to have all these skills – and manage the lighting, too. But I had come into television as dusk fell on the old regime when a reporter would be able to call on a three-man crew (camera, sound and lights) before heading off to the edit suite, where a dedicated editor would be waiting. What incredible luxury that now seems!

The early stages of any transitional period are tricky, but I wish the bosses had chosen someone else as a guinea-pig. When I arrived at Heathrow to meet my cameraman – who was also going to have to be my editor and producer for the India tour – one look at the huge quantity of equipment should have made me realise that we were being asked to do the impossible. But I was too inexperienced in TV reporting overseas to appreciate just how big a mistake somebody upstairs had made. I was about to find out.

By definition, a royal tour always involves a great deal of travelling, often to two or three countries in quick succession. It's not uncommon to take three or four flights in a day, and if it's a royal couple on tour they may go their separate ways – doubling the workload for the accompanying journalists. All this requires a great deal of planning, and we work closely with our rivals – ITN and Sky – to ensure that every event is covered by at least one of our cameras.

As I discovered on that visit to India, we travel with a mountain of equipment: cameras, tripods, lights, edit packs and satellite phones. We are the scourge of fellow passengers as we turn up at airports with fleets of trolleys groaning under the weight of all our luggage. My cameraman, Dan, was already loading the first of ours on to the conveyor belt when I got to Heathrow.

'Good Lord!' I said. 'Do we really need all this?'

'I'm afraid so,' he replied, lifting another hefty silver box, ready to be checked in.

Bowing to the inevitable, I put down my suitcase and gave him a hand. So *this* is the glamorous world of foreign travel, I thought to myself.

On the plane, Dan confided to me that he'd had only a couple of weeks' practice at editing and wasn't feeling too confident. I knew, too, that he'd had a bit of a drink problem in the past, and this was his first big assignment since returning to work. Suddenly, I started feeling pretty shaky about what lay ahead.

We arrived in Delhi late at night and, amid the chaos of the seething airport, managed to find a van to carry all our equipment to the hotel. Even in the darkness, the scents and sights of India filled me with excitement. As our van hooted and fought its way through streets blocked by crazy lines of old yellow taxis and battered tricycles, an enormous elephant strolled by, its back covered with a brilliantly coloured, shimmering cloth.

This, I thought, is fantastic.

The next morning, things seemed somewhat less fantastic. Dan had set up his editing equipment – and it wasn't working. Neither of us had much of a clue how to mend it. But at least we weren't alone. Most of my colleagues from the ratpack were staying in the same hotel, and a media centre had been opened to help us with details of the coming six days. We had a briefing with the Prince and Princess's press secretary, and I began to realise just how complex the logistics were going to be. Normally – and ever since that tour – I have a producer with me to sort out all the operational difficulties (deploying the cameras, organising where we can edit, and how we are going to get the report back to London, to mention just a few). This time, though, it was all down to Dan, who frankly had enough problems of his own, and to me.

There was no turning back now. The Prince and Princess were on their way, and we had to jump in a press bus and go out to the airport to film their arrival. Delhi looked even more wild and exciting by daylight, and I began to feel more cheerful. It was a boiling-hot afternoon, but the Princess looked cool and elegant as she followed her husband down the aircraft steps. We filmed their every move, did some interviews and the dreaded piece to camera, and hurried back to the hotel. Time was flying by, the bulletin deadline was approaching – and we had yet to edit the report.

It wasn't Dan's fault that he knew only the rudiments of picture-editing. It certainly wasn't his fault that he was slow at it. He'd been a cameraman all his life and that was his skill. He'd never had the least desire to edit, but now he was landed with it. And I was left with a major problem. India was a notoriously difficult place to work in – and we were going to have to do it with our hands tied behind our backs.

With his fingers trembling and my nervous voice quavering, we finally managed to put together a scrappy, roughly edited piece in time to dash to the local TV station. When we're abroad, we 'hire' a ten-minute slot on a satellite feed to London. It's expensive and it's pretty non-negotiable: miss it and you've lost your chance and your money. We jumped into the nearest taxi, clutching our precious tape.

Almost instantly, the car got snarled up in the pandemonium of Delhi traffic. The driver swore he knew a short cut to the TV station, but after fifteen minutes of dodging rickshaws, buses and camels I began to have my doubts. Dan was sweating and looking at his watch every ten seconds.

'This is going to be really tight,' he said with an air of desperation. 'We've only got eight minutes until the satellite's up.'

'How far now?' I demanded, trying not to shout at the driver.

'Oh – you must not worry, missie,' he said in the singsong tones of Peter Sellers doing one of his famous impressions. 'Believe me, you will be getting there with no trouble at all.'

Well, I thought miserably, I've already *got* trouble, and plenty of it.

At last the taxi stopped outside a large building, which seemed to be on the outskirts of the city. I chucked a bundle of rupees at the driver and waved at his smiling face as Dan and I ran up to the gates. They were locked.

'Four minutes to go,' he groaned.

We shouted and pulled on the padlocked chain. After what seemed like an eternity, a security guard sauntered over and enquired who we were. There is, thank goodness, a kind of magic about the mantra 'BBC' that opens doors around the world. He questioned us no further, and in seconds Dan and I were racing through a maze of corridors.

With about a minute to spare, eventually we stumbled into a room that looked like a partially used warehouse. Half a dozen men were standing around drinking tea or sitting on what looked like upturned packing cases. No one seemed to be expecting us.

'Have you got comms up yet?' asked Dan, hoping they had already established communication channels with London to alert them of our incoming report. They looked at us blankly.

'We've got a tape to send to the BBC,' I joined in. 'It's got to go right now.'

They jumped up and started rejigging wires and cables; one of them began dialling through to London on a phone that looked as if it had come straight out of a period costume drama. A great deal of shouting, pleading and praying followed as they tried to work the technical wizardry that would send my report winging through the air. For several minutes it seemed like a hopeless task. Then, against all odds and with seconds to spare until the line went dead and the satellite slot was gone, we succeeded in sending the pictures. But they just couldn't master the sound. After all that effort, we'd managed to send only a half-finished silent movie! Despondently, Dan and I trekked back to the hotel. I filed my voice track on the phone, knowing that it would sound crackly and dreadful.

I rang the desk in London and told them my tale of woe. They made sympathetic noises but I still felt a dismal failure. I vowed there and then never to allow myself to be put in that kind of situation again.

The next day we had a choice: to follow Prince Charles to a business lunch or to fly with the Princess to the Taj Mahal. There was, of course, no contest. We made sure that at least one camera was with the Prince, and then piled on to the bus for the airport. Dan and I struggled again with all our equipment. He'd decided that the only way to try to meet our deadline was to take the cumbersome edit pack on board the plane and do our best to cut our piece on the short flight back to Delhi.

Crumpling under the weight of the tripod and the lights – which Dan had insisted on bringing – I took in my first sight of India's most famous landmark. The white marble of the Taj Mahal was gleaming in the sunshine against a cloudless blue sky. It was good to be there – weighed down or not. And though we didn't yet know it, this was to be a day on which the Princess would send out a potent, symbolic message about the barren state of her marriage.

She came into view in the far distance, a small figure in red and purple, dwarfed by the immense grandeur of the building. About forty cameras were trained on her as she walked slowly towards us, her head cocked to one side in a familiar pose. She stood by an ornamental pond as the cameras whirred, said nothing, and disappeared off into the mausoleum. We relaxed and everyone was gossiping when, suddenly, she emerged to walk very deliberately to a white bench in front of the Taj Mahal and to sit with her back turned to us – strikingly alone. The message was unmistakable. Here was one of the world's most beautiful women, seemingly deserted at one of the world's greatest monuments to love.

I looked round at Dan just in time to see one of our Fleet Street friends nudge him into action. Distracted for a moment, he had come within a hair's breadth of missing one of the most famous shots of Diana's short life.

Looking back now, it's clear that the Princess must already have embarked on – or been on the verge of – telling Andrew Morton the wretched truth about her marriage. Most of the time, though, she was still putting on a convincing show of unity with her husband. Even on this trip – just four months before the Morton book exploded the fairy-tale myth – there were times when royal reporters far more seasoned than I was commented on how well she and the Prince seemed to be getting along. But on that day at the Taj Mahal, she had the perfect opportunity to relay her innermost thoughts to the world's press with just a picture – and a couple of words.

'What did you think of it, Ma'am?' we asked as she left.

She looked at us, paused and, with her head bowed, said quietly: 'It's so healing.'

I have to admit that I was still reluctant to believe that the marriage was as bad as some people made out. I wasn't convinced that her remark was an unambiguous reference to her suffering. Of course, we frequently asked her press secretary about the rumours; inevitably, we were told that everything was hunky-dory.

'Every marriage has its little ups and downs,' he would say. 'The Prince and Princess wouldn't be human if they didn't have them, too. But they're fine, honestly.'

An outright lie, of course. But, in retrospect, what else could he say? Should he have answered with: 'Well, yes, actually. All that stuff you read – it's true. The Prince and Princess have been leading separate lives for years. They've both got lovers and the marriage is dead in all but name.'

It was an impossible situation for the press office. Until the couple themselves decided to end the marriage, the façade had to be maintained. And so it was that, when we flew to Jaipur to watch the Prince play polo, the great 'missed kiss' episode was similarly dismissed by the Palace – and naïvely played down by me.

Jaipur was reminiscent of something out of the Raj. Polo ponies with British royalty and Indian aristocracy on board careered around the field, cheered on by a noisy native crowd. In white tents alongside, European faces looked on demurely from beneath their sunhats as the champagne flowed and the canapés were consumed. I had never seen a polo match before, and found the whole thing profoundly confusing. But it didn't matter; my job was simply to gather the information and make sure we got the pictures we needed.

As luck, or skill, would have it, the Prince's team won. It therefore fell to the Princess to present him with the trophy.

The niceties of this situation had already been sussed by the ratpack: would they kiss in front of ten thousand people and the massed cameras? If they did, it was a great shot; if they didn't, it was a story. We were poised, jostling one another for the best position as the Prince stepped forward to receive his award.

The Princess handed him the trophy; he moved forward to kiss her cheek. At the last possible moment, she swerved – leaving him lurching awkwardly as his attempted kiss collided with the side of her neck. It was another very public coup for Diana.

It was also another very delicate situation to report. I didn't have much time to work out how far I should go in my analysis. The press buses were ready to roll again; I pleaded for a few minutes to do my piece to camera but, the moment the crowd saw Dan's camera, they gathered around in a crush, waving frantically and shouting just a couple of feet away from my microphone. It was a hopeless state of affairs. I cajoled them, pleaded with them and finally screamed at them to move away and let me work.

Somehow, the piece to camera got done – but only with several hundred overexcited extras in the background – and I didn't give proper emphasis to that calculated 'missed kiss' gesture by the Princess. She was saying to the world: 'This marriage is over. And I can't even be bothered to keep up the façade any longer.'

By this time I had made a unilateral decision to hire an experienced picture editor in Delhi to take the pressure off Dan. Our attempt to edit the Taj Mahal extravaganza on board the plane had been farcical, despite his best efforts. So now, at last, I was managing to get some decent reports back to the UK.

The final stop of the tour took us to Calcutta, a city of searing heat and abject poverty. Life seemed surreal as police outriders, sirens blaring, escorted our air-conditioned bus through the dusty streets, roaring past some of the worst slums I've seen anywhere in the world. We spent just a few hours there – time enough for the Princess to shed a tear as nuns at an orphanage sang her a haunting song, while abandoned children tugged at her hand.

That tour of India was certainly a sharp learning curve for me. In many ways, perhaps, it marked my coming of age as a royal correspondent. But first and foremost I was still a mum and – as the royal plane took to the skies – I reminded myself that I had just fifteen hours to get home if I were going to get back in time for Emma's second birthday. And so, while most of the ratpack stayed on for another night, I flew out of Calcutta on an absurdly circuitous route home. Getting back in time was now more important to me than any news story and I couldn't relax, even though all the hard work and stress were over.

I made it to Heathrow shortly after dawn on my daughter's birthday. I rang the doorbell in a state of exhausted triumph. Throwing off the fatigue of the royal tour and journey back, I went straight into supermum mode. It was a day for celebrations – and, thanks to the organisational skills of my husband, we had a wonderful party. I also discovered later that evening that I'd missed another milestone in my daughter's life. I had left her as a one-year-old, still in nappies. I had returned to find a two-year-old who, miraculously – with the daring and dexterous encouragement of her daddy – had cast aside her nappies for good. I felt a surge of excitement for their success; and a stabbing disappointment that I hadn't been there to see it.

'Could you come along to my office, please?' Another call from one of my bosses. Perhaps it had been unwise to go it alone and buy in that editing in Delhi. Now, no doubt, I was going to be brought to book. I walked along the corridor, rehearsing a feisty response to any complaint about the cost of extra editing.

'Ah – good to see you,' said the boss. I sat down, staring at the coffee machine.

'Would you like a drink?' he enquired – clearly trying to mollify me before the storm. I asked for a coffee and his secretary did the honours.

'Well done in India, by the way. It must have been quite tough.'

Quite tough! I laughed to myself. The man has no idea! I was preparing to launch into an explanation for going over the allotted budget when he said: 'Anyway, we've got something a bit different for you now. We'd like you to be one of our team for the general election.'

For once in my life I was gobsmacked. I enjoyed politics and was certainly interested in the election, but had never expected to be asked to take part in it. Now, here I was being invited to follow the Labour leader, Neil Kinnock, in his bid to get to Downing Street. Of course, I would only be very much a third string, following in the shadow of at least two bona fide political correspondents. Even so, it was a great opportunity, and I welcomed it with open arms.

The campaign proper was still some weeks away, and I notched up some useful practice at political interviews by presenting *Breakfast* news. After my years on the *Today* programme, it should have been relatively straightforward to handle a similar show on television. But the prospect filled me with some trepidation. Television is a more complicated medium. The presenter has to deal with numerous distractions beyond the debate being conducted: which camera to look at, whether the autocue is showing the correct script, and even whether the studio lights have made your face shiny.

I also discovered that the most peculiar thing happens to me when I'm nervous. I can control my voice pretty well, and I do my best to keep my feelings from showing in my eyes (not always with success), but I seem to have no jurisdiction whatsoever over my *nose*. Quite simply, when I'm nervous it runs! The first time I presented *Breakfast* news, I must have gone through half a box of tissues. Everyone assumed I had a cold – only I knew the truth. I had cause to call on quite a few more hankies during the next few weeks.

As election fever began to get a grip, we set off crisscrossing the country with Mr Kinnock. Sometimes we travelled on the campaign bus with political journalists from all the papers; sometimes we went by train, or plane, or car. In many ways it was the same as a royal tour – arriving early, leaving late, hurrying to the next destination. But it was more compelling because this was a race to Downing Street – and the whole country was immersed in it.

An unwritten convention dictates that the Royal Family keep a low profile during election campaigns. There should be no unnecessary distractions to take the public's attention away from the debate. I was *not* therefore expecting any royal stories to get in the way of my election duties. I was in for a big surprise.

On 17 March of that annus horribilis, the Labour bandwagon moved to Bristol. With his media pack in tow, Mr Kinnock set off from Paddington Station. We filmed him on board; we followed him on the hustings in Bristol; we faithfully recorded the speeches which, by now, were becoming ever so slightly familiar. At the end of a long haul, I pulled up outside my home at around midnight, knowing that there was another bout of election fever to confront in the morning. But my day was about to start rather earlier than I had contemplated.

Once again the shrill ring of the phone pierced my dreams. Desperately hoping that it wouldn't wake Emma, I stumbled across the bedroom and whispered crossly: 'Hello – what is it?'

'It's the news organiser here. Sorry to disturb you,' said an excited voice at the other end.

'What time is it?' I demanded rudely.

'It's 5 o'clock.'

'Oh,' I groaned. 'I didn't get in until late from Bristol. But never mind – what is it?'

'It's the *Mail*,' he said loudly. 'It says the marriage is over.'

My heart sank, and then bobbed up instantly, thumping in my chest.

'What does it say? Who's going for divorce? Charles or Diana?'

'*No*,' said the news organiser, exasperated. 'Not *them*. It's Andrew and Fergie – they're busting up, it seems.'

I could hardly believe my ears. How could this be true? The Duke and Duchess of York, apparently so well suited, so easygoing, so in love – and now, according to what sounded like a very well-sourced report, so set upon ending their marriage?

At times like this there is always a moment as you stand there in the dark, shivering slightly in your nightie, when you imagine that, if you simply put the phone down quietly, the full horror of this most inconvenient interruption to your life might just go away. Then you could creep silently back to the warmth of your bed and wait until morning to deal with the problem – like any normal person. Sadly, that's not how it works with news.

'Right,' I said in a voice stronger and braver than I felt, 'I'll be in the office in half an hour. By the way, I'm meant to be with Kinnock again in the morning – you'll have to sort out a replacement.'

I got dressed as quickly as I could, popped my head around Emma's door, blew a kiss towards her sleeping face, left the house and got into the car. I felt anxious about how I was going to confirm the report about the break-up, and annoyed that I was being called off the campaign trail.

By now there was a new press secretary at Buckingham Palace. Charles Anson had come from the private sector; he was debonair, charming and pretty unflappable. He was one of the 'grey men' that both Fergie and Diana publicly lambasted. Over the years I developed a good working relationship with him – even though, like most Palace courtiers, he could sometimes be infuriating. That morning I rang him at home as I drove to work.

'Ah, yes, good morning, Jennie,' he said in his usual languorous way. 'How *are* you?' He always sounded as if he meant it and that it would be churlish to neglect such niceties as a brief discussion on our respective states of health.

'Fine, thanks,' I said curtly. 'Charles, it's about this report on the Duke and Duchess of York. I'm on my way to the office and I've got to go on *Breakfast* news. Is it true?' I demanded.

'Ah, yes,' he said. For a moment I thought I was going to get an immediate, straightforward answer. 'I'm afraid there's nothing we can say about that at the moment, Jennie.'

'Well, are you denying it?' I sighed.

'As I said, Jennie, we really don't have anything to say at all at the moment.'

'So the Palace aren't confirming or denying it?' I badgered.

The conversation drifted on for a few more minutes, but Charles was set on his course and nothing would divert him.

There would be no comment from the Palace that day. Neverthe-less, I spent the next fifteen hours rushing between the BBC and the Palace, ringing contacts and filing reports on the mounting speculation that the marriage was, indeed, all over.

It didn't take long for the Palace to recognise that the tide was unstoppable. The next morning the cameras were lined up outside a school in Windsor to watch the Duchess, looking pale and distraught, drop Princess Beatrice off at nursery. Then came the phone call summoning me to the Palace, alongside four or five other royal correspondents. It was a rerun of the separation announcement of the Princess Royal – but this time it seemed more serious.

We were asked to arrive shortly before midday: appalling timing, as usual, for the *One o'Clock News*. It was going to be a fraught and frantic morning. Inside Charles Anson's office we were handed a piece of paper. It read:

In view of media speculation, which is especially undesir-able during a general election campaign, the Queen has authorised the following statement to be made:

'Last week, lawyers acting for the Duchess of York initi-ated discussions about a formal separation for the Duke and Duchess. These discussions are not yet complete and nothing more will be said until they are. The Queen hopes that the media will spare the Duke and Duchess of York and their children any intrusion.'

That was the meat of the matter. But the sting was in the tail.

'So will the Duchess carry on doing royal engagements?' we

asked as we sat around the table, urgently aware that we now had a major story on our hands.

'Well,' said Charles, 'in the circumstances it's thought best that she should not undertake any further royal duties as from midday today.'

The axe clearly had fallen; the Duchess had already been severed from her royal role.

The briefing went on a little longer, but we were all getting fidgety – much as we wanted more information, it was imperative to get to our cameras. I closed my notebook very obviously, and pointedly put my pen in my bag. Charles was still offering titbits of information, but I could sense the news desk a few miles across London willing me to jump up and race to the camera. Somewhat ungraciously, I made my escape.

'Thanks, Charles. I'll call you later,' I shouted as I flew out of the Palace and dashed across the road, competing in my own private Olympics with my rival reporters. We arrived at our camera positions in an honourable dead heat, but my heart was in my mouth as I tried to memorise the historic statement. I was on air almost immediately and succeeded, I hope, in giving the news as calmly and as fully as possible. The first live 'hit' over, I jumped into the edit van to start putting together a taped report. It was while I was busy doing that that my BBC colleague Paul Reynolds, who was covering events for radio, popped back into the Palace and came across Charles Anson again.

This time, the conversation was a good deal more candid. The Duchess had never really settled into royal life, Paul was told. She'd behaved badly on a number of occasions – putting a paper bag over her head on a flight back from the States, for example, and appearing in glossy magazines. The Palace also held the Duchess responsible for the leak that had appeared in the *Daily Mail*; it was even suggested that she might have employed the services of a professional PR firm.

Paul came out, somewhat breathless from all this, and went straight on Radio 4's *World at One* with his impressions of the mood at the Palace. It became his most famous moment of broadcasting: 'The knives are out for Fergie,' he said.

He couldn't have put it better. I was simultaneously aggrieved that I hadn't been there to hear the fuller, franker briefing, and aware that this story was getting bigger by the minute.

Indeed, it turned into another long day, cutting reports for the bulletins at Television Centre and then firing down to the Palace to go live. At times like this you run on adrenalin. There's no chance to stop, every minute is spent chasing interviewees or contacts or pictures. It's vital to plug every loophole: you don't want to see better shots on rival channels. Would the Duchess do the school run again? Where was the Duke? Should we have cameras with any other members of the Royal Family – would anyone dare ask them for a comment? I always feel as if I'm on an express train careering through a tunnel from which there is no escape. It is a period of intense concentration when all that matters is to have your product ready as we reach the next bulletin.

It went well. We met all our deadlines, the pictures were reasonable and the facts accurate. I drove home feeling overexcited, overtired and quietly satisfied at a job well done. I crawled into bed long after Emma was asleep. I hadn't seen her awake since the day I had set out for Bristol with Mr Kinnock. Jim said she'd seen me on television and called out 'Mummy' but hadn't seemed unduly upset by my absence. It was something she was getting used to.

I'd hoped to get back on the election campaign by the

end of the week, but Charles Anson's remarks had fuelled a story that was already hot. The morning after the separation announcement, he found that the headlines were more about *him* than the Duke and Duchess. That meant only one thing for me: another pre-dawn session standing outside the Palace reporting on the latest twists. Inside the Palace walls, there was much toing and froing as Charles Anson considered his position. Finally, after his offer to resign had been turned down by the Queen (though we weren't told of this) he issued an apology:

I very much regret that what was said should have been interpreted by the media to the detriment of the Duchess of York, to whom I have offered my personal apologies. I have also apologised to the Queen, and both Her Majesty and Her Royal Highness have been kind enough to accept these apologies.

It was a carefully worded statement, attempting to shift the emphasis on to the way in which the media had reported what he had said. But it was a small triumph for the Duchess of York, and a cracking news story, which ran all day long. I got home late on Friday night, looking forward to at least one day off before I went back on the election trail. That's exactly what I got.

The final couple of weeks of the campaign took me around the UK several times – to Scotland and Wales, to the Midlands and to Sheffield. It was there, just a few days before the election itself, that Labour held its now notorious glitzy celebrity rally. It was a night when the lines between politics and showbiz became fatally blurred. I had a seat in the balcony of the auditorium, looking down on the cheering, whistling crowds who seemed drunk on the prospect of a Labour victory as they swayed to the sounds of ear-splitting rock music. It reminded me of when, as a twelve-year-old, I'd seen the Beatles in concert for the first time: hysteria constantly threatened to bubble over and immerse the whole audience. The music reached a crescendo as Neil Kinnock and his Cabinet-in-waiting trotted on to the stage, arms waving in perilously premature celebration.

I must admit that I thoroughly enjoyed the evening, but it went down in history as a grave error of judgement by Labour's managers, and perhaps signalled the beginning of the end of their hopes of election victory. During the last few days of the campaign, the message remained grimly upbeat – but they knew they were going to lose.

As dawn broke on that post-election morning, I stood shivering outside Neil Kinnock's house in London. I'd spent polling day itself in Wales and then driven back in time to have a hot bath at home before going to work in the office all night. It's always great to be a part – however minimal – of national occasions, and I had no complaints about working a thirty-hour shift. But as I kept vigil outside the Kinnocks' home, it seemed even more draining to be with the losing side. John Major was the man of the moment and only too delighted to face the cameras. Our man was heartbroken and had no intention of coming outside.

I began to feel impossibly cold, largely due to fatigue, and my mind focused only on the thought that a relief reporter would eventually show up. When, in the early afternoon, he did, I thankfully called an end to my brief incarnation as junior political correspondent and collapsed into the car to drive home.

As I left, I saw a puff of smoke wafting up from the Kinnocks' garden. The unmistakable smell of a barbecue drifted across the road. Clearly, Mr Kinnock was seeking solace in the bosom of his family and friends. I was only too happy to head off to mine.

CHAPTER FIVE

Annus horribilis:
it's not over yet

I t had been a hectic start to the year and I was looking
forward to calmer waters. Emma was fourteen months
old and thoroughly enjoying her new-found mobility. She
would run around in her Andy Pandy romper suit, looking
impossibly tiny, and could already talk for England. My trip to
India and the demands of the election campaign had given Jim
a crash course in being left holding the baby. He was now a fully
fledged househusband and doing a brilliant job. He took Emma
to playgroups and to the swings in the park – almost always a
sole male among flocks of young mothers. And he was finding
it deeply fulfilling. But with the election over we all felt we
could do with a short holiday, and I began thumbing through
some books about cottages to let in the West Country.

Life, though, is never simple – especially in my business – and
this, after all, was the annus horribilis. I was still relishing a brief
respite from it all at home when, four days after the election,
the news broke that Princess Anne was to file for divorce. It was

nearly three years since she'd separated from Mark Phillips, and he'd recently been embroiled in allegations that he had a love child in New Zealand. Perhaps this had spurred the Princess on – but it had always been made plain that there were no plans for divorce unless one of them wanted to remarry. We sent our cameras out in pursuit of Tim Laurence. I'd written to him some months earlier explaining, as discreetly as possible, that there could come a time when we would need some decent footage of him. All we had in the can was one shot of his face disappearing behind his front door. He'd responded in the most eloquent terms, but it was one of those letters which you could immediately sense was going to get you absolutely nowhere. Of course, he wasn't going to pose for any pictures for me; it simply wouldn't be appropriate, he explained, and in any case he couldn't imagine why I should need them.

So it was that, on the day the Princess announced her intention to divorce, her future husband was seen yet again retreating behind the safety of his front door.

The story dealt with, I resumed my preparations for our holiday. An advert in a bird-watching magazine had caught my eye with its wistful poetry. It read: 'We have cirl buntings in our cow-shed at the tide's edge. Come and visit us.'

We did – and it was magical. The sight of the sea cheered me no end, and it was a delight to view all that the Devon countryside has to offer through the eyes of our little girl. I had no idea then that we had stumbled by chance on our future.

Back home, aching limbs reminded us that we'd needed a new bed for a long time, and on one of my days off we set out to do the rounds of the stores. An hour or so later, we were somewhere in Islington, trying out a particularly comfortable pine bed, when my pager rudely bleeped at me.

'Diana . . . suicide story. Ring news desk urgently,' the message read.

This was extremely inconvenient. We had reached a critical point in our bed-buying programme and did not wish to be disturbed. We'd driven there in one car, and I would have to leave husband and daughter stranded, or jump in a cab and manage without a vehicle for the rest of the day. Given my husband's severe displeasure at the disruption that had already occurred, I chose the latter option.

In the cab I rang the office and gathered as many details as possible. They were few and far between. Several newspapers were carrying reports that the Princess had attempted suicide by throwing herself down the stairs six years earlier. There were also suggestions that she had slashed herself on other occasions. Why the office had chosen not to contact me first thing about this I shall never know. Perhaps it was because it all seemed so incredible. I freely admit that my first instinct was to view it as a headline-grabbing ploy by the publishers of a book we all knew was about to be serialised, a book by one Andrew Morton. Stories of suicide attempts – even in a fairy-tale marriage that was so seriously flawed – seemed sensational. I had to try to establish whether there were enough facts for me to broadcast. Unsurprisingly, there was no help to be had from the Palace. Calls to the press office brought forth only the response that they were not about to comment on a book they had not yet seen. But the very fact that they didn't deny the story out of hand was certainly worth putting on air.

That episode heralded the start of an extraordinarily intense cloak-and-dagger period of royal reporting. The race was on to find out what was in Morton's book, *Diana – Her True Story*. Even more imperative was to find out his source or sources. I set off to interview Andrew Neil, then editor of the *Sunday Times*, which had bought the serialisation rights. He let us film the front page of his paper as it was being prepared – but only from a distance. The detail of the lead story was under wraps. He was adamant that Morton's account had been independently verified by his paper, that it was fireproof and that it had come from the heart of Diana's circle. The pressure on the Palace to confirm or deny the veracity of the book was becoming irresistible. If the Princess *had* colluded with Morton, the damage to the monarchy could be untold. And the impression that she did, indeed, have her hand on the tiller was gaining momentum fast.

In pursuit of the truth, I called all the contacts I could muster. One, a household name who was a personal friend of the couple and whose integrity I'd always respected, told me he'd recently stayed with the Prince and Princess. 'Everything was fine between them,' he said. 'They were both very relaxed; there was no atmosphere. It's a very happy marriage. This stuff in the papers – it's the worst case of media hype, you know. It's all rubbish.'

That's just one example of how very confusing it was to be a correspondent at the centre of all this, charged with trying to convey an accurate account. In most briefs in journalism there is a far more direct route to the heart of a story. You simply call up the person in question and discuss the rumours, reports or allegations with them. Clearly, you then have to use your judgement to decide whether they have told you any or all of the truth. You may also feel it necessary to corroborate it through other sources, but at least you're not always solely dependent on the word of a third party. As a general reporter and news presenter I've been lucky enough to meet all sorts of movers and shakers in society. A perk of being the newsreader on the Sunday-morning show *Breakfast with Frost* is that you *do* have breakfast with the guests afterwards. I've enjoyed some splendid discussions over scrambled egg and bacon with Prime Ministers, Chancellors, and a bevy of other government and shadow ministers. But it is rare, indeed, to have an opportunity like that with any of the Royal Family.

Instead, as a royal correspondent you depend on the press office at the Palace and on a friendly relationship with private secretaries, or friends and relatives of royalty. That means you never get your information from the prime source; it's always at one step removed and, inevitably, runs the danger of being diluted or distorted to some extent.

The row about Morton's book was becoming stormier. There were demands to know who was behind the revelations, but no one at the Palace was saying anything. On the Sunday that the serialisation began, Prince Charles was playing polo at Cowdray Park. I went along, too. It was a damp and misty afternoon and I'd only just arrived when my pager and phone went into frantic mode.

'There's a statement from the Palace.' The news organiser's voice sounded urgent. 'They say Diana had nothing to do with the Morton book.'

'OK,' I said. 'I'll call them straight away.'

The polo match had started, but there was no time to watch. My cameraman concentrated on getting shots of the Prince, while I rang the Palace. On a Sunday it meant bothering the on-duty press officer at home. The message was brief and to the point.

'The Princess did not cooperate in any way whatsoever with Andrew Morton's book,' I was told.

'Well, did she authorise anyone else to talk on her behalf?' I asked.

'As I said,' came the reply, 'the Princess did not cooperate in any way at all. She did not authorise any interviews.'

I filed a report to that effect; perhaps I even believed it. I certainly wasn't in a position to deny it. Of course, we now know that nothing could have been further from the truth. The Princess had misled her brother-in-law, Sir Robert Fellowes – the Queen's private secretary – who had dutifully reported to all who needed to know that Diana had not cooperated with the book. It was the moment that strained their already fragile relationship to breaking point. But Sir Robert took her at her word, and the world was informed that the Princess was not the voice behind this explosive book.

At the same time I was, of course, doing as much of my own research as possible. For several days now I'd been compiling a computer file which I rather dramatically called 'The Chase'. It was a list of the sources that Morton might have used, with their addresses and phone numbers – and a record of my progress in tracking them down. We managed to get a shot of one of those sources, Rory Scott, standing at his front door. He confirmed that he'd given an interview to Morton. Another source told me over the phone that she had spoken out in good faith; the idea had been to show everyone that the Princess had overcome extraordinary trauma in her life and was better and stronger for it.

'I was told it would be helpful if I talked to Morton,' she whispered conspiratorially.

This seemed the clearest possible indication that the Princess had, at the very least, encouraged her friends to go public. The next day James Gilbey – named as the source for the revelation that the Princess had attempted suicide – issued a statement saying his interviews with Andrew Morton had been treated fairly and accurately. It was becoming more and more difficult to swallow the Palace line – oft repeated – that the Princess had not cooperated with the book. The strain she was under was beginning to show. Later that week, faced with kind words and sympathy at a hospice in Merseyside, she struggled in vain to hold back her tears. Was she crying because the book was untrue? Or was the full impact of what she had done beginning to hit home? From where I was standing, she remained an enigma – and the extent of her involvement in the book was still a mystery.

There was a fair bit of strain at my end, too. I seemed to be called into the office constantly, the phone at home was forever ringing, and Emma had by now learned to answer it with those haunting words: 'Has Mummy got to go to work?' But the saving grace was that Jim was always there for her – no matter how erratic her mother's life was becoming.

It was June and, as always, the Queen's Birthday Honours List was announced. Covering this was a task I used to dread. The list would be delivered from Downing Street shortly after midday with an embargo on revealing any of the names until midnight. That sounds quite reasonable – twelve whole hours to get it sorted – but it was always a desperate race to get finished in time. For it was never so much 'a list' as a tome – page upon page of names to be scoured through, as we searched for the famous among the simply worthy. Once the celebrities had been found, there followed the even trickier job of trying to track them down for an immediate interview. With a producer, I would work my way through agents and relatives, theatre companies and business directories – frantic to contact my quarry before ITN or Sky got there. In June 1992 some of the names that leaped out from the page were Jeffrey Archer, Michael Caine, John Cleese, Ian Botham and David Gower. All had been awarded an honour of some kind and, despite hours of phone bashing, very few of them were available for interview. Eventually, with a small sense of triumph – minimal, in fact – we secured an interview with the soon-to-be-Lord Archer. Many weary hours after we'd started our research, and many more since we'd got out of bed, the report was finally ready for transmission.

At least I'd got away from the royal saga for a day, but now there was a new chapter to tell. Andrew Morton had finally agreed to the interview I'd been asking for since the day the story had broken. I drove to his house, which, as it turned out, was only a mile from mine. It was a warm day and we sat in his garden. He seemed nervous; so was I. This was my golden opportunity to find out once and for all just how much credence to place in his book. I'd received an advance copy the day before and had stayed up half the night reading it. I'd written two pages of questions to challenge Morton. Why should we believe this was the Princess's 'true story'? How did he know the intimate details of rows between husband and wife? *Had* he spoken directly to Diana? Wasn't he simply interested in dishing the dirt – and making a million?

Conducting a television interview is a bizarre business. While the cameraman sorts out all the technical details, the interviewer does his or her best to put the interviewee at ease. You chat about mutual interests or the topic under discussion but without telling them the questions. That's not for some Machiavellian reason; it's simply because their spontaneous answer is almost always the best. And then, as the lights go on and the camera starts to roll, you both go into 'performance mode', no matter how natural you try to make it seem.

Andrew Morton was a fellow journalist: he'd been a royal reporter just like me. I didn't believe he'd have written this book without cast-iron evidence that it was true. But I also knew that he was going to protect his sources – as every journalist must. He parried every question I threw at him; there was an urgency about his insistence that this was a portrait of a young woman who was on the verge of leaving the Royal Family.

'I can't emphasise it too much,' he told me. 'There is chronic instability in the House of Windsor. I tell you, we are going to lose the Princess by default if something isn't done. She is at the end of her tether.'

He said that Camilla Parker Bowles had hung over the marriage 'like a dark cloud' for many years. That the Princess's tears in public were nothing compared with her tears in private and that her friends had chosen to speak out because they couldn't bear her misery any longer.

It struck me that this was all rather melodramatic, and I had nothing to back it up beyond Andrew Morton's word. I filed a long report and went home feeling distinctly uneasy. Could it really be that the House of Windsor was in danger of toppling right over? Was I about to witness the end of the monarchy? Suddenly this job had become anything but frothy and frilly. Questions were being asked about the very substance of the monarchy and whether it was still relevant to twentieth-century life.

In Prince Charles's camp there was, understandably, an air of barely contained panic about the book.

'Don't underestimate the problems this is giving us,' I was told in an off-the-record briefing. 'That was one hell of a brick she threw. It's a very difficult time for us all.'

Gradually, though, the dust began to settle and I spent much of the next few weeks presenting *Breakfast*. By now my nerves had calmed down and my nose had stopped running. All too frequently, though, we presenters found ourselves challenged to hold the programme together in the face of adversity. On one particularly memorable occasion, I was confidently reading the lead story off the autocue; it was about Bill Clinton's nomination as the Democrats' presidential candidate. The words are reflected on to the camera lens, and an autocue operator manually scrolls down the script, keeping pace with the presenter's delivery. On this morning, the machine suddenly froze. I stumbled, stopped and – trying to look calm – hastily looked down at my printed script. The tricky bit here is whether you can find the right place on the piece of paper. It becomes even trickier when, like me (and many other newsreaders), you wear contact lenses for distance and could really do with a pair of reading glasses for close-up work. Through the blur of the print in front of me, I took a stab at where we were and continued. Normally, this kind of social embarrassment lasts no more than a few seconds. Before you know it, you've managed to lurch towards a taped report, giving everyone a two-minute breather during which, with any luck, the autocue will be fixed. Not that day! To my horror, I looked up again to see that the script, although no longer frozen, appeared to have taken on a life of its own. The whole *Breakfast* programme was whizzing crazily around before my eyes as the scrolling process went into overdrive. What's more, it was flashing by backwards. My nose started to run. Between sniffles, my co-presenter and I struggled on without the autocue for a good fifteen minutes as frenzied phone calls were made to our technical support teams. After what seemed like an eternity, they eventually came to our rescue and repaired the offending machine. Normality was restored to the studio and we slowly recovered our spirits, but it had been a most unpalatable experience.

On the royal front, there was at last some happier news: in July 1992 Lady Helen Windsor married Tim Taylor. People often imagine that I'm invited to occasions like this. Sadly, nothing could be further from the truth. But I *am* rewarded by being required to stand outside chapels and churches, often for hours at a stretch, waiting for the big event. And, in truth, it *is* fun to be part of an occasion like that – however peripherally. Lady Helen's wedding was a joyful day, although, inevitably, a considerable amount of press and public attention was centred on the body language between Prince Charles and his wife. And with good reason. For, as we were to discover, this annus horribilis was far from over.

It was the middle of the night and Emma had already woken me twice; I felt angry and victimised to be forced into consciousness again. As I groped my way over to the phone, my sole ambition was to silence its intrusive din.

'Yes?' I hissed spitefully.

'It's the desk here,' came the irksome reply. 'Really sorry to call you so early, but there's an incredible story about the Duchess of York, and we need you in as soon as possible.'

'What is it?' I demanded.

'She's plastered all over the papers topless – with her toes being sucked by that financial adviser of hers, John Bryan.'

It took a few moments for this to sink in. From the bed came a groan and Jim's husky voice: 'What the hell is it this time?' He sounded inordinately grumpy. 'And whatever it is, make it happen somewhere else.'

This was not a suggestion; it was an order. I could hear Emma stirring in her room. Please don't let her wake up again, I silently beseeched any gods who might be listening.

'I'll be right in,' I whispered down the phone. 'Tell a producer to find all the recent shots of the Duchess that we've got.'

Fumbling in the dark, I grabbed some clothes from the wardrobe and crept downstairs. I switched on the radio, but didn't dare turn up the volume beyond barely audible, swiftly got dressed and slapped on some make-up, praying all the while that Emma wouldn't be disturbed. Clutching my keys, I closed the front door behind me and tiptoed to the car.

Over the years I have established that, given a tailwind and an atrociously early start, I can drive to work in seventeen minutes flat. It is a journey across London of some eight or nine miles – and, when the world is awake, it is not unusual to be incarcerated in traffic jams for well over an hour. On that morning I was at the office faster than you can say 'Buckingham Palace'.

I stared at the papers in disbelief. The royal story was becoming more outrageous by the minute. The pictures of the Duchess and her beau were manifestly unregal. They were on holiday at a villa in the South of France. It was secluded – but not enough to escape the attention of one of the band of paparazzi who prey on royalty and celebrities. The couple had been snapped relaxing together by the swimming pool. The Duchess was indeed topless and, in one of the pictures, she appeared to be proffering her foot, Cinderella-like, to her bald companion, who was taking a decidedly intimate interest in it. They were pictures any woman would dread being published. For a member of the Royal Family – albeit an estranged one – they were devastating.

'What do you think we should do with them?' the editor of *Breakfast* asked me. 'Can we show them, do you think?'

Therein lay our dilemma. This was obviously a story of

some interest, and it was unlikely simply to blow over. The Duchess would shortly be seeing the pictures for herself – along with the rest of the Royal Family sitting around the breakfast table at Balmoral. And she was certain to face repercussions from such a monumental embarrassment. But there was also a viable argument that her privacy had been invaded. If we put the pictures on television, we could be judged to have done the same.

It didn't take us long to agree that this was a story I would have to tell without the aid of the pictures themselves. In other words, I had to head off to the Palace to be interviewed live about the offending photos and likely consequences. Along with every other TV network, we also dispatched a camera crew to Balmoral in case the Duchess chose to submit herself to the public gaze.

Unsurprisingly, she endured her humiliation in private for the duration of her short visit to Scotland. She left after three days, giving us all a glimpse of her retreating figure as she climbed the aircraft steps to fly back south. Outside her home in Surrey, the cameras were ranged to film the fallen Duchess as she was driven through the gates. It seems a heartless thing to do to a fellow human being – but this is a tough business, and the rules are straightforward. People in the public eye have to accept the consequences of their actions. Many of us thought that Fergie had put the final seal on her isolation from the Royal Family. To an extent, it was true. But few of us – even in the royal ratpack – had reckoned on the Duke of York's astonishing love and loyalty. For years after their separation – and indeed after their divorce – we were told behind the scenes that the Duke still adored the Duchess and would take her back at the drop of a hat. As they gradually metamorphosed into the happiest divorced couple in the land, the constantly recycled rumours that they were about to remarry posed quite a quandary. But contacts assured me that life as a member of the Royal Family had exacted too high a price from the Duchess; she was unwilling to subject herself ever again to that level of private and public scrutiny. She would live with 'her bestest friend', Andrew, but never return to the royal fold.

No sooner had the Duchess left Balmoral, keeping me busy with news stories on every bulletin, than our sleep was ruptured once again. This time the papers had zeroed in on the Princess of Wales.

'They've got a tape of a phone conversation Diana had with a bloke,' the news organiser told me as I endeavoured to force my eyes open. 'It sounds like her and they've printed a complete transcript. He calls her Squidgy!'

Squidgygate had broken, and I was beginning to wonder just what depths the royal saga was going to plumb. We'd had separations and so-called suicide attempts; now we were down to toe-sucking and bugged phone calls.

'Sorry to wake you so early,' the news organiser went on, irritatingly awake, 'but we need to decide what to do about it.'

'Don't worry,' I said morosely as my brain slowly began to grind into action. 'I had to get up in half an hour anyway because I'm presenting *Breakfast*.'

This was a tightrope I was constantly walking, trying to balance my presenting and reporting duties. It was always a risk that a royal story would break when I was reading the news. Often the news desk would simply ask another correspondent to cover the story, but sometimes, if my 'expertise' as a royal correspondent was deemed indispensable, a hapless secretary would have to ring round fellow presenters and ask them to step into my newsreading shoes. At three in the morning, that is not easily done.

There was, in any case, a moral dilemma about this story, just as there had been with the pictures of the Duchess and John Bryan. If this were indeed a genuine conversation between the Princess and a friend, was it ethical to broadcast its contents? Wouldn't that constitute an invasion of privacy? The news organiser and I rehearsed the arguments for and against, and decided to refer the problem to a higher power. In the meantime I got dressed and went into *Breakfast* rather earlier than planned. While others mulled over the rights and wrongs of reporting Squidgygate, I applied myself to researching the topics lined up for me in the *Breakfast* programme. There was a sterling crisis to analyse, a hurricane alert and a discussion to chair about the effects of the brain drain on the quality of British science. Plenty to be getting on with while the royal story simmered.

It took much of the day for the bosses to reach a decision on the leaked tape. On *Breakfast* there was, at least, the legitimate option of referring to the story in the newspaper review. But there was still debate about whether we should go any further. During the course of the next few hours, I managed to get hold of a copy of the tape. It sounded very much like the Princess, talking to her friend James Gilbey. No one knew how it had come to be recorded or why it had been released to the newspapers, but it reinforced, in no small measure, the Princess's acute disillusionment with the family into which she had married. Buckingham Palace had also been provided with a copy, and my urgent phone calls to the press office eventually produced a response. It wasn't exactly conclusive, but it was an official line.

'It's simply not possible to say whether the tape is authentic,' I was told.

It was little enough to go on, but it gave us a newsworthy 'top line'. I put together a carefully constructed report which alluded to the Squidgy tape without betraying its contents.

By now rumour was rife about the origin of the tape. Was this a plot by MI5 to discredit someone who had become a troublemaker in Palace eyes? Or was it the sordid work of a radio ham seeking to capitalise on his eavesdropping? The world of royal reporting was becoming more conspiratorial by the minute. Every week, if not every day, brought events so bizarre that they were barely believable. Frankly, I couldn't have made it up if I'd tried. What, I wondered, could possibly happen next?

CHAPTER SIX

Annus horribilis: the final episode

I f this was an annus horribilis for the Queen, it was turning out to be an annus exhaustus for me. I'd taken on far too much presenting work, knowing only too well that there are always embryonic and ferociously ambitious newsreaders prowling in the wings. So whenever I was asked to plug a gap in the *Breakfast* rota or present the bulletins on what should have been a day off, I accepted with alacrity. As a result, I seemed to be working every day, sometimes as royal correspondent, sometimes on general news and often as a presenter.

Gradually, I noticed that people were beginning to stare at me in the street. In my vanity – and I'm as vain as most (my husband would say more so) – I'd imagined the exhilaration of being mobbed in the supermarket by adoring fans. Thankfully, I've never reached those dizzy heights but, when people first began to point and whisper, it struck me as both flattering and distinctly odd. Even today I find that a little bit of fame is a peculiar thing. Perhaps if you're a megastar it's more clear cut, but when you're a face that people only recognise if they happen to see the BBC news on a regular basis, the whole experience is far more haphazard. In a single day you can find yourself signing a dozen or so autographs and then being brought down to earth with a wallop. Not so long ago I caused a very small stir in a shopping centre when I popped in on my way to work.

'Oh, hello, Jennie.' A voice broke into my thoughts. I looked up, expecting a familiar figure, but I'd never seen the lady with the smiling, eager face.

'Well,' she continued, unabashed, 'you look a lot thinner in real life – and a lot younger. What do they do to you there?'

I explained that television makes you look fatter and that, in any case, I'm not in the least photogenic and should never have gone into TV in the first place. By this time, quite a crowd had gathered around me as I stood ambushed outside Marks & Spencer, and I spent the next few minutes signing autographs.

When I arrived at Television Centre, I went straight to the Research Centre to pick up a CD for a musical report about Ascot.

'Yes?' said the librarian, looking up at me from his chair.

'Hi,' I replied cheerily, still buoyed by my five minutes of stardom at the shops. 'I need some music from the 1950s for a sports piece I'm doing. What have you got?'

He ferreted around and then ambled off to find something suitable. A few minutes later he returned clutching three CDs. A small mountain of BBC paperwork followed, at the end of which he looked up at me again and said: 'Name, please.'

'Er, Jennie Bond,' I replied.

'Is that B-O-N-D?' he queried.

'That's it.'

'And what department are you?' he asked, twiddling his pen in his fingers.

'Newsgathering,' I said flatly.

I left with my CDs, feeling somewhat deflated but suitably chastened. For more often than not in this news business you're only as famous as your last bulletin – and sometimes, as I'd just experienced, that fame doesn't even stretch to your own back yard.

With all this work in 1992, the summer was almost over before Jim and I decided we could take a holiday. We are both confirmed Francophiles; my degree is in French, and Jim once spent a couple of years as a correspondent in Paris. It was probably my experience as a student language teacher in France that led me to become a journalist. I was twenty at the time, and fate decreed that I should be sent to the South of France for my year out from Warwick University. I was a 'cool chick' in those days – at least, I considered myself as such. With flowers in my long, bottle-blonde hair (which had to be ironed regularly to keep it poker-straight) and skirts that ended at the top of my thighs, I thought I'd died and gone to heaven when I arrived in the hugely trendy resort of Juan-les-Pins, just down the road from Nice. My sole function as an *assistante* at the lycée was to encourage the pupils to speak English; my classroom duties extended to no more than nine hours a week. It was not an onerous job. Or, at least, it shouldn't have been.

My first mistake came within seconds of setting foot in the classroom.

'*Bonjour, mes enfants,*' I declared. And there ended my effort towards any formality. 'Don't bother about calling me Mademoiselle – Jennie will be fine.'

Major misjudgement! A clear admission that I, the teacher,

neither demanded nor, from this moment on, commanded any authority over the class.

And so it turned out. There were occasions in the coming year when I lost all control over my students. One young boy, I remember, frequently insisted on riding around the classroom on his bicycle. Another lit a small bonfire under his chair. Several made it their life's work to rifle through my handbag for cigarettes whenever my back was turned. In a desperate attempt to hold their attention, I decided to offer them the choice of what we would discuss in English each day. Another enormous error.

'Jenneee,' they would shriek. 'Tell us about ze way you all 'ave ze drugs in Londres. It eez a fab citee, eh?'

I tried, in a responsible way, to explain the ready availability of narcotics in Britain in those days as well as the dangers. Jimi Hendrix had just died in a blaze of publicity, and I told them what a waste of a great talent it had been.

One morning the knock on my bedroom door was not – as it had sometimes been – one of my pupils trying to wake me up to tell me I was late for class. This time it was a summons from the headmaster. I dressed hurriedly and took myself to his study.

'Mademoiselle Bond,' he began gravely, peering over his reading glasses. He spoke in French very slowly, as if I wasn't bright enough to keep up. 'We have had complaints from the parents of your pupils.'

'Oh,' I said, thinking they'd discovered that teaching was not one of my most impressive strengths.

'Yes,' he continued grimly. 'They say you have been corrupting the children.'

Now this sounded serious. I sat bolt upright. 'I've been doing what?' I demanded, puzzled and perplexed.

'They say you've been teaching them all about drugs.' His voice was brittle with anger. His face was turning puce.

My heart was in my mouth. The awful realisation dawned on me that my words of warning about drugs had lost a great deal in the translation between classroom and home.

'I have not been teaching them about drugs,' I replied in faltering French. 'These are young people of sixteen and seventeen, and I simply answered their questions in a responsible manner.'

'Well,' he shouted, 'from now on you do not answer any questions unless they are about rabbits or the countryside.'

His choice of topic struck me as bizarre even then – and has intrigued me ever since. But I didn't query it. Relieved to have escaped with no more than a warning, I scurried back to the relative safety of my classroom and maintained a crashingly boring curriculum for the rest of the year. Indeed, it was so boring that towards the end only two or three pupils would turn up for my class. Unable to suppress the rebel in me completely, I used to escape with them to the beach. We'd talk in English all the way there and back, and I'm sure they learned far more than if we'd stayed in that stuffy classroom. But the lesson I learned in that memorable year was that teaching is excessively hard work, and I am definitely not cut out for it. When I left university a year later, I decided instead to follow in the path of a couple of friends who had gone into journalism. I judged – correctly – that it was a far less arduous option.

And so it was to France that we headed for our annus horribilis holiday. There was just one task to tackle before we left: laying the foundations for an extraordinarily lavish Wendy house that we'd recently ordered for Emma. It was not so much a toy as a miniature Swiss chalet, large enough for an adult to stand in, with an upstairs gallery where you could sleep, not to mention window boxes and a porch. It cost a fortune and reproaches me still from the bottom of our garden: a potent reminder of how foolish a new parent can be. Someone more experienced might have foreseen that Emma would never use it for fear of coming across a spider. Before we set off across the Channel, Jim laid some hefty paving stones as a base for our acquisition. This was not a wise course of action for a man who has suffered chronic back pain for many years.

The next day we set the alarm for 4 a.m. and there was a tingle of excitement in my bones as I realised that, this time, the jarring tones of the radio were not summoning me to work. This was worth getting up for. This was a call to holiday. I didn't have time to notice Jim's groans as he got out of bed; I was too busy dressing Emma and doing the last-minute packing. We were in the car and off by 5, heading for the ferry to Cherbourg and on to a favourite hotel on the Brittany coast. It was as we got to Portsmouth that Jim confessed the full extent of the pain he was in. Suddenly, his foot became stuck as if glued to the accelerator, his leg paralysed with pain. It was only with the utmost difficulty that he prised his foot off the pedal in time to brake at some traffic lights. It was a frightening experience. I suggested we abandon our holiday plans and turn back for home. He insisted it was just a twinge.

On the ferry, things went from bad to worse. The pain in Jim's back was excruciating; I booked us into a cabin and he lay down, assuring us that all he needed was to relax his muscles for an hour or two. Emma and I left him in peace and explored the boat. When we arrived in Cherbourg, I took over at the wheel and drove for a half-hour or so, but my poor husband was obviously in agony. I found a hotel in a small seaside town, hoping that a night's proper rest might do the trick, but it was far more serious than either of us had reckoned.

By the time the ambulance came, Jim was unable even to walk. The hotel corridor was so narrow that he had to crawl to the stretcher, pulling himself along the floor on his elbows. Holding Emma tightly in my arms, I watched the ambulance drive off, tears streaming down my cheeks. *Why* had we been so stupid? *Why* hadn't we turned round in Portsmouth and headed home? I rang the office in a panic, hoping for help if we had to charter an air ambulance to get Jim back to London.

Fortunately, it didn't come to that, but the holiday ended where it began: a few miles outside Cherbourg. The painkillers and treatment at the hospital put Jim in a better humour, while Emma and I spent lonely days at the beach between visiting hours. We became the focus of attention at our little hotel: a mother and toddler sitting together at dinner every evening discussing the affairs of the world. After nearly a fortnight, Jim was discharged and able to limp straight on to the ferry home with us. I returned to work, exhausted.

As the year wore on, speculation about the dire state of the Waleses' marriage was running rampant. I fixed up a lunch with the Princess's private secretary, Patrick Jephson. We met in the elegant surroundings of a London hotel; I'd taken him out once before and enjoyed his company. Patrick told me that the strains of the summer had been considerable, but that a number of deep discussions had taken place and there were now signs of some improvement in the Prince and Princess's relationship. He said they had taken the decision to try to stay together. Even then, this nugget of information seemed implausible. In retrospect, it is obvious that he was simply trying to keep the lid on an impossibly volatile situation – one that was heading ineluctably towards divorce. But who was I to argue? I filed his suggestion away in the back of my head as a possible, though unlikely, piece of this complex royal jigsaw puzzle.

I had to wait only a few weeks to discard Patrick's offering. The whole game was finally given away when the Prince and Princess embarked on what turned out to be their last tour together: to South Korea. It has always been a matter of regret to me that I didn't go on that trip. The reason was partly BBC finances – it was only a four-day tour and would be expensive to send me – and partly office politics. A respected and senior correspondent in the region had proposed covering the visit, and would use it as a springboard to report on the broader issues of relations between North and South Korea. I didn't feel in a position to quarrel with this. I was also secretly relieved not to have to leave Emma again. As it transpired, the senior correspondent was called away and someone else from the regional office covered the royal story – without any reference to the broader issues. I was deeply annoyed, particularly as photographs of the unhappy Prince and Princess – dubbed The Glums – quickly made front-page news. But there was nothing to be done, and I watched the denouement of the marriage unfold from a distance.

About a month later I was sitting in the press secretary's office at Buckingham Palace discussing upcoming royal events when one of the Queen's most senior courtiers put his head round the door.

'Oh, sorry, Charles,' he said. 'Didn't realise you were busy . . . Just wanted a word, when you've got a moment. Hello there, Jennie.' He nodded in my direction. 'All well?'

I nodded back and smiled at his retreating figure. As Charles Anson and I resumed our meeting, I thought no more of this brief interruption. A few minutes later the courtier returned.

This time Charles went out into the hallway to talk to him. When he came back, he explained that there'd been a slight security alert, but that there was nothing to worry about. Almost simultaneously, my pager bleeped bossily at me.

'Ring the desk. Urgent,' it read.

'Excuse me a second,' I said to Charles, groping in my bag for my mobile.

The phone was answered almost instantly.

'Hi, it's Jennie here,' I said. 'What's up?'

'It's Windsor Castle,' replied the news organiser. 'It's on fire.'

'Oh, my God!' I shouted. 'How bad?'

'They can see the smoke from the motorway. Where are you?'

'Well, you won't believe this,' I moaned. 'I'm in Buckingham Palace, and no one told me the bloody Castle was on fire! I'll be right there.'

I glowered at Charles and ran out of the Palace. As I drove towards Windsor, I suspected that by the time I arrived there'd be nothing much to see; perhaps a blackened window or two, but no real damage. First reports on stories like this were all too often exaggerated; the fire was certain to be out by now.

It was therefore with a sense of true shock that I saw the smoke billowing from the roof of the Castle from at least a mile away. I rang the desk to tell them as I raced along the motorway, my heart thumping, supremely aware that this was a colossal news story. It also occurred to me that I was wearing an uncommonly splendid pair of red suede ankle boots, with three-inch stiletto heels. Quite apart from the fact that they were brand new and I was probably going to ruin them, they were starkly unsuitable for the job in hand. But there was nothing I could do about that now.

I parked at the bottom of the hill and ran up to the Castle. Cameramen were converging on Windsor by the second, and it took a few moments to find the BBC crews. Our outside-broadcast truck was on the way, but it would be an hour or so yet before we could send pictures direct. In the meantime, dispatch riders were ferrying the tapes back to TV Centre as quickly as possible. The air was thick with acrid smoke and, despite the best efforts of dozens of firefighters, new pockets of flame kept springing up through the Castle walls. To my untutored eye, this was a fire that was very far from under control.

I began gathering what facts I could. Considering that the fire was still raging, the media were given surprisingly good access. We were ushered into the courtyard overlooking the wing of the Castle that was worst affected. A press officer gave us the latest information: St George's Hall was gutted, but a human chain of volunteers – including Prince Andrew – had succeeded in saving many of the artefacts. Paintings, pieces of armour, weapons and works of art had been passed along the chain to safety. The Queen wasn't there when the fire broke out but, we were told, she was 'very upset'.

In my absurd stilettos, I tottered up and down the hill half a dozen times that afternoon. It was 20 November – the Queen's wedding anniversary – and the fire seemed to rage all the more vigorously in the gloom of a wet winter's day. At least twice, just as I'd staggered to the bottom of the hill, a producer rang me to say there was about to be another briefing at the top. Breathlessly, I retraced my steps and arrived, on one of those occasions, in the nick of time to listen to a graphic account of the fire from none other than the Duke of York.

'I was doing some research in a room in another part of the Castle,' he announced to the bank of cameras and reporters. 'The horror is that it took hold so quickly. Everywhere is full of smoke and flames – it's a nasty mess in there.'

'We were told that your mother was very upset. How is she now?' I shouted.

'Her Majesty', the Prince answered pointedly, 'is profoundly shocked. I have spoken to Her Majesty and she is devastated.'

It seemed a peculiarly formal way to speak about your mother, but we all appreciated that the Prince had at least taken the trouble to talk to us.

At the bottom of the hill the edit van and our satellite truck were now set up and waiting for me to deliver the goods: a script and some instructions about which pictures to use. We had some stunning shots, but there were so many to look through – and so little time before the *Six o'Clock News*. A crucial advantage on occasions like this is to have a picture editor who is meticulous about logging all the shots as they come in. You may find you have ten or fifteen tapes in the van; there's often simply not enough time for the reporter to look at them all and write a script. I was lucky on that day, and, as I climbed into the van, I could see that the picture editor already had several tapes neatly lined up and logged. I slid the door closed and entered that period of intense concentration and suppressed panic which – hopefully – ends with a report ready for broadcast. We breathed a sigh of relief as our piece successfully led the news but, as we shivered in the damp and cold darkness, the fire was still raging behind us, and the *Nine o'Clock News* was only two and a half hours away.

I ran back up the hill to get the latest information and bring yet more shots down to the van. I hadn't eaten since breakfast

– nor had anyone else. We'd had one cup of coffee brought to us at the van and I felt dehydrated, but that was probably just as well because there'd been no chance to find a loo either. When youngsters ask me what they need to do to become a journalist, I often tell them: 'Make sure you've got a strong bladder.'

The edit for the *Nine o'Clock News* turned out to be far more desperate than the earlier one. As vital seconds ticked away and we still had the final shots to lay, my head began to throb. I scribbled the last few words of my script in my rain-sodden notebook and dug deep into the chaos of my handbag in search of some powder. I had to go live on the news immediately after my report and I knew I looked a wreck. But this was no time for vanity.

'Lay those shots and send it as quickly as you can,' I barked at the picture editor as I jumped out of the van, my stilettos sinking inexorably into the mud.

Flames shooting out of the Castle's Brunswick Tower made a dramatic backdrop to my live spot. I had no idea what I was going to be asked by the presenter back in the warm studio, but I remember standing there, in my ruined red boots, trying not to tremble with tiredness and cold. I just hope that I was reasonably articulate. Eventually, after giving a brief update on *Newsnight*, we were released from duty and allowed to wend our way home. It had been a sad day at the Castle in many ways, but once again I had been privileged to have a ringside seat on a snippet of history.

The house was silent when I arrived home. Jim and Emma were sleeping peacefully; they probably hadn't even watched the news. Their lives had been busy, no doubt, with playgroups and expeditions to the park. And that was really far more important for them. It also put things very firmly in perspective for me.

Back at the Castle the next day, the drizzle had turned to driving rain, making the blackened mess look even more miserable. We spent another long, cold day there as firemen struggled to deal with dozens of hot spots inside, and smoke continued to drift up into the grey sky. Matters were made worse when the Heritage Secretary, Peter Brooke, declared that the government would foot the bill for the restoration of the Castle. His words provoked an almost immediate public outcry. To my eye, the whole gloomy scene was encapsulated in one small, involuntary action by the Queen as, in Wellington boots and headscarf, she surveyed the damage to her home. As she picked her way carefully across the courtyard, which was littered with debris, she sneezed violently, her head jerking forward to rest, briefly, on her chest. For a moment she looked like any other vulnerable elderly woman, weighed down by the woes of a personal tragedy.

That impression was emphatically reinforced four days later, when the Queen arrived at Guildhall for a celebration lunch to mark her forty years on the throne. The argument about who should pay for the damage to the Castle had thundered on – almost as ferociously as the fire itself. Harsh comparisons had been made between the misfortunes of a Queen who had lost part of one of her homes and families who were left with nothing after a fire. It was a bruising time for the monarchy.

To my surprise and delight, I was invited to the Guildhall lunch as a guest as well as a reporter. It necessitated a rapid search for a hat, which I duly secured in time to jump in a taxi. As I stepped out at Guildhall, a television crew rushed up to me: 'Good to see you, Valerie,' they said. 'Could we have a word about today's event?'

I laughed to myself, knowing exactly what had happened. Yet

again I had been mistaken for Valerie Singleton. It's a recurrent theme in my life, and – having chatted to Valerie about it – I find she experiences the same problem in reverse. I suppose we do look similar and, as I have always regarded her as a very handsome woman, I'm flattered by the comparison.

Having set the camera crew right about my true identity, I went into Guildhall for what turned out to be another historic event. I'd been forewarned that the Queen's speech would be 'of interest', but no one had suggested that it was going to be dramatic.

As she stood up to speak, a diminutive figure in the grand hall where the great and good of the City of London were gathered, her voice was hoarse and cracked. Evidently, that sneeze at Windsor had been the precursor to something more serious.

'My Lord Mayor,' she began. 'Could I say first how delighted I am that the Lady Mayoress is here today.'

I had switched, instantly, from guest mode to correspondent; my pen was poised, my notebook ready. She went on to talk about her memories of Guildhall – the routine stuff of a speech on such occasions. But, abruptly, she changed tack.

'Nineteen ninety-two is not a year on which I shall look back with undiluted pleasure,' she said in her small, wounded voice. I scribbled furiously and looked up anxiously to the balcony to check that my cameraman was recording every syllable. 'In the words of one of my more sympathetic correspondents, it has turned out to be an "annus horribilis".'

This was an unusually personal remark for the Queen. It was also the perfect sound-bite. She, of course, would have been powerfully aware that the annus was about to become even more horribilis, as lawyers for her eldest son and daughter-in-law put the finishing touches to their separation terms.

'I sometimes wonder', she continued, 'how future generations will judge the events of this tumultuous year. I dare say that history will take a slightly more moderate view than that of some contemporary commentators.'

This was an admission of how sharply she had been stung by the stream of criticism directed at the Royal Family during the course of that torrid year. No one stirred in the great hall; everyone was spellbound by the Queen.

'There can be no doubt', she went on, her voice straining, 'that criticism is good for people and institutions that are part of public life. No institution – City, monarchy, whatever – should expect to be free from the scrutiny of those who give it their loyalty and support, not to mention those who don't. But we are all part of the same fabric of our national society, and that scrutiny, by one part of another, can be just as effective if it is made with a touch of gentleness, good humour and understanding.'

This was a recognition that the monarchy was not beyond rebuke, though clearly the manner of that rebuke had been hurtful. By now my pager, silently strapped to my waist, was vibrating. Word had already reached the news desk that this was a weighty speech, one that would lead the evening bulletins. I ignored the urgent throbbing of the machine and went on scribbling until the Queen had finished. She sat down to sympathetic and heartfelt applause; everyone knew they'd witnessed a unique occasion. I had to get out as fast as possible.

'Sorry – must rush. Lovely to have met you,' I apologised as I grabbed my possessions and brushed past my fellow lunch guests.

Once outside, I phoned the news desk; they wanted as

much as I could give them as quickly as was feasible. For the rest of that day my feet didn't touch the ground, as the Queen's annus horribilis speech became part of the annals of my broadcasting career. I eventually arrived home, tired and rather dishevelled, my battered Guildhall hat in my hand. It had been a long lunch.

There was to be no respite that year, either for the Royal Family or for the correspondents who followed their every move. The public baying, if not for royal blood then for royal money, had not abated. Two days after the Guildhall speech, my pager brought me screeching to a halt on the way to a meeting with some friends. It was a message from Charles Anson at the Palace. I rang him immediately.

'Jennie,' his voice was as deceptively soothing as always, 'I thought you'd like to know that the Queen has asked the Prime Minister to consider ways in which she might voluntarily pay income tax.'

Whoosh! Out of the car window flew all my plans for the rest of the day. My choke chain was strangling me again. Silly me! Of course, I wasn't going to be allowed to meet my friends; of course, I couldn't expect to go home, put my baby to bed and have supper with my husband. Oh, no! I was being dragged to work again.

I turned the car towards Television Centre and listened to Charles telling me more about the tax plans and the proposed change in the Civil List. Every now and again I pulled over to the side of the road to make some notes. The Palace insisted that the proposals had been hatched some months previously and were not in any way a kneejerk reaction to the public clamour about who would pay for the restoration of Windsor Castle. Few believed them.

In the dying weeks of the year, my choke chain began to work overtime. On 4 December the report into the Windsor Castle fire was published, which kept me busy all day. It was a Friday and the end of a long week, but it was satisfying to finish with a story that made the headlines. I drove home after the *Nine o'Clock News*, looking forward to the weekend. My parents were coming to lunch on Saturday and we were planning a quiet day. Now, I don't consider myself to be particularly dense, but it took me an inordinately long time in this job to learn the hard lesson of never making promises to my family and friends.

At least, this time, the call came at a reasonably civilised hour. We were having breakfast; Emma extricated herself from my knee and raced over to pick up the receiver. I carried on with my coffee, certain that it was my mother checking the arrangements.

'They want Mummy,' said Emma accusingly. My heart sank as I walked over to the phone, already planning the cancellation of the day's activities.

'Sorry to disturb you on your day off.' The familiar tones of the news organiser confirmed my fears.

'It's the Princess Royal. It looks as if she's getting married again. Could you check it out, please?'

I put down my coffee and started making calls. It was the usual scenario from the Palace. Nothing was being said officially but, on the other hand, they weren't denying the reports. There were clear indications that I would not make a fool of myself if I ran with the story. The details, it seemed, would be announced later in the week. I rang my parents and told them not to bother coming, kissed Jim and Emma goodbye and, rather resentfully, set off for work. Once again, we found ourselves strapped by a lack of pictures, and poor Tim Laurence appeared again before millions of BBC viewers in the only shot we had of him – sidling out of camera range behind his front door. But at least we persuaded some of his neighbours in Winchester to talk to us.

'Splendid news,' they chorused. 'He's a first-rate chap.'

Sunday brought new revelations about where the wedding was likely to take place. The hot money was on Crathie Church near Balmoral. Abandoning all hopes of a weekend, I trundled into work again to report on the latest developments. On Monday, the Palace confirmed the arrangements and we managed to secure a brief interview with the bridegroom's proud mother: I was off and running again with another news story. There was also a mountain of planning to be done for the wedding, which, we learned, was going to be held in just five days' time, on Saturday. It all seemed extraordinarily hasty but, if the Princess had had her way, none of the media would have been told at all. We booked flights to Aberdeen and rooms in a hotel as close as possible to Balmoral.

Tuesday promised some respite, or so I thought. The papers, though, had a different idea.

'Queen Mother snubs Anne,' they trumpeted in unison. 'She refuses to attend Scottish wedding.'

The story demanded my attention throughout that day. The official line was that the Queen Mother hadn't yet decided whether she would be able to go to the wedding. There were suggestions that the flight would be too much for her – and yet she frequently flew to her homes in Scotland. There were vehement denials that her absence would be any kind of snub to her granddaughter, but there was a diplomatic silence when I suggested that it was the thorny issue of divorcees remarrying that lay behind her reluctance to travel. The Queen Mother is first and foremost a traditionalist. I have been told that, even after the divorce of her own daughter, three of her grandchildren and numerous other relatives and friends, she insists sometimes that 'she has never met a divorced person'. In the event, the whole debate became irrelevant, because the Queen Mother did indeed fly north for the Princess's wedding.

By Wednesday – my tenth straight day of work – I was feeling a little weary. But from the second my pager started bleeping at me I quickly realised that this was not a day to complain of fatigue. The office was buzzing with rumours. The source of these rumours was Westminster, which, as we all know, leaks like a sieve. Reports there were rife that the Prime Minister would be making a statement to the Commons that afternoon that would be of national – and royal – significance. I rang the Palace. Everyone, it seemed, was 'in a meeting'. I kept on ringing. Eventually, Charles Anson came on the line.

'Charles, what's going on?' I demanded. 'Our political people say Major's going to be announcing something big this afternoon. What's up?'

'I can't confirm anything right now,' he replied, sounding rather more urgent than usual. 'But it is likely that the Prime Minister will have something to say.'

'Everyone says it's about the Prince and Princess of Wales,' I cut in. 'Is it separation at last?'

'Well, I can't tell you that, Jennie. But it is certainly a possibility that it might be about the future of the Prince and Princess.'

The newsroom went into full-alert mode. We began sending camera crews out to all the obvious locations. Incredibly, the Princess was on an official engagement in Tyneside. We made sure we had enough cameras on her. We sent crews far and wide and started drawing up lists of possible interviewees to assess the implications of a marriage breakdown. I kept close to my phone; Charles had told me he would call with more news when he could.

At 1.45 he rang to tell me that, although nothing had yet been confirmed (a caveat which I took with the intended pinch of salt), we could be talking about a formal acknowledgement that the marriage of the Prince and Princess was over in all but name. We could 'quite possibly' be about to hear that separate living arrangements were being organised.

'It's no secret', confided Charles, 'that the marriage has been in severe difficulties for many years now.'

It may have been no secret, I thought, but this was the very first time that the Palace had acknowledged it. He then instructed me to come to the Palace at 2.45 that afternoon for a briefing, which would not end until after 3.30. That, of course, was the appointed time for statements to the Commons. And this, I quickly realised, was a carefully coordinated operation between Downing Street and the Palace.

My stress levels were running high as the taxi dropped me off outside the Palace gates. I had just enough time to check that everything was ready across the road, where the TV crews from all the British, and several foreign, networks were putting up their lights in preparation.

'I'll be out the second they let me,' I told the cameraman and producer. 'We're going to be locked in the room until Major has finished talking in the Commons. Make sure we're ready to roll just as soon as I get back here.'

With a deep breath I marched back across Constitution Hill to the Palace. The police at the gates were expecting me.

'Afternoon, Miss Bond,' they said, with a look that seemed to say: 'We're all in for a right song and dance now.'

My fellow correspondents from BBC Radio, ITN, Sky and the Press Association were gathered in the tiny waiting room just inside the Privy Purse door. We were all experienced journalists, and friends as well. Normally, we'd be laughing and joking with each other; on that afternoon, though, we were lost in our own thoughts, each of us considering how we would measure up to the task of reporting the moment of history we were about to witness.

Shortly after 3 p.m. we were ushered into Charles Anson's office by one of the footmen. This added an air of extreme formality to the occasion (usually Charles would come out to greet us himself). And there was no mistaking the gravity of the mood inside. Waiting there, like two adversaries in a courtroom, were the Prince's private secretary, Richard Aylard, and the Princess's, Patrick Jephson. I knew both of them well, but this was no time for pleasantries. Between them sat Charles Anson, now charged with one of the most delicate assignments of his career as the Queen's press secretary.

As John Major rose before the House to tell MPs and the watching world that the fairy-tale marriage was over, we heard the same message from the men who had been in the eye of the storm. After the basic facts had been given, we were invited to ask questions. All of us felt the weight of responsibility that was on us; it was imperative that we extracted as much information as possible about the consequences of this sombre turn of events. But the answers had been meticulously drafted in advance and were read from prepared sheets of paper.

'Were there any third parties involved?' we asked.

It took a moment or two for them to locate the answer. When the right paragraph had been found, we were assured that there was no one else involved in the marriage breakdown. Other questions elicited equally studied responses, some of which were quite hard to digest. Despite the acrimony of recent months, we were told, the Prince and Princess remained 'fond and supportive' of one another and, in theory at least, the Princess could still become Queen.

Only when the signal had been given that the Prime Minister had finished speaking were we allowed to bolt out of the door and sprint to our camera positions. It was impossible to stay calm; my heart was pulsating so violently I'm surprised the microphone didn't pick up the noise, my nervous nose was threatening to soak my notes, and the crowds of onlookers around our cameras were growing by the minute.

Somehow, I got through that first report. As always, once you get started you find you have plenty to say, and this was a story that was not short of drama. But there was no time to pause for thought; the *Six o'Clock News* had to be tackled next, and then the *Nine o'Clock News*. I felt drained of all energy by the time I came to the end of those commitments. But before I could even think of going home *Breakfast* rang to demand their pound of flesh for the morning. There would be no time to rest or remind Emma that I was her mummy until the shock and furore of the royal separation had dissipated. And I had to fly to Scotland in forty-eight hours.

Those hours flew by in a blur of bulletins, each with its own demands on my time and knowledge. When we finally got on the plane, I was relieved to escape from the maelstrom of life around the Palace – if only for a couple of days. I'd had about fifteen minutes to throw some clothes into a suitcase, kiss Emma goodbye and rush to the airport. By now I was running on neat adrenalin; I seemed to have been on every bulletin for the past fortnight, and the next target was a piece about preparations for the wedding. From the airport we went straight to Ballater, the nearest town to Crathie Church, to see what we could find.

The wedding of the Princess Royal was the only bright spot in a year of unmitigated gloom for the Royal Family. The media were kept at arm's length, however, and I saw nothing of the bride or groom. Instead, I spent that chill December day in the back of our outside-broadcast truck, just down the hill from the church, compiling my reports from the pictures that were brought to us from a film crew commissioned by the Royal Family. I was absurdly tired after the traumas of the past two weeks, and I fear my script was uninspired. One of my young bosses had come up from London to lend a hand and, as the early winter night drew in, she gamely organised some food and coffee for us in the truck. Meanwhile, as the minutes ticked by to our deadline, I was hoping she hadn't noticed that I was struggling with writer's block. Halfway through my script, I simply could not think of anything else to say about this low-key wedding of which I had neither seen nor heard anything. A silence fell among the assembled cameramen, producers and technicians in the truck. In the middle of them, I sat with my pen poised over the scribble that passed for a script; the picture editor twiddled with his machine, pointedly waiting for me to deliver some pearls of wisdom to match the footage. But the more they stood and stared – desperately trying to appear nonchalant – the worse the block became. I put down a few words just to break the tension. They were nonsense. I crossed them out. No one dared say anything as slow panic crept through us all. At this rate we were going to miss the satellite feed to London.

Nowadays, if I have trouble with a word or a sentence, I simply ask for suggestions from the rest of the team. Someone will always come up with an idea which at least gets my brain rolling again. But on that Saturday I sat in stubborn silence, frozen in a state of impotence, and doubly embarrassed because one of my bosses was there. Eventually – and in the nick of time – I snapped out of it and found a form of words to finish the script. The wedding report winged its way to London, and I sat back feeling more relieved than I was willing to allow anyone to see.

The annus horribilis had left the Royal Family wounded and weakened. It had left me truly blooded as a royal correspondent – and shattered. But it had one final sting in its tail. Two days before Christmas, the Queen's Christmas message was leaked to a newspaper. It is a matter of tradition, and great pride to the Queen, that her seasonal speech remains a closely guarded secret until Christmas Day. She was said to be 'very distressed' by the leak – so much so that she authorised legal proceedings to sue the paper for breach of copyright. It was a desolate end to a year that had proved an emotional roller-coaster for everyone involved.

CHAPTER SEVEN

In search of calmer waters

While the Royal Family retreated to Sandringham to lick their wounds over the festive period, I collapsed into the bosom of my own family. Christmas is a magical time when you have a two-year-old in the house. Suddenly, Rudolph rides again, and all the fairy lights, the tinsel and the carols have renewed meaning. Although generally I try to leave the stresses and strains of the job at the front door, I'm not always successful and, after the year I'd just had, it was particularly hard. Nevertheless, I threw myself into the joys of Christmas, which we always share with my two sisters, their offspring and our parents. I come from a close and loving family who have been a constant source of encouragement as they watch me flit around the world.

Surrounded by nephews and nieces, with a mountain of presents under the Christmas tree, I sat by a huge log fire in my sister's farmhouse and watched Emma's face sparkling with sheer uncomplicated happiness. The traumas of the past twelve months seemed a million miles away. A contented family life is a crucial safeguard against a job that can threaten to consume you. My parents have always been stalwart supporters of everything I do; they've sat through hundreds of hours of news bulletins just to catch a glimpse of me, and offered me lavish praise – or, occasionally, gentle criticism. They've listened to me moan and whinge, berate my bosses or royalty and have offered me tea and sympathy. But an equally important perspective comes from Jim and Emma, who rarely watch anything I do. They remind me that my professional disappointments and disasters are of conspicuously little relevance to the vast majority of this country.

This was reaffirmed a few years ago, in Ireland, when Prince Charles was making an important speech at Dublin Castle. He was due to start at 9 o'clock, just as the main evening news went on air. My producer and I took a calculated gamble that, as long as the rest of my report was finished, we could squeeze in a few seconds of the Prince's address at the last moment. The editor of the *Nine o'Clock News* agreed that it was a risk worth taking. We planned the operation with precision; we had a good idea of what the Prince was going to say and, the instant he had said it, a producer would whip the tape out of the camera and sprint to our edit van parked immediately outside the Castle. We would finish the edit by 9.15, bounce it over to London on our satellite, and it would make its allotted slot in the bulletin at 9.21.

By 9 o'clock, tension in the edit van was running high. My report was ready for broadcast – except for a terrifying black hole that awaited the Prince's words. At 9.07 a clatter of footsteps and a burst of heavy breathing signalled the arrival of our producer, who'd run the length of the Castle to bring us the tape. My picture editor worked like a demon; the piece was finished a couple of minutes ahead of schedule and we fired it off to London. A sense of elation swept through the edit van; we hugged one another and sat down to watch the last ten minutes of the news bulletin. At 9.21 I felt the flicker of excitement that still courses through my body whenever a report of mine is about to be broadcast. I leaned back to enjoy it. But in the London studio, Peter Sissons introduced a report about something quite different. I began to feel edgy: had they simply moved my piece down the running order or was there a problem that no one had told me about? As the minutes ticked by with no sign of the Prince, the awful realisation dawned on me that something had gone drastically wrong.

'And that's all from the *Nine o'Clock News* tonight,' said Peter. 'Good night.'

The closing music rang through the edit van as we sat in glum silence, staring at one another.

'What the *hell* can have happened?' I asked blankly as I wrenched the phone off its cradle and furiously dialled the news desk.

The answer took a while to establish. In the end, an unfortunate picture editor in London admitted that there had been a minuscule satellite glitch on the tape. Although, as he later conceded, it would have been perfectly acceptable to broadcast, he had taken it on himself to try to fix it. In so doing, he had accidentally erased part of my voice track and had spent the final ten minutes of the bulletin frantically trying to salvage something of the piece. To no avail. The report was ruined, and all our efforts had been wasted.

I sat on the steps of Dublin Castle and wept. After a few moments of self-indulgence, I decided to try to cheer myself up by ringing home. Jim answered the phone; Emma had just gone to sleep after a wonderful day they'd shared together – playing and reading, walking and talking. He told me all about it in great detail, waxing lyrical about the joys of fatherhood. It was about twenty minutes into this rather one-sided conversation that he finally asked: 'And how about you? Everything OK?'

By then my minor mishap of a missed television report seemed unimportant.

'Oh,' I replied, trying to sound carefree, 'I was doing a report about the Prince in Dublin, but it didn't make it.'

'Well,' said my ever-tactful husband, 'I didn't watch the news, so I didn't miss it. In fact, I didn't even know he was in Dublin tonight.'

I blew my nose, wiped the last tears away and chuckled to myself. He was quite right, of course. It was a complete delusion to imagine, as I briefly had, that 90 per cent of the population were sitting, aghast, in front of their televisions debating why Jennie Bond's report about the Prince of Wales had failed to appear on the news. Thanks to my husband's nonchalance, my perspective had been restored.

It wasn't long before the royal roadshow veered off the rails again. The first misfortune came before 1993 was even one week old: Princess Margaret developed pneumonia, and I was dispatched to my chilly post on the pavement outside the King Edward VII Hospital for Officers. There I joined the usual troupe of royal reporters and photographers, and we spent a convivial few hours exchanging Christmas stories as we stamped our feet in a fruitless effort to keep warm. Luckily, though, the Princess's illness proved not too severe, ensuring that my sojourn at the hospital was not prolonged.

A week later a bombshell suggested that the annus horribilis was set to become plural: Camillagate exploded on to the front pages. Once again, someone had tapped into the mobile phone system and hit the jackpot. The private and extremely intimate conversation between Prince Charles and Camilla Parker Bowles that was now splattered over acres of newsprint was not only embarrassing but also highly damaging. Although some commentators defended the Prince, saying the tape showed a man who was loving, humorous and sexy, others denounced him as filthy, disgusting and not fit to be King. This was the Prince's Squidgygate – with bells on.

My dawn chorus – the phone and pager – had duly summoned me to work. Just as with the recording of Diana's conversation with James Gilbey, we were faced with the dilemma of how to tell the story without infringing the Prince's right to privacy. We gave it a great deal of thought – and with good reason, for over the next few days the Prince and Mrs Parker Bowles were asked by the Press Complaints Commission whether they felt their privacy had indeed been invaded. I wrote my script with immense care and had to submit it to the newsroom hierarchy for approval. It was a delicate balance, but I hope we succeeded in analysing the impact of what had been said without going into specific details of the conversation. I drove home late, imagining the horror of such a deeply personal exchange becoming lurid public property. I felt sorry for the Prince, and wondered how he would ever find the courage to face the crowds again.

But most news is extraordinarily ephemeral. After the inevitable and very funny rash of cartoons and jokes about the Prince – most of them featuring him reincarnated as various female sanitary products – the story more or less faded away. But it *did* leave residual damage. The Prince, who after the formal breakdown of his marriage must have dared to hope that the worst was over, now faced an uphill battle to regain respect. At the time of the separation, the world had been told that there were no third parties involved. Now, though, the depth of the Prince's feelings for Mrs Parker Bowles was a matter of public record, there for the entire world to see. Those feelings were clearly long-standing, for the conversation had been recorded a full four years earlier. He hadn't yet admitted it publicly, but no one could now seriously doubt that the Prince had committed adultery.

After such a prurient interlude, it was a welcome diversion from matters royal to find myself presenting the news with increasing regularity. As my face became more familiar, so, too, did the viewers. They began to write to me with disarming frankness. One of my earliest and most treasured letters came from an anonymous contributor whom I always imagine to be a man. It was curt and painfully to the point. He wrote:

Dear Madam,
I believe you are Jewish. Has anyone ever told you that
you resemble a wart hog?
Yours sincerely . . .

Faintly hurt, and then vastly amused, I ran to some of my Jewish friends (as it happens, I am not Jewish) and beseeched them to tell me that 'a wart hog' was some form of goddess in Hebrew mythology. Sadly, they were unable to do so, but I still regard it as one of the finest letters I've ever received.

Another that I kept for many years took a similar and even more fantastic animal slant. Though it stung me, I have to admit that it captured perfectly the look I sometimes unwittingly adopt when the tension of the job gets through to my face: 'I'd like to point out that you look like a horse that has eaten a bucket of sour plums soaked in iced vinegar.'

It is clear from these letters that my tactic of trying to think friendly, witty thoughts immediately before going on air does not always have the desired effect. But you'd go berserk if you believed everything 'the viewer' writes; the only salvation is to remember that the abusive letters are no more credible than those that extol your dazzling beauty and charm.

Despite the horrors of the annus horribilis, we had managed to take our short break in the West Country. It was a part of the world that sang to our souls. Now, in the slightly calmer waters of a new royal year, we decided to revisit the house where we'd so happily stayed – along with the cirl buntings in the cow-shed. This time, though, we were going in the middle of a raw February, hardly conducive to any extended bird-watching. But it was *so* good to be out of London, and the wood-burning stove kept us snug while the stormy seas lashed the coast outside.

We'd struck up a pleasant friendship with the owners of the house, so when they suggested that we should take a look at a run-down old barracks hut on their land that they were planning to sell, we were delighted to go along. On a bleak, grey day we walked up the hill to the long wooden hut, sitting in its own five-acre valley by the sea. Inside, it was all but derelict: indeed, the rats had already begun an assault on some of the rooms. Nevertheless, Jim and I were transfixed by the beauty of the valley and the views down to the sea. We looked at one another and had a simultaneous thought. With a liberal splash of tender loving care, this could be an idyllic holiday home.

The remainder of our stay in Devon was ruined. We spent sleepless nights talking over whether it would be madness to spend our life savings on this strangely wonderful piece of land with its bizarre dwelling. It was compellingly remote; it was at least four hours' drive from London; my pager and mobile phone didn't work down there – and I was meant to be permanently on call. It was a crazy proposition, but as the days passed we realised it was irresistible. We threw caution – and all our money – to the wind and put in our bid for the old barracks hut.

Instantly, life moved up another gear. Though we were incredibly lucky to be the prospective owners of a second home, it was one that needed a huge amount of work and meant we'd now be busier than ever. Exhausted by the emotional trauma of gambling away all that we had in the world, I returned to work just in time to head off to Nepal for Diana's first solo overseas tour since her separation.

This time I made sure that I had a picture editor, a producer and a cameraman. We flew out from Heathrow with our platoon of silver boxes, and I immersed myself in a mountain of notes and press releases about the far-flung kingdom of Nepal. I never feel properly prepared for a royal tour unless I have done my homework, and the flight out is the ideal time to study the politics, history and economics of our destination.

Kathmandu: the word breathes adventure and speaks of the exotic. I didn't know what to expect and, as always, I relished the new sights, smells and sounds of a land I had never before visited. As the press bus drove us from the airport to the hotel, my eye was drawn not only to the architecture but also to the tiny roadside shops where a forest of suede and leather jackets hung from awnings. One, in particular, made an impression – a vivid green suede coat, which would soon prove more than a match for my willpower, and which still has pride of place in my wardrobe. This, though, was no shopping trip. There was a great deal of news interest in the Princess's visit even before she set out: was this the start of a new go-it-alone career for her, or were we about to witness her last major foreign tour? The news desk's appetite was whetted still further when she arrived amid a welter of new allegations about her relationship with James Gilbey, the man featured in the Squidgygate tape.

As her plane touched down, the band struck up a series of tunes, including 'Colonel Bogey', but there was no national anthem. The Princess was met by Nepal's Crown Prince and given the highest honour for a visiting dignitary: a reception committee made up of five virginal girls, representing the living goddess, the Kumari. Legend has it that if the Kumari is ever in a bad mood, it is an ominous sign for the country. In the days preceding the Princess's visit, however, the goddess was said to have been in an excellent mood. The welcome seemed to me to have gone off very smoothly; the Crown Prince was assiduous in his attention, schoolchildren in colourful uniforms waved their flags and the Princess was smiling. But I soon discovered that my fellow reporters were getting hot under the collar about the lack of the national anthem. Was this a deliberate snub to the Princess? Was it a Palace directive aimed at downgrading her visit, now that she was separated from the heir to the throne? Frantic attempts ensued to get a response from British officials on the ground. They insisted that there had been no snub; this was a working visit and, as such, did not require the same level of protocol. Nevertheless, the missing anthem was headline news in the papers back home. In the absence of any concrete proof for either side of the argument, I took the safest route of reporting both viewpoints without reaching any conclusion myself.

Most people seem to imagine that the job of a royal correspondent is breathtakingly glamorous. And it *was* bewitching to be in

Nepal with the Princess of Wales. Sadly, though, there is always so much to worry about that we see precious little of where we've been and, after the sixth hotel in seven days, we remember even less. Part of my job is to help ensure that we get good, clear shots of the Royal Family. To achieve that, one piece of equipment is essential: a ladder. But standing on a ladder in the middle of a large and excitable crowd while balancing a heavy camera on your shoulder is not easy. It's up to me to protect my cameraman while he concentrates on the action below. The crowds move quickly and with frightening force as soon as their royal quarry appears, and it's vital to keep that ladder steady. The result of this is that I spend an astounding proportion of any royal tour with my arms firmly wrapped around my cameraman's thighs. The view ahead is generally his backside – unless, of course, he's facing the other way. And that sight is my main memory of many fine cities around the globe.

A royal tour also involves a great deal of planning, both in the UK before we leave and on the ground. We usually fly out a day or two ahead, partly to do previews of the tour but also to attend briefings from royal officials. Because the Palace operates a pool system at so many locations, our producers – from the BBC, ITN and Sky – have to battle it out for hours, deciding whose camera will go where. They also have to organise transport to get the dozens of tapes back to base as quickly as possible so that they can be copied and used by all of us. We try to book three hotel rooms that are either adjoining or at least on the same floor, so that our picture editors can work alongside one another. There's always a great deal of frantic sprinting between the edit suites as deadlines loom. If there's time, we also drive out to the television station to check that it has everything we'll need to feed our reports by satellite. It's important, too, to get

Charles and Diana at the Opera House in Sydney, 1988.
My first royal tour (TIM GRAHAM)

Diana, potently alone and feeling
unloved. At the Taj Mahal 1992
(PHOTOGRAPHERS INTERNATIONAL)

The missed kiss that said it all. At a
polo match in Jaipur 1992
(PHOTOGRAPHERS INTERNATIONAL)

'It's Windsor Castle,' the news organiser said. 'It's on fire.'
(PHOTOGRAPHERS INTERNATIONAL)

In a small, cracked voice the Queen stood up to say
it had been an 'annus horribilis'. Guildhall 1992
(TIM GRAHAM)

The Queen and President Yeltsin
in Red Square, Moscow 1994
(CAMERA PRESS)

Diana the show-stopper; this time in Tokyo. 1995
(TIM GRAHAM)

In search of the perfect script. Writing and editing a report
in the picture editor's hotel room. Moscow 1994.

The Queen with Bishop Desmond Tutu
and President Mandela. South Africa 1995

an idea of how long the journey to the TV station will take – and to make allowances for rush-hour traffic.

No matter how firm the correspondent's resolve to finish a report well before the deadline, ensuring a calm and unflustered drive to the satellite point, you can bet your bottom dollar that most of us will be editing up to and beyond the 'final and non-negotiable' cut-off time designated by the producer. As the seconds tick by, the correspondent and picture editor work as a tightly knit twosome – intent on making the report as perfect as possible, despite the entreaties of the producer simply 'to get to the bloody end'.

'Is someone holding the lift?' I shout, desperate to save a few valuable moments and oblivious to the needs of other hotel guests. 'And can you check that the driver is ready to go?'

We look at our watches, forlornly hoping that somehow time has stood still. It hasn't. The producer is getting dangerously agitated. The lift bell is pinging alarmingly as the cameraman valiantly refuses to let the door close. Finally, we put down the last shot and, with an overwhelming sense of relief, I reach my payoff: 'Jennie Bond, BBC News, Kathmandu [or wherever].'

Now it's up to the rest of them to get out of this mess I have got them into. The editor grabs the tape, hurtles out of the door and along the corridor to the waiting lift. The producer, brow furrowed, is carried along in the slipstream. I look out of the hotel window and see the taxi below, its engine revving. My team jump in, and the car screeches off across town to the television station. Alone now in the sudden calm of the room – jam-packed with equipment and littered with tapes, coffee cups and the remains of room-service snacks – I consult my watch again. The satellite booking starts in nine minutes. They have a seven-minute drive ahead, provided the traffic is light. It's going to be touch and go.

I can recall more than one occasion when the gridlock was so bad that my picture editor and I simply abandoned the taxi, grabbed the tape and galloped on foot to the satellite point. And the problems aren't over once you arrive. A multitude of technical hitches can crop up – none of which I either understand or am able to solve. Sometimes there are complaints from London that the picture quality is poor. That provokes a rash of twiddling and tweaking with buttons and switches in an effort to improve the vision. Sometimes it's the sound that's distorted by the satellite link. Further frantic fiddling follows. All the while, the clock is ticking and the time-slot we've bought is shrinking. The whole performance gives rise to so much tension, on top of the stress of the rest of the day, that I have long since given up going to the feed-point with the editor and producer. Instead, I repair to the hotel bar. It's rare, though, that we miss a feed altogether. We may have to extend the time allocated to us on the satellite but, one way or another, we usually get our reports through to London.

So it was in Nepal. The Princess, buoyed by the support of the Overseas Development Minister, Baroness Chalker, who was with her, went about her work with enthusiasm. On the second day she flew to a remote area of eastern Nepal to see the difference British aid projects were making to a tiny mountain village. Sadly, there was only room for a handful of media in the helicopter, and the only other way to get there was a twenty-hour drive followed by a two-day trek. In situations like this we have no choice but to accept that the pictures are the priority. Two or three cameramen were given helicopter seats, and the rest of us had to rely on the eyewitness account of a single reporter whose name was drawn out of a hat.

We waited by the swimming pool at the hotel in Kathmandu.

It was rather too nippy for my tropical tastes, but pleasantly relaxing to lie there knowing there was nothing to be done until the party returned from the hills. When they did we sprang into action, dubbing the pictures – which turned out to be stunning – and taking notes about all that had happened from the briefing given by the pool reporter. The Princess and Baroness Chalker had walked for three-quarters of an hour from the helicopter landing point to reach Majewa Village, eight thousand feet up. The scenery was breathtaking – as the pictures showed – but everyone, the Princess included, had found the going tough at that altitude. They'd been greeted by dancing girls who'd given them garlands, and the Princess had taken a peek into one of the primitive, mud-floor houses. As she came out, blinking in the bright sunshine, she'd uttered the immortal words: 'I'll never complain again!'

It was good television, and we worked late into the night editing and sending our report. The final evening brought the bonus of a chance to chat with the Princess herself about her impressions of the visit. Media receptions are a regular feature of most royal tours abroad. They're a prime opportunity to meet the people who are the focus of so much of our working lives. But they are also frustrating, because the very fact that they're held during the course of a busy tour means that the media are up to their eyes in work. It is, therefore, all too often a matter of making a mad dash from the edit suite to snatch half an hour at the reception. You then do your utmost to secure an introduction before it's time to race back to the edit suite.

Some receptions are more formal than others, but the Princess always injected a sense of fun into hers. She never looked anything other than sensational, and would work her way around the room, chatting and giggling with the reporters and photographers who, at other times, she would pillory for making her life a misery. She was naturally flirtatious, and knew some of the press better than others, but was keenly aware of each of us. This was my first proper encounter with her, and I was fascinated. She was vivacious, more articulate than I had expected and impressively tall. She talked about the trek up the hillside, and laughed at the memory of the small press party who'd found the going even tougher than she had.

'You should have seen them panting and puffing,' she said. 'I thought they were going to pass out.'

Events like this rarely lend themselves to more than a few minutes of jovial small talk, and they're no doubt something of an inconvenience to royalty after a day spent glad-handing hundreds of strangers. Nevertheless, they provide journalists with a rare opportunity for direct dialogue with the people we normally have to deal with through a third party. As such they are valuable.

I flew home from Nepal to a belated wedding anniversary celebration, a three-year-old exulting in the novelty of going to nursery school and a husband fretting about the inevitable complications over our house purchase. Slotting myself back into family life, I assumed my share of the trials and tribulations.

Less than three weeks later, Britain was shocked by an IRA bomb attack in the centre of Warrington. Two blasts ripped through the shopping centre, killing a three-year-old boy outright and injuring more than fifty passers-by. Four days after the attack, Prince Charles announced that he was going to visit the survivors. I threw some clothes into a bag, kissed the family goodbye and headed north. It was a bleak assignment. Warrington was still reeling from the sheer horror of what had happened. Outside the General Hospital, a small crowd did their best to raise a cheer as the Prince's car drew up. There was little he could do or say that would be of any practical help either to the bereaved or the survivors of such an atrocity. But at times of crisis, a visit by a senior member of the Royal Family seems not only to boost the local community but to be symbolic of the nation's sense of outrage and sorrow.

For the media, events like this demand extreme sensitivity. We are there to record the grim facts and their repercussions, but we have to make careful judgements about how far to go without intruding on personal grief. A line of cameras awaited Prince Charles as he left the hospital two hours later. Any comment on the bombing itself would clearly be a political minefield for him, but he *did* make a point of expressing his admiration for the survivors he'd seen. One, in particular, a thirty-three-year-old woman who had lost one of her legs in the explosion, had made a deep impression on the Prince: 'She simply made my day,' he told us. 'Despite her appalling injuries she has such a wonderful, positive attitude.'

I filed my report and, with the producer and crew, set off to our hotel for the night. It was too late to drive home and, in any case, the news desk hadn't yet decided whether we would be needed again the following day. Our mood was unusually subdued; you can't cover stories like this without experiencing the effects. Before turning in for an early night I phoned home – feeling more than usually blessed to have a healthy, happy family.

The next day brought cruel news for the relatives of another of the Warrington victims. It was also a day that stands out in my memory as one of the most humbling of my career as a reporter. I had been sent back to the General Hospital when the news organiser called me.

'Can you leave what you're doing and get over to Walton Hospital in Liverpool as quickly as you can?' she asked. 'There's going to be an announcement about Tim Parry any minute now.'

Twelve-year-old Timothy Parry had taken the full force of the IRA bomb blast and had been hanging on to life by the most tenuous thread. The news that there was to be an announcement was ominous. I drove to Liverpool as fast as I could, shouting to other motorists whenever I stopped at traffic lights to check that I was heading the right way. I arrived at the hospital just as word came through that Tim had died. I felt an emptiness seep through me. Of course, I couldn't claim to know anything about him or his family, but this hideous, unjust loss of a life full of such young promise made me shrivel inside. The suffering of his parents was unimaginable.

It was their extraordinary grace and dignity in the face of appalling tragedy that mark that day out in my mind. Within an hour of his son's death, Colin Parry gave a news conference at which he described the agony his family had been through since the bomb had shattered their lives. But it was his determination to cling to the hope that some good would come from their loss, combined with his poignantly honest tribute to his son, that wrenched the hearts of press and public alike.

'We produced a bloody good kid,' he told the cameras. 'One of three. Tim could be an impudent little pup. But he was a great kid.'

Later, I interviewed Colin Parry at his home. His son's presence was all around us: his football memorabilia, his posters and pictures. And Mr Parry remained as civil, measured and inspirational as he had been in the immediate aftermath of Tim's death.

It had been a wretched week – and it wasn't over yet. The next day I had to cover another heart-rending event: the funeral of the youngest bomb victim, three-year-old Jonathan Ball. At such an intensely personal occasion, you can only hope as a journalist that, by tucking yourself into a corner, you can do your job without inflicting further pain. I sat in an edit van hidden away behind the church and watched most of the proceedings on a televison monitor. But I got out to watch the pathetically small coffin pass by – reducing police officers and cameramen to tears. It is not easy to write a script in such circumstances, but deadlines pay no heed to sensitivity or emotion. A report like this, with music and tributes, demands extra care and dexterous editing. *That* takes time, and we were right up against the clock as we filed my piece to London. I hope, though, that despite the pressures of the job my words did justice to the innocent child and his family who were the focus of such a numbingly distressing episode.

'The service ended with a tape recording of Michael Jackson's song "Ben",' I reported. 'It had been requested by Jonathan's family because Ben had been the favourite teddy bear of the little boy his father called "his beautiful angel".'

I returned home feeling unsettled by the suffering I had witnessed.

Before long it was time to kiss goodbye to my family again and fly off on another royal tour: to Hungary with the Queen and the Duke of Edinburgh. The press party was small but select; Diana was still the biggest story around, and a visit to Europe by the Queen could not compete. To save money, the BBC had recruited a local cameraman and producer in Budapest, so it was rather a lonely flight out. But as soon as I got to the hotel one or two familiar Fleet Street faces popped up, and I felt comfortably back with 'the pack'. Almost immediately, we were treated to a briefing by Hungary's sprightly septuagenarian leader of the time, President Göncz. His enthusiasm was infectious. The Queen had chosen Hungary for her first full state visit to a former Warsaw Pact country – and he was feeling fiercely proud. With a twinkle in his eye, he insisted that there would be no 'smiles on command' for the Queen. His new and budding democracy would not, he declared, force people to line up and cheer. But he was obviously in no doubt that they'd do so of their own free will.

He was right. When the Queen and the Duke arrived in Budapest, thousands of Hungarians turned out to see them, cheering wildly and waving their flags. Sadly, the interest from my newsroom was rather more subdued. Though we conscientiously followed the Queen wherever she went, gathering the pictures and recording pieces to camera, I had a devil of a job to get any of it on the television news. Radio showed a bit more interest, and I was able to regale listeners with stories of the lavish hospitality offered to the Queen and the Duke throughout their stay. Everything, it seemed, was done in a grand manner. When they were invited to partake of a 'simple picnic' the menu included a spit-roast calf stuffed with a turkey, stuffed with a chicken, stuffed with a pigeon which, in turn, was stuffed with quails' eggs. And all that came *after* a first course of goulash.

No wonder, then, that after such a meal the Duke joked with some British tourists in the crowd that if they stayed in Hungary much longer they'd soon become 'pot-bellied'. It was a throwaway remark made on the last day of the visit and, in my view, was not intended to cause any offence. But my newspaper colleagues were hungry for a story.

'You're *surely* not going to run with that?' I implored them as they darted around trying to establish precisely who had been the recipient of the Duke's jest.

'You can't *seriously* claim he was trying to insult Hungarians – just *look* at all the food he and the Queen have been confronted with in the past couple of days.'

One or two wavered, agreeing with me that it wasn't one of the Duke's true, classic gaffes. But it was too late. The trail had been laid and the scent was too strong.

'Duke insults pot-bellied Hungarians' entered the realms of gaffe-land and is still regularly wheeled out as an example of his undisputed lack of tact. It was one occasion, though, when I stuck to my guns and – rightly or wrongly – chose not to file a story which I believed distorted the spirit in which the remark had been made. It's ironic that, at the start of the tour, I'd had a robust conversation with the Duke, during which he'd asked me how many press were in Budapest. I told him which papers had sent staff out to cover the visit. Hands behind his back, he peered around the room picking out some of the reporters he recognised.

'Mark my words,' he said gruffly as he moved off. 'They'll make mincemeat of it by the end of the week.'

I flew home clutching a Hungarian toy witch for my little girl and wondering if my bosses would initiate a witch-hunt into why I had failed to file the pot-belly story. But news moves furiously fast; if it had ever been noticed, it was now long forgotten. In any case, very few people in the television newsroom seemed aware that I'd even *been* in Budapest.

'Diana's going to talk about bulimia.' My bleeping pager ripped into my day and flashed the message at me accusingly. Abandoning plans to pick up Emma from nursery, I jumped in the car and pointed it towards the office, phoning as I went. I had no time to get to Kensington, where the Princess was attending a conference on eating disorders. Clearly, I should have known about her speech in advance and been there; now it was a case of making up lost ground as effectively as possible. When I arrived at the Beeb, the recording of the conference was already coming into TV Centre. The Princess was on her feet and taking her place at the rostrum. She shrugged her shoulders, took a deep breath and launched into one of the most powerful and personal speeches she had made to date.

'I have it on very good authority,' she began – her huge eyes flashing as she looked around the hall in a carefully choreographed performance – 'that the quest for perfection this society demands can leave the individual gasping for breath at every turn.'

She spoke from the heart, and she spoke well. Without directly referring to any of her own problems, she left no one in any doubt that they were listening to a graphic self-portrait. She looked determined, and her confidence grew with every word.

'From early childhood,' she went on, 'many people feel they are expected to be perfect; feelings of guilt, self-revulsion and low self-esteem create in them a desire to dissolve like a Disprin.'

These were sentiments with which Diana was, sadly, only too familiar. It seemed to me to be a brave decision to use her fame to give an insight into the world of anorexics and bulimics like herself who were, as she put it, 'locked in a spiral of secret despair'. Others might argue that it was a speech of gross self-indulgence. Either way, it was a class act – and she had the audience spellbound as she lifted the veil on the suffering and self-doubt that had afflicted her behind Palace walls.

The news desk loved it. Not only did we have a member of the Royal Family baring her soul, but the Princess had also raised some highly relevant social issues that we could explore from a variety of worthy angles. It was a producer's paradise. Within an hour, we'd found case studies of young women who were taking up to 110 laxatives a day in their quest to stay thin. We had more statistics about eating disorders than anyone could ever wish to know. With a fifteen-minute speech, the Princess had shone a spotlight on a problem that had badly needed publicity. When she wanted to be, she could be a supremely effective operator.

At home, the focus of attention was far less altruistic. The contracts had finally been signed, and our new home in Devon had become a reality. Discarding his role as househusband like the merest negligee, Jim jumped on his motorbike and zoomed off to the West Country. The plan was for him to make the bleak and filthy barracks hut vaguely habitable in time for half-term. We knew it was a risk to leave me without any childcare, but I booked a couple of days' leave and crossed my fingers.

Emma was finally drifting off to sleep when the phone rang. It was the night editor of the *Today* programme.

'The Queen Mother's been taken to hospital in Aberdeen – she's choked on a fish bone or something.'

My heart skipped a beat; this was my worst nightmare. Visions of flying to Scotland with Emma in my arms flashed by. Who would look after her? How would I manage?

'I'm afraid I haven't got any childcare just at the moment and I'm actually on leave,' I explained. 'Can't you find Paul Reynolds?'

'He's in Bosnia,' came the gruff reply. 'We need you in the studio in the morning.'

I was snookered. I'd forgotten that Paul, my radio counterpart, was abroad. 'Well, I've got a three-year-old and no one to look after her. What do you suggest I do?'

There was no sympathy from the editor. He wanted a royal correspondent, and he wasn't about to be swayed. I felt annoyed and alone but, eventually, we reached a compromise that they would send a radio car to me. I could then broadcast from outside my house, and pray that Emma would keep quiet during the interview. Curiously, my television bosses were more understanding and agreed to handle the story from Scotland, at least for the time being. But *Today* was adamant that I was required.

I set the alarm for 5.45 a.m. and curled up in bed, feeling tense and perversely awake. A few hours later, the radio car, bristling with antennae and aerials, ensured that I wasn't alone in enduring an early start. The whole street seemed to be up. I'd had to coax Emma out of bed, but now she, too, was raring to go. Too raring. It was abundantly clear to me that any interview I did on *Today* would include liberal ad hoc comment from my delightfully chatty daughter. Something had to be done and time was running short.

I was in the radio car and on the point of donning my head-phones – which, along with the various buttons and switches, were proving a source of endless fascination to Emma – when to my enormous relief I saw the familiar figure of our builder strolling down the road. He was someone whom Emma knew and liked. I leaped out of the van and grabbed him, thrusting my darling daughter into his arms.

'You've no idea how wonderful it is to see you,' I shouted. 'She's all yours for a while; make yourself at home – the door's open.'

My encounter with John Humphrys passed without incident

and, fortunately for us all, the Queen Mother recovered after four days in hospital – just as Jim returned triumphantly from Devon. A week later, all three of us set off, this time by car, to spend our first holiday in our new home. Bouncing down the bumpy track, on the very edge of the ocean, it seemed an awesome proposition that this exquisite piece of land was now ours. Buzzards circled overhead and, occasionally, we could hear the high-pitched screech of peregrine falcons. The long wooden house sat staring at the sea, wondering, no doubt, what the next chapter in its colourful life was about to bring.

'Is this where we're going to live now?' Emma asked as we drew up at the foot of the valley.

We explained that this was to be her home for the best times of the year, but that my job meant we still had to live in London. On that first night we all slept in the same bed, in the middle of the lounge, with ragged blue wallpaper not so much peeling as collapsing limply off the walls. In the morning we peered out through the grimy windows to the sea beyond. We knew at once that, even though we had a mountain of work ahead, the view alone would make it all worthwhile.

Back in London, it was soon time for the opening of the capital's latest and biggest tourist attraction: Buckingham Palace. The outcry over the cost of repairing the fire damage to Windsor Castle had led the Queen and her advisers to declare the Palace open to the public for a couple of months each summer. And we, the ladies and gentlemen of the press, were invited to a preview. You might imagine that this would be a leisurely affair, with every opportunity to linger in the labyrinthine galleries and explore the ornate chambers. Indeed, as far as Palace officials were concerned, it was. The news desk had other ideas. My deadline was set precisely twenty minutes after I had entered the Palace. My colleague from Sky Television was in the same boat. Together, we submitted ourselves to the security checks at the entrance, and then – like hares sprung from the trap – bolted through the various rooms, eyes on stalks, gleaning what little information we could as we scurried on to the exit. We emerged, more or less simultaneously, blinking in the sunlight and searching for our cameras. Earpieces in place, microphones strapped on, we went on air on our respective networks – breathless, inarticulate and with only the faintest idea of where we had been or what we had seen. Fortunately, we'd both had the foresight to pick up guidebooks, which proved an invaluable reminder of some of the highlights that had flashed before us. To this day, most of Buckingham Palace remains a blur of red and gold in my mind, and every summer I promise myself that one day I'll find time to look round it properly.

While thousands of tourists tramped through the corridors of the Palace, the Princess of Wales was becoming more and more dissatisfied with her life. She'd been distraught by a series of pictures secretly taken while she was working out at a gym. They'd been splashed all over the Sunday papers, and she felt betrayed and exploited. She was also unsure about the direction her life was taking now that she was officially separated. And she was about to spring another surprise on the world that would send us all galloping to meet our deadlines.

It was December, and I had a day off. Or so I thought. It promised to be rather a memorable one because I was taking Emma for her first grown-up hairdo. For three years I had snipped away at her tresses whenever the need had arisen. The results were pitiful, and now it was time to admit the necessity of a hand more skilled than mine. After picking her up from the nursery, we headed straight for the local hairdresser's. Perched precariously high on a special seat, Emma looked like a tiny china doll, wrapped as she was in one of the salon's long black gowns. She held my hand tightly as the young stylist carefully swept her hair back and turned on the water. The three of us had just negotiated our way through the first shampoo – with a certain amount of anxiety from Emma – when my pager sounded. I winced, annoyed to be disturbed at such a critical point in the proceedings. The message was not encouraging.

'Ring Charles at Buckingham Palace. Urgent.'

It was not a message that could be ignored. Emma was looking worried. She demanded an assurance that I wasn't going to leave her. It was something I couldn't provide.

'Just stay with the lady and be good while I make a quick phone call,' I implored.

At the other end of the salon, where the phone signal was stronger, I rang the Palace. 'Charles Anson, please,' I demanded, as my mind raced through the contingency plans that might be hastily required. I was pretty sure that Jim hadn't gone out, so it would be a straightforward parenting swap: him to the hairdresser's and me to the office.

'Yes, hello, Jennie.' The press secretary's dulcet tones infused me with a sense of calm that was almost always misplaced.

'I thought you ought to know', he went on, 'that the Princess of Wales will be making a speech this afternoon that you'll find of some interest.'

'What's she going to be saying?' I asked.

'Well, I can't tell you that but, for guidance, I can say that it'll be about her future role.'

Emma was calling for me from the other end of the salon. Her hair hung damply around her frightened face. She knew the signs only too well: her mother was about to abandon her again. I winkled a few more details out of Charles and, as I did so, a flood of calls started coming in on my phone. The office had got wind of the speech as well; it seemed the Princess was about to announce some kind of withdrawal from public life. It was almost 12.30; the *One o'Clock News* wanted to interview me in the studio and I was stuck at the hairdresser's on the other side of London. Life had turned manic again.

Trying to sound calm, I told Emma that I was going to find her dad and that he would come and watch her have her hair cut. She looked at me reproachfully. I called home. The phone rang interminably, as the seconds ticked by and my heart beat faster. I dialled again. No reply. Why hadn't he *told* me if he was going somewhere? I rang again; it was now just twenty minutes until the news. Suddenly, the old reporter's instinct came to me; I called a neighbour and asked if they could see any sign of Jim.

'Ah, yes,' came the reply, 'I can just see him down there at the bottom of your garden.'

'Well, can you tell him to go and answer the bloody phone?' I screamed. 'I'll ring straight away.'

Eventually, I managed to tell my husband that he had to get in his car *immediately* and take over childcare duties at the hairdresser's. It was almost 12.55 by the time he arrived. I waved goodbye to our bemused daughter and ran to my car for a crazily irresponsible race to the BBC. I drove far too fast, cutting corners, as I listened to the radio news, desperate to catch any more details about Diana. At traffic lights, I ransacked my mucky make-up bag and clumsily plastered on some blusher, lipstick and powder. A couple of miles out from the BBC, I hit a traffic jam; it was only small, but *any* delay now was drastic. I swerved out into the road and took an illegal right turn, the wrong way round some bollards. It was sheer madness, but I arrived at the studio at 1.22 p.m. – and, trying to appear calm and collected, went straight on air at the very end of the bulletin.

When the Princess made her speech that afternoon, it turned out to be every bit as dramatic as my drive into town. Dressed in a sombre green suit, looking pale and nervous, she stood up to address the charity Headway. But her words were directed at the cameras and the world outside.

When I started my public life twelve years ago, I understood that the media might be interested in what I did. I realised that their attention would focus on both our public and our private lives. But I was not aware of how overwhelming that attention would become, nor of the extent to which it would affect both my public duties and my personal life in a manner which has been hard to bear.

Her appeal was for time and space, commodities which, she complained, had been lacking in recent years. In pursuit of that, she was announcing what amounted to a comprehensive withdrawal from public duties. The Princess, it seemed, was hanging up her tiara. The story led all the bulletins that night.

CHAPTER EIGHT

Pot shots at the Prince

With the Princess of Wales now largely absent from the stage, the scene was set for Prince Charles and his team to mount a rescue mission. Not of any maiden in distress, but of his own image. It had taken a battering during the breakdown of his marriage, and 1994 – the twenty-fifth anniversary of his investiture as Prince of Wales – presented the perfect opportunity to recoup some ground. Jonathan Dimbleby had embarked on a documentary about the Prince's work, and the Palace spin doctors were busy.

'This is not,' they insisted, 'any kind of repackaging or relaunch of the Prince. It's an opportunity for everyone to see the big picture.'

With that objective, they'd drawn up a hectic schedule for the coming year, with a strong emphasis on trips to Wales as well as several visits overseas. The first was a two-and-a-half-week odyssey to Australia and New Zealand.

I set out from home, bound for Sydney, with the usual

patchwork of simmering excitement and intense sadness in my heart. I was going to be away for more than three weeks: the longest by far that I had ever left Emma. As soon as I reached Heathrow, I was swept up in the complex business of checking in all the equipment and securing the correct bits of documentation. I'd brought a mountain of notes to read on the plane, and thoughts of home soon settled quietly into the background.

Twenty-four hours later, as we flew over the red earth at sunset, Australia looked just as wondrous to me as it had the first time round. At Sydney airport our cameraman – an Australian aptly named Bruce – was waiting to help us with all the boxes and luggage. It was a summer's evening in January, and soon we were sitting in a pleasant hotel bar just across from the Opera House with glasses of wine in our hands and an unknown adventure ahead. It seemed to me to be not a bad life.

My first job in the warm sunshine of the next day was to prepare a preview of the Prince's visit and attempt to gauge the level of interest among Australians. The republican argument was running strong and the Prime Minister, Paul Keating, was in the forefront of it. Bondi Beach seemed as good a place as any to begin my quest to decipher public opinion. I kicked off my shoes and revelled in the sensation of the hot sand under my feet; the ocean looked unbearably enticing but, already, I could feel the pressure of the looming deadline. I waded into the crowds of sun-bathers and surfers, brandishing my microphone and demanding to know their opinion about the Prince's impending arrival in their country. The overwhelming sentiment was one of apathy. One memorable newspaper headline proclaimed: 'Indifference to this royal tour has now reached fever pitch'. Events, though, would soon conspire to ensure that, whatever their views about royalty, few Australians could ignore the fact that the man who might one day be their King had come to visit.

It was 26 January – Australia Day – and the Prince had a packed programme ahead before making a keynote speech in the evening. It had been flagged as the speech of the tour, in which he would address the issue of Australia becoming a republic. Naturally enough, there was considerable news interest in what he might say. It was late afternoon by the time the royal entourage and accompanying media arrived in Sydney's Tumbalong Park for the final event before the speech. Rather like us, the Prince was looking a little weary as he sat watching an open-air prize-giving ceremony. It was unlikely to feature in any of our reports, but Bruce kept the camera rolling just in case. As a group of children sang on stage, word spread through the ranks of reporters that transcripts of the Prince's big speech were being distributed in the conference centre across the park. We began a slow stampede there, all of us driven by the nagging thought that we would arrive just as the last copy was handed to someone else.

Fortunately, there were plenty to go round and, having safely netted one, I decided to head straight back to the hotel to file a piece for *Breakfast*. Though I couldn't break the embargo on the speech, I could at least hint at its tone, which was, essentially, one of affectionate understanding and regal neutrality. The decision about becoming a republic, the Prince was to declare, lay solely with the Australian people, and Britain would respect their wishes. I calculated that if I hurried I could be back at Tumbalong Park before the Prince began his address. I hailed a taxi. It was only then that I realised that I'd left my handbag beside the camera, which was still at the prize-giving. I had no money and no choice: I had to race back across the park, through the crowds, to retrieve the bag.

Annoyed with myself for wasting time chasing after my possessions, I threw off my shoes and set off at a run. The ceremony was still going on, watched over by Bruce. I whispered in his ear that I'd been stupid enough to leave my bag behind and bent down to get it. It was just as I stood up that I saw and heard something that sent shock waves through my body – and made headline news around the world. The crack of a pistol ripped through the park, followed swiftly by another. At the same instant, a young man catapulted himself out of the audience and on to the stage; he seemed to be flying through the air – on a dangerously direct path to the Prince. His body tore through the microphone stand, sending it crashing to the ground with an electrifying clatter. In a split second, a sleepy afternoon ceremony in the park had been transformed into a real-life drama. I remember thinking out loud that we were witnessing an assassination attempt on the Prince of Wales. The stage was now a seething mass of police and security men; the gunman was pinned to the floor, and the Prince, looking bewildered rather than frightened, was shielded by his protection officer, Colin Trimming, who had unceremoniously shoved him to the side.

I looked at my cameraman. He was one of the few to have filmed the whole incident – and, as it turned out, to have captured it brilliantly. Many of the others had moved off to the next 'rota' position seconds before the gunman had struck. Now they came racing back, ashen-faced, frantic to find out what they had missed. Many reporters had missed it, too; they were still at the conference centre studying their transcripts. For once in my life, I'd been in exactly the right place at precisely the right time

– and it was all because I'd been absent-minded enough to forget my handbag.

The sense of shock took a few moments to settle. Gradually, though, the facts began to emerge. This had not been any kind of assassination attempt; the gun was no more than a starting pistol and the 'assassin' was a student intent on drawing attention to the plight of Cambodian boat people. Nevertheless, it was a dramatic story and, back in London, the news desk was already clamouring for me. My producer, Heather, dispatched me off to the hotel to start filing reports, while she stuck with the Prince, who by this time had decided to continue with the prize-giving.

As all too often in Sydney, the taxi driver had the greatest difficulty understanding English. He'd clearly been in the city only a few weeks longer than I had and his knowledge of the layout was sadly lacking. Eventually, frustrated by the hassle and delay, I arrived back at the hotel and burst into the picture editor's room. The equipment was all set up, and I could hear the commands coming in from London. I was needed immediately on both *Breakfast* and *Today*.

'Here's the lip mike; put on the headphones – you're on next,' said my picture editor before I'd even sat down.

I did each programme in turn, describing in detail all that I'd seen. I felt breathless and nervous, but ploughed on. The next instruction was for a straight report for immediate use; there was no time either to write a script or to prerecord it. I simply launched into what I hoped was a coherent and cogent live analysis of what had happened. The demands kept coming, and it was nine in the evening before I came up for breath. At last – the chance to make some calls. There were a number of loose ends to tie up. We had to establish where the gunman was and get a camera there; we needed to find out about his family and friends – would anyone talk about him? The police were about to give a news conference, and the Prince had been making his big speech; every development had to be covered. As far as London was concerned, there was a full day's work ahead, and the main bulletins were all drawing up wish-lists which they were relaying to Heather. I was also expected to report for radio. One thing was certain – there'd be no sleep for any of us that night.

We were all tired and still suffering from jet-lag, but we were kept wide awake by the prospect of cutting a four-minute piece for the *One o'Clock News*, with an update for the Six *o'Clock News*, which also wanted a live spot from Tumbalong Park. Heather had her work cut out organising engineers and satellite links to beam me back to London from a deserted park in the middle of the night. I concentrated on writing the first piece, which went reasonably smoothly, and then began gathering the extra elements for later. We sent a crew to the police station where the gunman was being held; we tried to track down his family and neighbours; we recorded the news conference given by the police chief. First the minutes and then the hours flew by with alarming speed; suddenly it was time to get down to the park – but I still had to send a report for Radio 4's main evening bulletin. I left my picture editor to put the finishing touches to my television piece, dashed down to my room and plugged in the infernal machinery. I scraped together my notes and produced a hastily scribbled account, of which I was far from proud. But my heart was pounding; we were getting desperately late for our live spot in the park. I knew I looked a mess but stopped only to seize a clean dress and tore out of the hotel.

Heather had a taxi waiting. I jumped in, rifling through my bag for my earpiece, rehearsing what I might say on the news.

The taxi chugged through the empty streets, the Asian driver seemingly oblivious to our need for haste. Soon it became terrifyingly clear that he was also oblivious to the whereabouts of Tumbalong Park.

'You need to turn right at the end of this road,' we chorused, hoping that our recollection of the route was better than his.

It was then that we cottoned on to the gruesome truth: he didn't understand a word we were saying. He stared straight ahead and kept on driving. After what seemed like an eternity going round in circles, we saw what we thought was the park – just across some traffic lights. The driver stopped; we waited in silence. The red light glared at us, stubbornly refusing to change. We started fidgeting; this was getting desperate. Our entreaties for the driver to ignore the light fell on deaf and uncomprehending ears. We jumped out and ran.

It was an immense relief to see a small satellite truck waiting for us, with two Australian engineers on board. At last, I thought, we're in safe hands. Bruce, our cameraman, had also turned up in case he was needed but, reassured by the sight of the truck, he set off home for a change of clothes. I followed the cable that led from the truck to the live position in front of the stage where, hours earlier, the whole drama had unfolded. Now the park was pitch-black and eerily quiet. Mystified for a moment – and then horrified – I discovered that there wasn't a camera at the end of the cable. We were on air in fifteen minutes and the most essential piece of broadcasting equipment was missing. My stomach churned. I raced back to the engineers, who said there'd obviously been a mix-up about who was going to provide the camera. We didn't argue; we rang Bruce, who came screaming back to the park, grabbed his camera from the boot of his car – hitting his head so hard he almost knocked himself out – and set up ready for the live piece.

I put in my earpiece. I could hear London talking – but it was someone at ITN calling out for Nick Owen, their royal correspondent and a dear friend of mine. I shouted back that Nick wasn't there but that I was ready, so could they please get the BBC across the line? Chaos ensued. No one at the BBC seemed able to hear me; people kept calling in my ear that my office had to ring the IFB number (whatever that was). It was two minutes to six and my story was the lead item. In desperation, I held up a piece of paper to the camera with 'CALL IFB NUMBER' scrawled across the page, hoping that someone technical would see it. With thirty seconds to go, I finally heard the studio in London talking to me. The news wasn't good. My picture editor, who'd gone to the TV station to send our completed story, had come up against his own problems. At this eleventh hour, my report was still coming into London – and they would almost certainly have to run my 1 o'clock piece instead. I felt like crying.

In the end the 6 o'clock piece ran at 9; the live spot was a success, and – a couple of minutes later – Nick Owen came panting into the park. He, too, had come up against the dreaded 'Sydney cabbie syndrome'. His driver hadn't even got close to Tumbalong in time for his bulletin. He'd spent the past half-hour cruising around town, totally lost. I was still shaking with the tension of it all but, to his eternal credit, Nick simply put his arm around me, pointed up to the night sky and said: 'Look, old thing. Here we are in Australia in the middle of the British winter and there's the Southern Cross. We're bloody lucky really, aren't we?'

Of course, he was right. The immediate crisis was over; all the main news outlets had been served. And we were still breathing.

But this was no time to sit and natter; dawn was breaking and I had to get on a plane with Prince Charles for a day in the bush. While the gunman protester acclimatised himself to his new surroundings in a police cell, we struggled on through what turned out to be a forty-hour stint without sleep.

Despite the hard work, Australia continued to weave its magic on me. We flew to Tasmania and the beautiful port of Hobart. It was cooler there – which displeased me – but the countryside was stunning. And one day we got to see rather more of it than we'd bargained for. Prince Charles was off to the west of the island to visit a remote fishing village called Strahan. The royal hacks were following in a rather ropy-looking light aircraft that had been chartered on our behalf. The skies were cloudy (according to the guidebooks it rains on 240 days of the year in this region) and, unsurprisingly, the flight was bumpy. It was when we came in to land on a scrappy piece of tarmac that several of the press party began to turn pale. Perilously low in the air, the plane circled round a couple of times, as if the pilot was considering how best to tackle the problem of reuniting his aircraft with the earth. As we banked sharply, I looked around the cabin and saw a look of terror on the face of one of my colleagues. His knuckles, by now attached to the armrests as if by super-glue, had turned white. Suddenly, the Australian pilot screwed up his courage and swooped down towards the ground. We seemed to be approaching imprudently fast and, more significantly, one wing tip was alarmingly close to the tarmac as we came in on the tilt. Somehow, with a screech of rubber and a massive jolt, we landed askew and slithered along the bumpy runway. As the plane shuddered to a halt, there was silence in the cabin at first, followed by loud joking, which served to alleviate the barely suppressed hysteria.

The pilot got out and inspected his wing tip. Chuckling to himself, he took off his cap, scratched his head and, in his native drawl, declared: 'That wasn't the best landing I've ever made. Everyone OK?'

Strahan is picturesque in the extreme, with a cluster of wooden houses overlooking the harbour. Almost everyone in the 600-strong community had turned out to take a peek at the Prince. The pub had put up a brash sign announcing that 'Princes Are Welcome'; he rose to the challenge and dropped in for a glass of whisky – prompting a manic clattering of ladders and cameras as his merry band of media fought to get the shot of the day.

From there, the Prince was heading to an old mining community called Queenstown. In its prime, it had been the site of one of the world's biggest copper and gold mines. Now, though, the town was bracing itself for wide-scale unemployment after the imminent closure of the last remaining mine. With a certain amount of trepidation, the three TV cameramen and their respective correspondents piled into an eight-seater plane that had been allocated to us for the journey. As we bounced through the sky, looking down on a bleak and lunar landscape, I was perturbed to see what looked like smoke gushing out of the seat in front. Soon, some of my colleagues noticed the same phenomenon around them. We shouted at the pilot, thinking – not unreasonably – that it would be as well for him to know that his plane was on fire. He gave us a withering look. 'Don't let that worry you,' he shouted above the engine noise. 'It's just a bit of condensation.'

At that point the landing strip came into sight. It appeared to be nothing more than a mountaintop. We decided that now was not the time to argue about the niceties of whether or not we were on fire. We sat tight as he came in to land – a manoeuvre which, to our profound relief, he executed perfectly. We jumped out and pulled our gear from the hold. The next task was to get down to Queenstown before the Prince. We looked around for the cars that had been booked to meet us. They were nowhere to be seen. In fact, there was no one and nothing to be seen for miles. Apart from the empty landing strip, the only sign of civilisation was a small wooden shed. Perhaps there was a small Tasmanian person inside who could help us? The shed door was open and swinging spookily in the wind. We peered inside; it was all but derelict. No one had been there for months.

So it was that three senior correspondents and their cameramen were stranded on top of a mountain somewhere in western Tasmania. As we peered into the distance, hoping for inspiration, we saw a convoy of grand-looking cars winding down the valley towards Queenstown. The Prince was on his way. Perhaps, we thought, we could hitch a lift – if we could just get as far as the road. But we were still half a mile away when the convoy swept by without so much as a glance in our direction. How the Prince would have laughed if he had seen us! We stood, tripods and cameras on our shoulders, and giggled. There was nothing else to do.

Halfway through the tour, the Palace decided to give the Prince a day off. And they came up with a sensational way for him to spend it: on a tropical island off the coast of Queensland. We were told there'd be the chance to film him, and so, with very little persuasion, the press party followed. Fraser Island, the world's largest sand island, was waiting for us – warm but sadly wet. Ignoring the rain, we set off to explore. We were shown the magnificent rainforest; we walked with dingoes on the beach and swam in a stunningly blue lagoon. That evening we disgraced ourselves by holding a karaoke competition in the hotel. Though I like to think that my crew and I upheld the honour of the Corporation with our rendition of 'Love Me Tender', I have to admit that ITN's 'Da Do Ron Ron' beat us hands down: largely due to their burly cameraman, who donned his producer's silk dress for the occasion. We ended the evening in the open-air jacuzzi under the stars, where we were joined by the Prince's new press secretary. It was a wonderfully relaxing day and certainly made up for the sleepless week we'd just endured. The next morning the Prince, who was staying in the same hotel, posed for the cameras and chided us all for keeping him awake with our singing. 'I can tell you one thing,' he laughed; 'you all need a lot more practice.'

It was no more than friendly banter, but it reaffirmed the impression we had all formed during the tour: that the Prince was concerned by the public debate about his fitness to be King and, whatever his advisers told us, he recognised that improving his image was important.

Ironically, it was his coolness under fire – both in Sydney and when we arrived in New Zealand – that made some people sit up and reassess his character. No one imagined that there could be two security scares on a single tour, but an ardent anti-royalist in Auckland proved us wrong.

It was a peaceful, sunny day towards the end of what had been a long and eventful visit, and the Prince was viewing the Whitbread Round the World yachts in the harbour. It wasn't likely to make a news story, but we were going through the motions, filming him as he went. He'd almost reached his car, and we were looking forward to getting back on the press bus, when, in what seemed to be an instance of *déjà vu*, a man lunged towards him, shouting wildly. This time, though, he didn't get very far, and the only weapon he was brandishing was an aerosol. He was wrestled to the ground and smartly sat on by security officers; the Prince was hustled into his car; and we were left with another hot story.

I left New Zealand a few days later after an extraordinary three weeks which had been a test of stamina for us all. I was more convinced than ever that I had been born in the wrong country: I thrive in sunshine and wide-open spaces – that's where I belong. Nevertheless, as we flew eastwards over oceans and continents, the pull of home and family began to win the tug of war. Before long, dressed for summer in the middle of winter, I swept Emma up in my arms, kissed Jim and transformed myself back into mother and wife.

Once again, I'd arrived home in the nick of time for Emma's birthday. Even though Jim had done most of the preparation, I found that merely supervising a party for half a dozen four-year-olds was every bit as exacting as reporting from the other side of the world. It was strange, too, to be making snowmen in Devon when just a few days earlier I'd been basking in the warmth of a Maori settlement that had given me the once-in-a-lifetime opportunity to sign off with the words: 'Jennie Bond, BBC News, Twangawaewae.'

Back at the office there was a lot of newsreading to be done. And one of those shifts turned into a day I shall never forget. It was 12 May, and I was in the make-up room enjoying being pampered and listening to all the gossip, when rumours began to spread that the Labour leader, John Smith, had been taken ill. Knowing his history of heart problems, the newsroom took this very seriously. The laughter in the make-up room instantly stopped; I got ready to go on air immediately if necessary. The newsroom was now buzzing with reports that Mr Smith had died. But we had no confirmation. Nevertheless, the decision was taken to break into the scheduled programmes with the information that we had, and I hastily made my way to the studio for a newsflash. It was to be more than an hour before I came out.

As the countdown to the newsflash sounded in my ear, the editor's voice broke in saying that confirmation had just come through that Mr Smith was indeed dead. I was to ignore the autocue – everything on it was now out of date; instead I would have to ad-lib the announcement of his death.

'Five, four, three, two, one – on air, cue Jennie,' I heard. Staring at words on the autocue that now had no meaning, I ad-libbed, I hope with dignity, the sad news. As I spoke, instructions came through my earpiece: 'Well done. Now introduce the obit, ad-lib again, there's nothing on autocue.' Hugely relieved that there was at least one tape ready for transmission, I did as I was told.

The video report about Mr Smith's life gave us a breathing space of three or four minutes to find someone at Westminster to interview. With seconds to spare, a political correspondent suddenly popped up on the monitor; we crossed to him and I fired questions at him until the editor's voice cut in once more – this time with the name of another correspondent who, by now, had arrived at the Labour Party's headquarters. So it went on. At times I felt as if I was spinning plates as I conducted one interview after another with every prominent member of the Party, never knowing what was coming up next. We continued for most of the morning until, at 1 o'clock, it was time to hand over the reins to the main bulletin team. I came out of the studio feeling sad that a man at the height of his powers had died, but satisfied that we had done our best to relay the facts sensitively, accurately and swiftly.

Two days later I was packing my suitcase again: bound for Russia with Prince Charles. The visit was seen as a precursor to one by the Queen. If it went well, she would follow later in the year. It was my second trip to St Petersburg; the first had been as a tourist with Jim, back in the days when it was called Leningrad. I discovered that it had lost none of its beauty; even in the chill wind of a Russian spring, the city looked exquisite, the grand palaces stunning. There was certainly no hardship involved for the royal hacks as we pursued the Prince around the sights, all of which he much admired. It was only when we ventured out of town that I found myself somewhat uncomfortable.

Tasteless as it no doubt is, I have a weakness for white shoes. I am particularly fond of white stilettos – preferably plastic – and in the summer I wear them incessantly. I don't buy expensive shoes; the cheaper the better. When, a couple of years ago, I came across a perfectly serviceable pair for £9.99, I decided to go for broke and splashed out on ten pairs in exactly the same style. My reasoning is that all shoes get battered – especially on royal tours – and I'd rather chuck away a cheap pair than get upset about ruining some that had cost a great deal more. It's also delightfully easy to clean my white plastic monstrosities, no matter where I am, simply by running them under the tap.

Through my own lack of foresight, however, I had not been aware that, on the day in question, the Prince and his entourage were going to end up in a seed potato field outside St Petersburg. I looked out of the press bus in horror as it drew to a halt in what appeared to be a muddy farmyard. Gingerly, I climbed out, avoiding one of the larger puddles. My cameraman handed me the tripod to carry. It weighed a ton. The field was newly ploughed; huge clods of earth stretched as far as the eye could see. The Prince and his people were striding out across it towards a tractor that was piled high with potatoes. As I picked my way daintily across the field, my stilettos sank into the soil and the white plastic turned a reddish-brown. When I finally arrived at the tractor, the Prince had already finished his potato inspection. He looked up at me, and then down at my feet. Barely suppressing a giggle, he said: 'Wrong shoes, I think, Miss Bond.' Feeling foolish and rather miserable, I did my best to laugh it off.

Soon, though, back in the UK, we all had something more serious than sartorial elegance to consider.

'We need you in here quickly.' It was the overnight news organiser, and the last editions of the papers had just landed on his desk. Bleary-eyed, I asked what was up.

'That documentary about Prince Charles – apparently, he admits adultery in it.'

The programme that Jonathan Dimbleby had been working on for more than a year had been kept a closely guarded secret. It was due to be broadcast the following week; evidently the publicity machine was now swinging into action. The unanswered question had always been whether the Prince would be given an easy ride or whether Dimbleby would tackle the taboo topic of Camilla Parker Bowles. It seemed now that he had and that the film was going to cause a sensation. News desks around the country, mine included, went into a frenzy. Calls to the Palace indicated that the rumours were pretty well spot-on. We started tracking down potential interviewees who might give their reaction; most, though, quite reasonably wanted to wait until they had seen the complete programme.

The story bubbled on for a week until, finally, I joined royal reporters from every paper and magazine at a press preview of the film. It was a bright summer's afternoon as we filed into the theatre, notebooks poised, to find out just what the Prince had said. Dimbleby explained that we were about to see much more than the speculation had suggested. His intention, he said, had been to create a rounded portrait of the man. But as he looked out into an auditorium full of cynical, hard-nosed journalists, he must have known that his film would forever be famous for just one dramatic exchange.

Dimbleby: 'Did you try to be faithful and honourable to your wife when you took on the vow of marriage?'

Prince Charles: 'Yes, absolutely.'

Dimbleby: 'And you were?'

Prince Charles: 'Yes. [Pause.] Until it became irretrievably broken down – us both having tried.'

It was a moment of high theatre. In the semi-darkness, the frantic scribbling of notes that had punctuated the entire showing became even more furious as we struggled to capture the Prince's admission verbatim. A shuffling of feet signalled that most of us were now itching to get to a phone. This was headline news. But there was, of course, a great deal more to the film. It gave an insight into the Prince's work, his philosophy and the inner man. It also illustrated the depth of his animosity for the media.

'Look at the level of intrusion,' he grumbled, 'the persistent, endless carping, pontificating, criticising, examining, investigating . . . the soap opera . . . trying to turn everyone into a celebrity . . . What's the point? I always think there's a camera hiding in the bushes somewhere.'

Why, then, many commentators justifiably asked, had the Prince invited a film crew to follow him around for more than a year? As one fellow journalist put it: 'The problem is that we already knew too *much* about the Prince of Wales, and now we know even more. There's an argument that he's beginning to invade *our* privacy, rather than that we're invading his.'

Armed with my impressions of the film – and fifteen pages of scrawled notes – I rushed to Buckingham Palace to tell the *Six o'Clock News* audience what they could look forward to that evening when the documentary was screened. It was gratifying for once to have facts that had come straight from the horse's mouth. For better or worse, the Prince had made his views plain; this time there could be no press office ambiguity about them. We didn't need the press office, either, to establish that the battle for supremacy between Charles and Diana was far from over. Faced with this headline-grabbing haemorrhage of her husband's innermost feelings, the Princess stepped out for an engagement at the Serpentine Gallery that evening wearing a black cocktail dress that guaranteed her a place on every front page.

For the next forty-eight hours I might as well have been abroad for all I saw of my family. I worked late into the night and was up at dawn to head back to the studio. The Palace insisted that the gamble of taking part in the documentary had paid off and that the switchboard had been jammed with messages of support for the Prince. Along with other commentators, I observed that, whether or not the film had succeeded in its objective, its one sure-fire achievement had been to focus world attention back on to the Prince's failed marriage. And that was where it stayed – even when, a day or so later, we all travelled to Caernarfon for what had been planned as the centrepiece of the royal year: the anniversary of Charles's investiture as Prince of Wales twenty-five years earlier. The garden party at Caernarfon Castle proceeded perfectly to plan, but beyond those walls many people, both in Wales and in the UK at large, were publicly questioning the Prince's fitness to be King.

The unmitigated gloom of the 'war of the Waleses' was relieved later in July by the wedding of Lady Sarah Armstrong-Jones to a genial young man named Daniel Chatto. And in August the Queen Mother's ninety-fourth birthday gave us all another opportunity to examine the life of someone who personified steadfastness and stability in the monarchy. But three weeks later who could blame the media for likening the royal saga to a soap opera? Now, we learned, a police investigation had been launched into nuisance phone calls allegedly made by Diana to a millionaire art dealer. Oliver Hoare was handsome, married and a friend of the Princess of Wales. According to the *News of the World*, dozens of calls had been traced back to her. Suddenly, the soap opera had become a whodunit. The following day, the story was given new 'legs' – as we say in the trade – when the Princess adopted a daring strategy to try to establish her innocence.

My phone rang shortly before 5 a.m. Fortunately, Jim and Emma had decamped to Devon for the summer holidays, so there was only me to disturb.

'Diana's given an interview to the *Mail*,' said the news organiser. 'She says she didn't make those calls. *Breakfast* want a package from you and a live in the studio.'

It's far easier getting up and out of the house in a flash when you're alone. I left a trail of destruction behind me – discarded clothes, coffee cups and half-eaten fruit – but there was no one to worry about as I hurtled towards the office.

The papers made fascinating reading, although I had time only for a breathless romp through them. The Princess had poured her heart out to Richard Kay of the *Daily Mail*. As they sat in his car at a pre-arranged spot in a London street, she had tearfully insisted that she had not made the nuisance calls. This, in itself, was quite a story. But the *Sun* had its own scoop: a freelance photographer had snapped the Princess getting into Richard's car – and the results were all over the front page.

It was a pivotal moment for Diana. Having castigated the media for failing to give her the time and space she'd needed, here she was hopping into a tabloid reporter's car. She'd cut herself free from the Palace machinery and was fighting her corner on her own. But she had made herself more than ever a magnet for the ranks of press and TV cameras that were once again trained on her every move.

A month or so later she did turn to the Palace press office for protection when a sensational book claiming to tell the story of her love affair with a cavalry officer hit the shops. Charles Anson, the Queen's press secretary, weighed in on the Princess's behalf with scathing condemnation: it was a 'grubby, worthless piece of work', he snorted. The public would have to judge the motives of people who were 'quick to peddle gossip of their acquaintances with the Royal Family'. The Palace, he declared, was not going to waste any more time on this 'tawdry little book'.

Most royal reporters suspected, and some already knew, that Anna Pasternak's offering, *Princess in Love*, was a genuine account – albeit romanticised – of a true love affair. James Hewitt was the cavalry officer in question and, as we were all to discover in the Princess's *Panorama* interview, she had indeed loved him very deeply. The story sent me scurrying to work to try to make sense of why the Princess wasn't planning any legal action if she and the Palace were so outraged by the book.

The year was proving almost as turbulent as the annus horribilis. From the pistol shots in Sydney, through the drama of the Prince confessing adultery while his estranged wife apparently wandered the streets making nuisance phone calls, the royal ratpack had claimed acres of newsprint and bulletins. But it was far from over yet. Hot on the heels of Anna Pasternak's book, Jonathan Dimbleby published his lengthy biography of Prince Charles. It was serialised in the *Sunday Times* the day before the Queen left for her historic visit to Russia, and it was a show-stopper.

With astonishing naïvety, the Prince's advisers had not only given Jonathan Dimbleby full editorial control but had failed to foresee the inevitable consequences of allowing the book to be serialised. The headlines that morning were lurid:

CHARLES: MY AGONY AFTER BEING FORCED INTO A
   LOVELESS MARRIAGE
CHARLES: I'VE NEVER LOVED DIANA
PHILIP DROVE ME TO MARRY DIANA

I'd spent the previous week planning and preparing for the Queen's trip to Russia. It was an important event, regarded both by her and the government as one of the most significant state visits of her reign. I'd been due to fly out that weekend and, like the Palace, didn't welcome this distraction. But now, with just twenty-four hours to go, everyone's attention had switched from the Queen to her son.

The *Sunday Times* held back its story until 1 a.m. I waited up at home until the newsroom rang me with the details. It was stunning material, portraying the Prince's inner feelings in far more depth than anything that had gone before. My plan had been to hear what was in it and then get a couple of hours' sleep before going into the office. I shouldn't have bothered. As I crept into bed beside Jim, script lines for the morning buzzed around my brain; I made mental notes of all the pictures I'd need and then started compiling lists of everything I still had to pack for Russia. At 4.30, about ten minutes after I had finally drifted off, the alarm jolted me out of bed.

By 5.15 I was in the newsroom wading through the papers. The book clearly suggested that Prince Charles had felt pressurised into marrying Diana by his father, who had bullied him as a child. The Prince told Jonathan Dimbleby that his marriage had become like a Greek tragedy: 'It's agony to know that someone is hating it all so much. It's like being trapped in a rather desperate cul-de-sac . . . I never thought it would end up like this. How could I have got it all so wrong?'

I could happily have spent the rest of the day reading all the extracts and analysis: one paper viewed the book as 'the longest abdication note in history'. But time was running short, and I had to put together a long report for the early morning news before going into the studio to be interviewed by David Frost. He quizzed me about the contents of the book and I hope I was coherent and concise, but it certainly wasn't an appearance that merited any special press coverage. It was therefore with some astonishment that I found myself featured a few days later as a diary item. Sadly, it was not for my incisive comments to David but for those tasteless, trademark shoes: 'Imagine the surprise', guffawed Peterborough in the *Telegraph*, 'when the camera suddenly tilted down to reveal Jennie Bond's white stilettos, so out of character with her image!'

The repercussions of the Dimbleby book meant that I had to postpone my flight to Moscow. The story kept me at the office late into Sunday night. By the time I got home my eyes were drooping – and I still had my packing to do. While my husband – back from Devon – grumbled about being kept awake, I shuffled around the bedroom, throwing as many warm clothes as I could find into my suitcase. It was after two by the time I was finished; unsure quite when I would finally make it to Russia, I checked that I had my ticket, passport and money – and collapsed into bed.

Emma woke me a few hours later, and the shrill summons of the phone followed almost instantly. The office barked instructions at me while Emma crawled on to my lap, vying for my attention. I was to get on a morning plane to Moscow; it wouldn't get me there in time to see the Queen arrive, but I'd only be an hour or so behind. The producer and crew would have filmed everything and, if I worked fast, I should be able to file for the *Six o'Clock News*. This was a fine way to start a royal tour, I thought . . . late before I'd even begun!

Exit wife and mother, suitcase in hand, into the waiting taxi. En route to the airport, the metamorphosis into working woman took hold once again.

On the plane I raked through all my notes about the tour and quickly realised that my best hope of completing a piece in time for the early evening news was to write the script there and then. It's not a recommended form of journalism, but the deadline was so tight that I plumped for the prudent option.

'In the late afternoon of a chill autumn day,' I wrote, 'the Queen set foot on Russian soil. A moment of history, meticulously planned, designed to set the seal at the most senior level on post-cold war relations.'

As long as the weather reports were accurate that would probably do as an opener. By the time we landed in Moscow, I had at least the skeleton of a script that could be changed as circumstances dictated. It was then that I decided to take a gamble. Every reporter knows that your best work comes from your own eyewitness recollection of events. Even though I was hideously late and as yet had no accreditation or official pass for the tour, I was determined to see something of the occasion. The Moscow office had sent a driver to take me straight to a hotel, where they had set up the edit suite. I jumped in his car and, ignoring my orders, yelled: 'Take me to the Kremlin.'

He drove like a madman. We bounced over potholes and along special taxi lanes, where we seemed to be going in the opposite direction to everyone else. We screeched around corners and across major junctions until, there in front of me, I saw the golden domes of the Kremlin.

'Wait here for me,' I said firmly. 'I may need you again quickly if I can't get in.'

I've often found that when you're unsure of yourself, the most effective tactic is to approach the problem with an uncompromising air of authority. Taking a deep breath, I marched up to the doors of the Kremlin, oozing confidence with every stride. I gave the guards an icy stare, announced to their uncomprehending ears that I was from the BBC, and strutted past them unchallenged. In minutes I found myself, rather to my own amazement, in the splendour of St George's Hall, in the heart of the Kremlin, where I was reunited with my astonished media colleagues. Seconds later, I was able to witness the meeting between the Queen and President Yeltsin.

It was therefore with a sense of having seen *something* at least that I was hustled by my producer to do a piece to camera outside St Basil's Cathedral, one of the most fabulous backdrops in the world. From there, we raced to the edit suite and embarked on our battle to finish the piece in time. I looked and felt decrepit by now, but suddenly I discovered that I was expected to appear live immediately after my report. The row over the Dimbleby book was still big news. My luggage had vanished somewhere in a taxi, but I smoothed out my creased clothes, dabbed on some powder and managed to get to the camera with seconds to spare. The whole performance was updated and repeated for the *Nine o'Clock News*, which meant that it was well past midnight in Moscow by the time we'd finished. I finally checked into my hotel in the early hours of the morning and was delighted to catch up with my luggage. Unpacking, though, presented too much of a challenge. I lay down on the bed and the phone immediately rang. The next batch of demands was already coming in from *Breakfast*.

That's pretty much how it continued. The tour was historic and eventful. The security that had been so lax for my arrival at the Kremlin went into overdrive when the Queen and the Duke were taken to Red Square. To the consternation of the Palace planners, all but a handful of Russians were kept in the far distance behind cordons. To the Duke's irritation, the only people he found to talk to on his walkabout were from Birmingham.

After a couple of days the tour moved on to St Petersburg. A special plane had been laid on for the press, and we'd been given strict instructions to have our bags and equipment ready at the crack of dawn so we could take off on schedule. Precise plans had been drawn up to get us in the air well ahead of the Queen and safely on the ground to film her arrival in St Petersburg. She was in a much faster plane than we were, and the timings were critical.

It was when we were sitting on the tarmac at Moscow airport – some thirty bleary-eyed reporters, cameramen, editors and producers – that the first doubts began to surface. The tons of equipment and luggage we carried with us were still being loaded, painfully slowly. There was no heating in the cabin and we were shivering as we waited patiently. But patience is a rare commodity in the world of news, and the complaints weren't far behind.

'Come on, get us in the air. We'll miss the Queen at the other end if you don't get a move on.'

Still the plane sat stubbornly on the tarmac. One of the press officers from the Palace, who was travelling with us, did her best to ascertain what the problem was.

'They're worried we're too heavy,' she told us eventually. 'It's all the equipment. They want to know whether you really need everything you've got on board.'

A chorus of groans greeted her explanation for the delay. After all the bureaucracy and the dozens of forms we'd filled in, this was a fine time for queries. As the airport workers picked over our suitcases and edit packs, wondering which they could throw off, the unmistakable sound of police sirens permeated the cabin. That could mean only one thing – the Queen was on her way. The groans turned into loud protests.

'Let's get moving, for God's sake. She's nearly here and we've *got* to take off before her!'

Suddenly, the problems vanished. The hold was closed, the seatbelt signs went on and for a moment it looked as if we were off. But the plane didn't move. Through the half-frozen windows we watched as the Queen's convoy sped across the tarmac to her waiting aircraft.

'Come *on*,' we shouted. '*Go, go, GO!*'

But in our hearts we all knew that there was no way the airport authorities would let us take off now that the Queen had arrived. Miserably, we stared out of our chilly prison as the royal plane taxied effortlessly down the runway and soared skywards. The only thing flying in our cabin was an outpouring of expletives.

Eventually, though, we lumbered off in pursuit of the Queen, hoping somehow that we could make up time. As we flew north, the landscape turned truly Russian with a covering of early winter snow. There, far below us, a dark oasis in the sea of white, was St Petersburg airport – and the unmistakable sight of the Queen's plane, already on the ground. Our pilot began to circle in the sky, providing us with the perfect bird's-eye view of the welcoming ceremony below. It was not, however, the perfect camera position for a planeload of photographers – and our frustration at missing some colourful shots was boiling over.

'Look,' we grumbled loudly, 'she's getting in the car. For God's sake, will someone get us down there?'

Our Palace press officer did all she could to encourage the pilot to land, but it was only when the Queen's convoy was well on its way to her first engagement that we finally stopped circling. As soon as the wheels hit the ground, we were on our feet strapping cameras and tripods on to our shoulders, ready to jump off the plane and into the waiting press buses. We'd taken a joint decision to abandon all hope of getting to the Queen's first stop; instead, we'd go straight to the second venue, the Catherine Palace at Pushkin.

The bus driver looked bewildered as this overwrought and angry band of journalists clambered on to his vehicle. He seemed in no hurry to go anywhere.

'Go,' we barked at him, 'quickly – go – take us to the Catherine Palace as fast as you can.'

'*Nyet*,' he replied, shaking his head morosely. '*Nyet* Catherine Palace.'

The poor chap had been given his orders in advance, and he

was sticking to them. We would be taken to the Queen's first engagement whether we liked it or not.

'But she'll have left by the time we get there,' we roared. 'We *must* go to the Palace – now.'

Eventually, with some diplomatic persuasion from our press officer, the driver conceded defeat. Grumpily, he set off through the snow to Pushkin. The Palace looked glorious in its white setting, but to our annoyance we saw the Queen's car already parked inside the gates. A crescendo of clattering marked our arrival as we vied with one another for the quickest exit from the bus, ready for the stampede into the Palace. But none of us had reckoned on the immutability of the security guards.

In their thick, grey greatcoats and long, black boots, they stood, arms folded, in front of the locked gates.

'All right, mate,' said one of the photographers, nudging the chief guard playfully, 'let us through – we've got to film the Queen.' He reinforced this with a wink as he flashed his official pass.

The guard stared straight ahead, ignoring our pleas and our passes. We began a mass moan – the minutes were flying by, and if this went on much longer we'd have no shots at all of the Queen, and a good deal of explaining to do to our news desks. The Buckingham Palace press officer was equally frustrated. Stamping her feet, she explained that we were the entire British press party, sent out from London to cover the Queen's visit to this wonderful Palace and *would he please let us get on with our job*! Her words fell on deaf ears. Crossing his arms in a manner that suggested he was not to be trifled with, he said without a flicker of emotion: '*Nyet*. Queen here. No go in.'

These were clearly intended as his final words on the subject – and so it proved. Her Majesty's ladies and gentlemen of the press remained outside in the snow, while the Queen had a spectacularly solo tour of the tsars' old summer residence, unhindered for once by cameramen and reporters. She must have loved it.

I arrived home a few days later, bearing a strange assortment of Russian gifts to salve my conscience for having yet again been away from my little girl. It had been another bizarre and busy year, and as it drew to a close the Princess of Wales announced that she was taking on a new role – as patron of the British Red Cross Birthday Appeal.

A year on from her withdrawal from public life, the Princess, it seemed, was preparing for some kind of return to the world scene. The year 1995, I surmised, could turn out to be yet another blockbuster on the royal roadshow.

CHAPTER NINE

Getting to know Diana

For six years, the life of the Princess of Wales had impinged in no small way on mine. Whenever she chose to make a splash, I found myself dragged into the water with her. If she was busy, so was I, whatever my personal commitments. But it wasn't until 1995 that I truly began to know Diana on anything more than a superficial level. The seeds for this were sown in Japan.

The new year was just a few weeks old when she jetted off to Tokyo with a strong contingent of British press following in her wake. It was the Princess's first major overseas tour since her very public decision to cut back on her royal duties, and we were all curious to see how she would fare.

The crowds were sparse on that first day as she toured the National Children's Hospital, doing what she always did best: dispensing tender loving care. But by the morning, saturation coverage on Japanese television had brought thousands of people out on to the streets. Before long we were all reporting that Di-mania was back in town.

That evening, the Princess was in a buoyant mood when she hosted a reception for the media. As always, the timing was awkward for the travelling press; we were all involved in editing our reports or sending pictures back to London. Like the others, I abandoned my edit halfway through and took a cab to the British Embassy, determined to take advantage of this chance to chat with the woman who ruled so much of our lives. I arrived rather late, and the Princess was already moving from group to group, looking relaxed among the familiar faces of the British press – even though she was suffering from a headache. I joined in the banter and hoped she would come my way swiftly, so that I could race back to the TV station to finish my piece for the news.

Before too long she came over, hand held out in greeting. 'Hello, Jennie. It's good to see you.'

She looked elegant in a simple black dress and flat shoes. Even though I was wearing my usual high heels, I felt short, plump and dowdy beside her. I was surprised to find that I had her all to myself for a few moments, and I determined to make the most of it.

'Well, Ma'am, you've certainly kept my life busy over the past few years,' I said. 'It's been quite a roller-coaster, hasn't it?'

I wondered whether she would immediately switch the conversation to more neutral ground, but she seemed happy to take up my theme.

'Well, it certainly hasn't been easy,' she said. 'But I think – no, I *know* – that I'm much stronger now, much more in control of my life.'

I asked her whether she had read Jonathan Dimbleby's book.

She said she hadn't finished it yet; the newspaper headlines about it had hurt her too much. Her immediate and greatest worry had been for her sons.

We talked a little about the pressures of being a working mum; she seemed interested to learn that I had a child a good deal younger than hers. After six or seven minutes, she moved on and, feeling elated to have made some real contact with her, I flew out of the door and into a taxi. It was then that I realised that in my haste I hadn't made a note of the address of the TV station. My producer and picture editor were waiting for me there; our deadline was hideously close; and I was lost in the middle of Tokyo with a driver who spoke absolutely *no* English.

'Japanese TV building. Can you take me there?' I pleaded hopefully.

He looked baffled. I rang my producer's mobile, but there was no reply; obviously, there was no signal in the edit suite where he was working, deep in the bowels of the TV station. I remembered that it was called Nippon TV, which struck me as such a wacky name that I was afraid I'd got it wrong. Nevertheless, I repeated it slowly to the driver. At first he looked only flummoxed, but as I boldly experimented with the pronunciation a broad grin crept across his face. Muttering to himself, he threw the taxi into gear and sped off. I sank back into the seat, relieved to have resolved a problem that was of my own making.

It was only a short drive, and I jumped out of the taxi confident that I'd be able to finish my report in good time. As the driver waved farewell, I walked into the brightly lit foyer of the TV station. It looked strangely different at night. I headed for the lifts. They weren't there. Now it was *my* turn to be flummoxed. I looked around for the reception desk. *That* had moved as well.

I felt a chill run through me as the ghastly truth sank in: I was in the wrong place!

My watch seemed to be throbbing on my wrist as precious editing minutes were lost. I appealed to the young receptionist for some clue as to where I was. She stared at me apologetically, gesticulated to some signs written in Japanese and smiled sweetly. I ran outside, praying for inspiration. It was as I was standing, defeated, in the soft drizzle of a Tokyo night that I suddenly noticed the logo of Nippon TV on the building opposite. The taxi had dropped me off on the wrong side of the road. Feeling incredibly stupid, I rushed across and into the lift.

'You took your time,' moaned my producer. 'You'll have to get a move on if this is going to make the feed.'

Two hours later I was back in my hotel. The report had been safely sent to London and, in the welcome peace of my room, I was reflecting on my chat with the Princess. I poured myself a whisky and mused on how helpful it had been to talk to her. But there was so much more that I wanted to ask, so many mysteries she could clear up for me. After another whisky, there seemed to be an incontrovertible logic about putting my thoughts in writing. I found some hotel notepaper and scrawled a letter to the Princess.

Dear Ma'am,
It was so helpful to meet you today and to discuss recent events. But it strikes me as absurd that, even though our paths are certain to cross many times in the coming months and years, my only chance to snatch a few words with you is when we are on a tour.

Wouldn't it be sensible to meet one day over a cup of coffee and talk in more depth?

I prattled on for a page or so before signing the letter, addressing it to the Princess and putting it in my handbag. I decided to wait until the morning before making a final decision about giving it to her. To my surprise, the letter *still* struck me as a sensible idea the next day, when the effects of my late-night tipple had worn off. As soon as the opportunity presented itself, I handed the envelope to the Princess's press secretary and asked him to pass it on.

For the remainder of the tour I tried in vain to catch Diana's eye as we whizzed around Tokyo. Had she read my letter? Would she write back? Or had she thought it was an impertinent approach from someone who should know better? But she didn't look my way once, and I was left to wonder whether I'd ever have more than a five-minute chat with her in some other far-flung part of the world.

I'd almost forgotten about it when, a couple of months later, I received a phone call from one of the Princess's staff.

'Is that Jennie Bond?'

'It is, yes – how can I help?'

'The Princess has asked me to tell you that she has been considering your letter, and she'd like you to come to the Palace for a chat.'

'Well, that would be grand,' I replied, trying to sound calm but already feeling the excitement bubbling up inside.

'Would next Tuesday suit? Say at 11 o'clock?'

'That's fine,' I said. 'Please tell her I should be delighted.'

I put down the phone quietly and sat in the hubbub of the newsroom thinking of the golden opportunity that had just plopped into my lap. Finally, after years of following the vicissitudes of her life, I was going to have the chance to ask her some of the questions that had so often been posed. I began to write a list: Did she think that she and Prince Charles had ever been suited to one another? When had she found out about Camilla Parker Bowles? How had the Morton book come about? Who had been the driving force in the decision to separate? Was divorce now inevitable? The list went on for three pages.

I didn't tell anyone at work about the meeting. It was going to be strictly off the record. I had assured the Princess in my letter that I wouldn't be expecting to rush outside and broadcast an account of our chat. Its purpose was solely to help me understand the woman she was and to hear her side of the story. I began counting down the hours until Tuesday.

The day dawned bright and sunny. I felt excited and apprehensive. I didn't want to upset the Princess by firing too many questions at her, but I was determined to make the best use of this meeting. It could well be my first and last. I left the house with plenty of time to spare, terrified of getting caught in a traffic jam and arriving late. Instead, I flew through town and found myself in Kensington High Street a full half-hour early. I sat in the car, mulling over what I was going to say. At 10.50 I drove up the private road that leads to Kensington Palace. The police officer on duty recognised me and waved me through. He pointed to a black front door and told me to park opposite. I did as he said, and, gathering my notebook and handbag, I walked towards the door which, to my surprise, was wide open.

The sweet smell of jasmine hit me as I brushed against the bush just outside. I leaned forward and knocked. No one came. Inside the long hallway, scented candles floating in a glass bowl added to the aroma. Feeling faintly ridiculous, I called out: 'Hello, anyone in?'

Suddenly a butler emerged from the darkness. Paul Burrell

was all smiles as he welcomed me in and showed me upstairs, past a huge portrait of the Princess.

'Were you waiting there long?' he asked. 'Sorry – the Princess is all ready for you. Just make your way up.'

As I reached the top of the wide staircase, the door ahead burst open and the Princess breezed out smiling, with arm extended.

'You *made* it! Well done,' she said as she shook my hand. 'Do come in. What would you like to drink?'

'I'll have a coffee, thanks,' I replied, feeling unsure whether I should behave like a girlfriend who'd come round for a gossip or a journalist on the prowl for a scoop. I tried to strike a middle path.

We went into her drawing room. It was pleasantly proportioned, but not huge by any means. She motioned towards the two plush sofas, with cushions piled high, facing one another in front of the fireplace. The Princess was wearing a chic pink suit; she was immaculately made up and looked as if she had just had her hair done. As she crossed her long legs, I felt squat and shabby, sinking gently into the settee opposite her.

'Well, I read your letter, Jennie. And I decided you were right – we *should* talk more often. So here you are.' Her tone was friendly but businesslike. I decided not to beat about the bush. She knew I was a journalist and that this was no girlie meeting of minds.

'There's so much I want to ask you,' I said. 'I've reported about you for years and had to commentate on so much of your life, but it's often been hard to know what's true. Let's start at the beginning. Do you think you and Prince Charles had enough in common to make your marriage work?'

She looked a little taken aback at my directness, but she

answered in a steady voice. 'Well, I can tell you this: we loved one another very much when we got married, and we could have been the best team in the world.'

I asked her what she had felt when, in their 'engagement interview', Prince Charles – faced with the question of whether they were in love – had answered with the immortal words: 'Yes, I suppose so – whatever "in love" means.'

'Well, I wondered what on earth he meant,' Diana told me. 'And I asked him about it afterwards.' She didn't say what his explanation had been.

'So when did you realise things were going wrong?' I enquired, sensing that she was open to almost any question I wanted to pose.

'I always lived in hope,' she replied. 'But I felt – no, I *knew* – that there was something wrong *before* the wedding day. I'm afraid there were always three people in this marriage, right from day one.'

It was the first time I had heard this phrase, which was to become so famous after the Princess's *Panorama* revelations. But it was almost certainly something she'd said many times before. She spoke without any apparent bitterness.

'Look, I know now that Charles's feelings for Camilla were always going to be stronger than any marriage he might have made.'

At that point Paul Burrell came in with a tray bearing coffee for me and iced water for the Princess. I took the opportunity to look around a little more. There were framed pictures of William and Harry everywhere; it was a homely room in many ways, with a desk near the window where the Princess could work.

Over the course of the next hour or so, Diana answered all my questions without flinching. What she told me was obviously only her side of the story; the truth doubtless lay somewhere between that version and all that I'd heard from the other camp. But I admired her for having the guts to let me ask them. She told me she felt she had been thrust into the very public role of being a princess without having been prepared for it. She'd frequently been in tears, unable to face another crowd.

'Charles would just say: "Go over and start chatting to them." But how *could* I? All my upbringing had been not to speak unless I was spoken to.'

She said she remembered the feeling of emptiness in those early years. 'I would go out and give all I had got to people who were in need. When I got home, I felt the need to be refilled. But there was no one there to praise or replenish me. Eventually, it seemed to me that I had to go outside to be loved, because I wasn't loved inside the Palace.'

She confirmed that she *had* thrown herself down the stairs at Sandringham when she was pregnant with William. But she insisted it had simply been a cry for help, not a serious attempt to do herself any harm. She bristled at my suggestions that psychiatrists had been called in to help her. 'I wasn't unbalanced,' she said. 'The trouble was I was too *sane* for my environment.'

We discussed her relationship with other members of the family. She was full of admiration for the Queen. 'I love her and respect her hugely,' she said. 'I'll do *anything* for her . . . She's always shown me great kindness and been very supportive. And she adores William and Harry. I think she's a rather lonely woman, you know. She became Queen at such a tender age, she must have been like a startled rabbit wondering how to contend with this new role.'

To my surprise, the Princess claimed that she got on 'quite well' with Prince Philip, too. There had, she said, been a sharp exchange of letters between them. 'But I gave him as good as I got,' she insisted, 'and we sorted it out.' Warming to her theme, she said she felt rather sorry for the Duke because he was often ignored by the media. 'Think about anything they do,' she said, 'like a tour overseas. It's always the Queen did this and the Queen did that, but Philip was there, too. He must sometimes get fed up and think, What's the point?'

After all that I'd heard about the frosty relationship between the Duke and his daughter-in-law, this was an intriguing new perspective.

In response to another of my questions, Diana said she was very close to Fergie. 'We're really like sisters. We need one another because we're in the same boat.'

She had nothing but praise for the Duke of York. 'Andrew has got a lot to offer this country and one day he'll show it. Then his value will be recognised. He's such a lovely man; I've never heard him complain about anything. He's just great with his children – and with mine, too.'

I asked her when *she* had judged that her marriage had irretrievably broken down. Was it at the same time that Prince Charles had reached that conclusion?

'I'd say in the late 1980s or early 1990s,' she answered. 'Because there's always hope that something can be put together again, if you try hard enough . . . It was Charles's decision to go for a separation. I didn't press for it – it wasn't my place. It was discussed three times during 1992, and, on the third occasion, something was done about it.'

'And did *you* want it by then?'

'Yes, I suppose so,' she replied, eyes downcast.

I asked her whether she still harboured any hopes that her

ruptured marriage could be mended. She paused for thought for a moment.

'No, I don't think so,' she sighed. 'No. I've grown too much. I've learned so much and changed a great deal. But I don't want a divorce. I don't know if it will happen. *I* certainly shan't be asking for one.'

So would she fight it? I demanded. She was silent for a minute or so.

'I don't know. There's so much to work out. It's very complicated, you know. I wish I could tell you what's going to happen but I just don't know.'

'But you're young and beautiful,' I went on, 'and you've hinted that you'd like to have a little girl. Why not go for a divorce and hope you can start again while you still have time on your side?'

I wondered whether she would think I was becoming too personal, but she seemed happy to carry on our conversation.

'Well, that's one reason why I *might* consider divorce, I suppose. But there's no one in my life. I mean . . . who'd want to take *me* on?'

She looked at me with her big eyes, her impossibly long legs crossed elegantly, asking me to believe that no red-blooded males would chance their luck with her. I stared back incredulously.

'Come on, now – I'm sure they're beating a path to your door.'

'No, they're not,' she replied. 'There's so much pressure for anyone who gets involved with me – the paparazzi are everywhere. Last week in Lech, there were eighty cameras trained on us, you know.'

She'd been skiing with William and Harry in Austria and at

one stage had marched up to a cameraman, put her hand over his lens and shouted at him to leave them alone. It had been all over the papers.

'I feel raped by it all,' she continued, looking anxious and wounded. 'I use that word a lot, I know, but it's how I feel . . . raped by those prying eyes everywhere. I have to protect my sons. I suppose you could say it's my fault for taking them somewhere like that. Well, I won't do it again, I can tell you. There'll be no more skiing in Europe for us. I *had* to tell that cameraman he was making our lives hell. I was furious. It seemed to work, but why should I have to go up to him like that? Why can't they understand that William doesn't like the cameras? He'll get used to them – he'll have to – but at the moment he's very sensitive.'

She told me that whatever other problems she and Prince Charles had, they never quarrelled over the boys, who loved their father very much. She was determined that William and Harry should be brought up in a way no one else in the Royal Family had been. She had taught them the importance of queuing, for example, and had taken them on buses and trains.

'I shower my boys with love and cuddles,' she went on, glancing affectionately at the photos of her sons. 'I never had any as a child so I love to give it to them. They're wonderful boys, both of them. And this country is *really* lucky to have William in line to the throne . . . He's all right, William is.' Her face was etched with maternal pride.

Ever since the separation, there had been much debate in the media about whether the Princess could or would still become Queen. Technically, it seemed, separation was no bar; she would automatically become Queen in name when her estranged husband became King. Whether she would ever be *crowned* was a different question. I decided to find out her point of view on this. 'But if you don't divorce, you'll be Queen some day,' I suggested.

Diana laughed and raised her eyes to the ceiling.

'Yes, well that's definitely *not* something I'm looking for,' she said.

I asked about her feelings for her estranged husband. Did she hate him for what had happened?

'No, I've never hated him,' she said quietly. 'I feel disappointed in him, though. We could have done so much together! I think he's lonely, lost and confused. I've told Richard Aylard [the Prince's private secretary] that he'd better come up with a five-year plan for Charles – and quickly – because he's going to need it. I'm so angry with Richard,' she went on. 'He's got it so wrong. Charles should never have allowed that film and the book to go ahead as they did. I told my husband: "Speak out on some things if you have to, but for goodness' sake hold *some* of it back. Keep *some* things private, at least." I warned him not to allow the book to be serialised. I said it would be raped, and I was right.'

She was angry now, and went on for some minutes about the effect the publicity surrounding Jonathan Dimbleby's book had had on herself and her sons. She said Dimbleby had come to see her six months before the book was published, and she had asked him to show some discretion on sensitive issues. 'But he didn't,' she complained. 'He did it all wrong and made me out to be unbalanced and paranoid.'

So *what*, I asked, were we to make of her cooperation with that earlier, devastating book by Andrew Morton?

'Well, Jennie, what happened was that so many of my friends had seen me in floods of tears and so unhappy so often that they felt they *had* to speak out. They regretted it later, of course, because they were hounded by the press.'

She told me then about the evening she had so publicly visited one of the acknowledged sources for Morton's book, Carolyn Bartholomew.

'I felt so sorry for Carolyn,' she said, 'so I decided to go round. My head told me not to, but my heart said yes. So off I went. Wrong again! Of course, I should have listened to my head. I was horrified when I saw those cameras waiting. To this day I don't know how they found out I was going to be there – though I think my phones are bugged. So, inevitably, I got into trouble again.'

Her sense of outrage was beguiling. She was articulate, sure of herself and convincing. Before too long, though, I would learn that her version of those particular events was, to say the least, economical with the truth.

Another occasion on which she told me she'd got into trouble was her announcement that she was cutting back on her public role. 'I knew that if I just told the press office to put out a statement, people would say the Queen or Prince Charles had forced me to do it,' she said. 'So I decided to break the news myself. It took a *huge* amount of courage to stand up and make that speech, and I got my wrist slapped for it. But I felt *so* relieved when I'd done it . . . Now I can *choose* what I do. I'm sorry some of my charities have lost out but I'm *not* going back to the kind of role I had.'

What, then, of the future? I enquired.

'Well, I'm almost there – but not quite. I haven't worked out exactly what I want to do, but it's something involving people and something on the world scene. I feel I can help people because I've been through just about everything in the book –

except for being homeless or losing your job. I feel I have the knowledge and experience to help.'

With some pride she told me that people occasionally came up to her in the street or in a shop and started discussing their problems. 'One chap came up and told me he was gay and he'd just come out.' She smiled. 'He wanted to tell me all about it, so I listened. I'm good at that.'

Despite the hurt she said she'd endured during the previous fourteen years, she insisted that she had no regrets about having married Prince Charles.

'It's all been a learning experience,' she told me, 'and now I have so much to give. That's all I want to do – help people through shared experience where I can, or simply listen.'

She said she found that many people looked to her for an example. 'When we separated, lots of women came to me and said: "Now you've done it, I shall too." But I told them: "No – don't do it just because I have."'

She said she had learned to adopt a positive attitude to all that had happened to her. She consciously told herself to view events as something constructive and to go forward from there.

'One thing I'm certain of is that there are lots of people out there who need a bit of TLC – and I want to give it.'

Tender loving care. It was the very thing Diana had craved in both her childhood and her marriage. But in neither had she felt her wish fulfilled. As we spoke, I sensed that – despite her sophisticated looks and surprisingly assured manner – there was much of the young girl in her still.

'I know I act like the Princess of Wales,' she giggled, 'but I still feel like Lady Di. That's the real me. I love it when people shout that out at me. It's a term of affection, I always think.'

Since her separation and her decision to dispense with body-guards, she said she'd been having a fine time learning how to fend for herself again.

'I've been so mollycoddled.' She laughed, drawing her legs up beneath her on the sofa. 'The other day I went downstairs and got in my car – and found there was no petrol in it. I'd got so used to someone filling it up for me, I'd quite forgotten that you had to call at a service station once in a while.'

Diana sipped iced water as she worked her way through my questions. Some were so personal that I would have hesitated to ask them of my best friend, and a few of her answers still seem to me to be too private to pass on – even after her death. But she struck me as tougher, more focused and far funnier than I had imagined. Despite her humour, she also seemed to me to be a lonely figure, stranded in her ivory tower. She gave the impression of yearning for the anonymity she had once possessed, while being simultaneously addicted to the fame she had now acquired. She told me, though, that she *wasn't* lonely at all: she had lots of good friends. It was no doubt true. But, on that particular morning, as we chatted on until finally it was *I* who looked at my watch and said I'd better be moving on, it seemed a strangely isolated existence.

As I took my leave, I told the Princess that if she ever felt she could repeat any of what she had told me on camera, I would be the first in line to facilitate her wish. Sadly, though, when she eventually decided to bare her soul in public it was to someone else.

Any illusions that my new-found rapport with Diana would result in some special access in the field were quickly dispelled when, about a week after our meeting, we found ourselves in Moscow. The city was in the grip of some of its steamiest temperatures of the century as the Princess arrived on a brisk working trip. One of her main purposes was to visit Moscow Children's Hospital and, with the rest of the ratpack, I followed her from ward to ward, watching discreetly from a distance. It seemed to me that this was the perfect opportunity for the Princess to say a few words to camera about the hospital and her hopes of what her visit might achieve. I positioned myself carefully by the exit of her last port of call; she'd seen everything she'd come to see and had had the chance to form an impression of the medical care on offer. I waited with my cameraman.

As Diana rounded the corner, heading towards her car, I stepped forward with my microphone. It seemed – indeed it *had been* – only the other day that we had chatted so intimately together. Surely, now, she'd greet me with a smile and give me the chance to ask a question or two about the visit?

'Good afternoon, Ma'am,' I beamed, microphone poised. 'Could I ask what you think of what you've seen here at the hospital?'

The Princess put on her most regal face, drew herself up to her full, impressive height, and marched straight past me without so much as a backward glance.

I let the mike fall limply to my side. So much, I thought, for this new, frank relationship with Diana.

CHAPTER TEN

A year of travels and trauma

I f my relationship with the Princess of Wales was a source of confusion, my family life remained a welcome haven from it all. A few days after the trip to Japan, Emma was five. By now she had settled in happily at infant school. Suddenly, Jim had the whole day to himself, and although he missed her dreadfully he soon found that the hours between the school runs flew by in a haze of shopping, cleaning and washing. As a counterpoint to all these mundane tasks, he occasionally took advantage of his newly regained freedom by jumping on one of his motorbikes and going for a burn-up like some middle-aged rebel without a cause. At weekends and in the school holidays, we'd all gradually got used to the long and tedious car journey up and down to Devon, which we increasingly felt was our 'real' home.

The beach is a wonderful place to make friends – especially if you have children – and we had made more than we could ever have dared hope. Our bizarre wooden house, in its tranquil green valley, became the focus of our social life as we invited our growing circle of friends to join us for a sundowner or two on our deck overlooking the ocean. But I lived then, as I do now, with the constant fear that a major royal story would break, leaving me stranded at least four hours from London. I must be one of the few people for whom an essential item of beach equipment is my pager, clipped firmly to my bikini, while my mobile phone nestles in my towel. There was not, however, much opportunity to lie around on the beach in 1995. For it turned out to be a busy year for the Royal Family and their accompanying media, both at home and abroad.

Sandwiched between the outings to Japan and Russia with the Princess of Wales, the royal ratpack found itself heading to South Africa for a ground-breaking state visit by the Queen. Her return to the land where she had last set foot in 1947 with her mother and father was certain to be nostalgic for her, and deeply significant for the post-apartheid democracy headed by the irrepressible Nelson Mandela. I flew out a couple of days before the royal party, carrying archive film of that earlier visit so that I could prepare a preview piece.

Africa has always excited me; even its name breathes magic and unknown danger. As we flew over its vastness, I had my head pressed against the tiny window, craning my neck to examine the contours of the land and the snake-like shimmer of the rivers which, I whispered to myself, were doubtless bristling with crocodiles and hippos. Over the great African plains I strove to make sense of the microscopic dots far below, convinced that they were elephants and lions. The theme from the film *Out of Africa* reverberated around my head as, lost in hopelessly romantic thought, I imagined the lives of the millions of people for whom we were just a passing wisp of fumes, thousands of feet above. I couldn't wait to see Cape Town.

I wasn't disappointed. Few sights in the world can match that first glimpse of Table Mountain. As always, I was no sooner in a taxi than I started sounding out the driver about the impending arrival.

'Do you know that the Queen is coming here on Sunday?'

'Oh! We *do* know, we *do*.' There was genuine excitement in his voice. 'It means much, very much indeed to my country,' he went on. As we headed towards the hotel, he assured me that *everyone* knew the Queen was coming to South Africa; it was a visit that was seen as truly important, he said, because it meant that the country was back on the world map.

To my disappointment, the hotel I'd been booked into was certainly not on the *tourist* map. It was smack bang in the centre of the business area of Cape Town. The view out of my window was of other large hotels, with neon signs and pot plants on roofs. The sunshine was tantalising, but executives aren't expected to want to enjoy it; so there was nowhere to eat, drink or even sit outside. As a small measure of recompense, my room did offer a peek of the sea in the far distance and, on the other side of the hotel, whenever I took the lift I could enjoy a panoramic view of Table Mountain.

No sooner had I arrived than my producer phoned to set up a meeting with the rest of the team he'd brought with him from Johannesburg. It was time to start planning the fifty or so engagements that the Queen and the Duke would be undertaking during the week to come. We pored over the schedule with its mass of instructions about how many cameras and journalists would be allowed at each venue. Methodically, we worked through the long list until our eyes were glazing over and our minds were boggled.

Two days later, with the planning finally completed, I was

standing at the waterside overlooking Table Bay as *Britannia* steamed slowly into harbour, escorted by a noisy flotilla of small boats. It was 10 o'clock in the morning, a perfect autumn day in March, with clear blue skies, a sea breeze and brilliant sunshine. Whatever your feelings about the political correctness of Britain possessing a royal yacht, the sheer majesty of the ship was enough to bowl anyone over. And it seemed an entirely appropriate start to a state visit of historic proportions. Standing on a specially constructed wooden platform, battling to keep my hair under a modicum of control in the stiffening breeze, I broadcast live on *Breakfast* as *Britannia* glided gently forward, immaculate in every detail. The crowds, packed into every corner around the harbour, cheered and waved as the Queen came ashore to be met by their hero (and, I suspect, hers), President Mandela. It was the beginning of a hectic but incredibly happy few days for us all.

In the near half-century since the Queen had last stepped ashore in South Africa, the political and social map had been redrawn. She, like everyone else, couldn't fail to be inspired by the man who had led that revolution and who was now her host. The next day, at a reception on board *Britannia*, the Queen was at her most animated as she told us about her memories of her last visit and her joy at being welcomed back by President Mandela. As we stood on the deck, chatting in the late afternoon sunlight, she seemed exhilarated by her recollections of the past and fired by the promise of South Africa's future.

It is, though, the fate of royalty never – or at least rarely – to see life as it really is. On the second day of her visit, the Queen was taken to a township on the outskirts of Cape Town. Khayelitsha was home then to some half a million people living in conditions that could at best be described as squalid. Nearly a quarter of the children were stunted through chronic malnutrition, and the statistics suggested that there were more guns in the township than there were houses with water or electricity. Though she must have seen some of that desperate poverty from her car, the reality that the Queen was shown face to face was very different. She was taken to a newly painted, comparatively smart nutrition and welfare centre where, in a small oasis of green grass, lines of young girls in freshly laundered uniforms were waiting to greet her.

Fifty yards away, in a bare and dusty hut with no sanitation and little protection from the elements, a painfully thin and dirt-encrusted woman told me why she had sent her children to live with relatives in the countryside. It was hard to understand what she was saying: she had hardly any teeth and spoke virtually no English. But she acted out her thoughts well enough for me to grasp that she believed her children stood the chance of a life of less misery elsewhere. There was a barren emptiness about the tiny hovel she called home; her only companion now was her husband – or boyfriend – who sat on an upturned rusty bucket looking vacantly out at the commotion of the royal visit going on across the track. I thought it a shame that the Queen could not be shown more of that truth.

One of the most complicated days of the tour for the media was when we moved off from Cape Town, heading for Johannesburg, with an engagement en route in a township near Port Elizabeth. We phoned ahead and booked a room for the afternoon in a hotel in Port Elizabeth. We'd at least have somewhere quiet to edit a report before sending it to London and jumping on the next plane to Johannesburg. We got up early, loaded all the equipment into a small fleet of taxis and set off for the airport. We'd worked out our plan with military exactitude. As soon as we landed, the picture editor would take a taxi to the hotel, set up the equipment and await my arrival. I, meanwhile, would go with the rest of the press to the Queen's engagement in a township called New Brighton. Our cameraman, Glenn, had been given the job of filming the Queen's plane touching down at Port Elizabeth; he'd then come on by car to film my piece to camera in the township and, as soon as the Queen's engagement was over, we'd race to the hotel, write and edit the piece at breakneck speed, and then dash to the television station to send it by satellite. That should leave us with about fifteen minutes to get back to the airport for the connecting flight to Jo'burg. It was desperately tight – but feasible, as long as nothing went wrong.

The flight to Port Elizabeth was uneventful, and the beach looked glorious as we swept by in our press bus. If *only*, I mused, I could ask the driver to stop so that I could jump out and run across that white sand into the sea. Instead we drove on into another sea: of 20,000 excited faces jamming every approach into New Brighton as almost the entire population turned out to see the Queen. The bus inched forward through the cheering crowds, most of whom seemed convinced that we were part of the royal household.

'Come on, come *on*,' we yelled at the hapless driver. 'Sit on that horn – you've got to get us through before the Queen gets here.'

In a cacophony of shouting and horn-blowing, we eventually came to a halt outside a large hall festooned with flags and bunting. Impatiently, we clattered off the bus – all ladders and lenses – and, to the intense curiosity of the crowds, took up our assigned positions. I'd been given a rota pass for inside the hall and fought my way to the door. Inside, rather to my disappointment, things were much calmer as the assembled dignitaries awaited the royal convoy. About 500 people in their Sunday best were seated in neat rows, facing a stage. It didn't compare with the colour and chaos outside which, I thought to myself, would make *far* better television pictures. Then, in a corner of the hall, I spied an exotic-looking man brandishing a spear and boasting very little in the way of clothing except a loincloth.

'Who's he?' I asked a woman standing near by who looked as though she might know.

'He's the praise singer,' she said.

'Is the Queen going to meet him?' I enquired hopefully.

'She certainly is,' came the reply. 'He's going to lead her all the way up to the stage.'

I just had time to prime the pool cameraman about the praise singer's starring role when a crescendo of cheers outside signalled that the Queen had arrived in town. A few minutes later she was being greeted at the door by the leading citizens of New Brighton, for whom this visit had meant months of planning. As she turned to walk up the hall, 'loincloth man' – who, I'd now established, was a Khosa tribesman wearing native dress – leaped out in front of her and began ululating, flourishing his spear above his head.

She looked somewhat startled, but quickly regained her composure and realised that she was required to follow her Khosa escort up the aisle. With a wry look on her face, the Queen cut a diminutive figure as she fell into step behind him. The praise singer took his duties extremely seriously; the chanting and spear-waving became ever more frantic with each step. As they approached the stage, the shrill ululation echoing around the room, the Queen came within a couple of feet of where I was standing. With a sideways glance towards me and a twinkle in her eyes, she whispered: 'I *do* hope he's friendly.'

His role executed to perfection, the Khosa singer stood to one side and allowed the Queen to pass. She made her way on to the stage and sat down, with a suggestion of some relief. It didn't last long. No sooner had she put her handbag down and settled back in her chair than, from the wings, African drums sounded out a frenetic rhythm. Suddenly, eight buxom women, their bare breasts bouncing to the beat, leaped out on to the stage. Their energetic dancing was certainly a rousing performance even if, as I remarked later in my report, it was something of an unusual fare to set before the Queen. She watched with the politest interest and the merest tap of her toe.

As soon as the dancing and speeches were over, I beat a retreat to find Glenn outside. Time was racing by, and I was due at the hotel to start editing, but first I had to do my piece to camera. I'd composed the words in my head while I was watching the dancing; now I simply had to remember them and say them with conviction.

'OK, where shall we do it?' I asked Glenn, who was looking pretty hot and bothered after his drive from the airport. The crowds had grown even larger since I'd gone inside, and several thousand of them seemed to find the camera even more fascinating than the prospect of seeing the Queen. They swarmed around us like bees round a honey pot, talking, giggling, pointing and pushing. Every time I started speaking to camera, they crowded behind me, peering into the lens and laughing. I tried asking them sweetly if they could clear the background for us; for ten seconds or so a space would appear behind me, but the moment I began they converged on us again. I tried shouting at them to leave us alone to get on with our work, but to no avail. It was a hopeless situation. After several attempts at a clean piece to camera – with no mistakes from me and no problems with the background – I decided to cut my losses, take what I had and make a dash for the hotel.

'Let's go – where's the car?' I asked.

Glenn looked despondent. He shrugged his shoulders and cast his eyes around. It was mayhem, with bustling crowds and queues of vehicles everywhere. 'It's hopeless,' he said. 'We'll never get out of here in time for you to edit. Your best bet is to make your own way to the hotel. I'll follow on once I've got the car out.'

Well, that's just terrific, I thought. Here I am stranded in a township, up against an impossible deadline, with no idea where I'm going and no transport to get there anyway. In my white stilettos, I picked my way across the dusty park, hoping for inspiration. It came in the shape of a South African police officer.

'Are you all right there?' he enquired.

'Not really,' I blurted out, thinking – rather like the Queen – that I hoped he was friendly. 'I'm from the BBC in London and I have to get to the Hotel Elizabeth as fast as possible. Are there any taxis around?'

He shook his head. 'No, lady. I'm afraid you don't stand any chance at all round here.'

I felt desolate. After all the effort we'd been to, and the promises I'd made to the news desk to get a piece to them for the *One o'Clock News*, a simple lack of wheels had felled me. He must have seen how upset I was.

'Look, how desperate is this?' he asked. 'Do you want *me* to give you a lift?'

Untroubled now about whether he was friendly or not, I seized this unexpected solution to my dilemma.

'That would be *brilliant*,' I gushed. 'You are an absolute *saviour*. Where's your car?'

He pointed to a large, yellow armoured police van and said: 'Get in.'

And that was how I came to be screaming through the streets of Port Elizabeth in a police van, with its siren wailing and lights flashing. As we raced along, blitzing through red traffic lights, I bounced around in the passenger seat, lurching from side to side as we careered around corners. I spoke only to apologise for my lack of conversation.

'Sorry . . . can't talk . . . got to write this script . . . but you're very kind. Thank you so much.'

We arrived at the hotel in about ten minutes flat. I shouted my thanks as I jumped out of the van and flew through the doors. My picture editor was waiting in the hotel reception, looking agitated and annoyed.

'Where *have* you been? Did you get arrested? This is going to be next to impossible. Have you written your script?'

As we ran through the hotel corridors to the edit room, I tried to explain what had happened. But none of that mattered any more: we simply had to start editing and pray that we could get finished in time. We worked at a furious pace; the piece was finished in half an hour flat – which is about a third of the time we'd ideally take – and we set about packing up all the equipment again. Glenn arrived back in time to lend a hand; we threw it all into the car and sped off to the television station with our hearts in our mouths: the satellite slot was about to start. Incredibly, we got there with three minutes in hand and, through the wonders of modern technology, my report winged its way through the air to London.

'My God! We *did* it!' I cheered as we got the all clear. 'I *really* thought we'd had it when I was stuck in New Brighton.'

'Well, don't get too excited yet,' said my producer. 'We've still got to get to the airport.'

They were closing the check-in for our flight when we arrived, and they were far from pleased to see all our luggage. But they loaded it on, and we sat back to enjoy the journey, feeling smug that against the odds our report would already have run on the news back home.

Or so we thought. In fact, when I phoned through to the news organiser in London later that day from Johannesburg, I relearned another of the hard truths of this business.

'Hi. It's Jennie Bond here. We really bust a gut to get that report to you. I hope the *One o'Clock News* liked it.'

'Oh, Jennie, yes, thanks very much.' I could detect a sense of embarrassment in his voice. 'They *really* appreciated it, but I'm afraid it was a very busy news day here – so they dropped it.'

News editors are paid to make ruthless decisions and, on the day, a story will always be measured against what else is happening in the world. Of course, I knew the rules; but it didn't make the outcome any less painful. I went to bed livid.

There was plenty of news interest, though, as the tour moved on through Johannesburg and Soweto to Durban. And on the final night I very nearly had a scoop. President Mandela had come to Durban to say farewell to the Queen, and a spectacular finale had been arranged. The grand City Hall was floodlit on a balmy African evening and, as I waited for the President and his royal guest to arrive, I felt a mixture of sadness and exhilaration that a demanding week's work was almost over. In the semi-darkness of the forecourt, a band of fiery Zulu dancers were rehearsing their warrior jumps and gesticulations beneath the stars. The drumbeat coursed through my body; I had to force myself not to join in. The danger and excitement of Africa seemed more compelling than ever.

By luck more than judgement, I'd secured myself a particularly fine spot at the top of the steps leading into City Hall. Nelson Mandela would have to walk right by me – and to my astonishment I discovered that my cameraman and I were the only news team there.

'Let's try to blend in with the background,' I told Glenn. 'I don't want the security guys to notice we're here, because I'm sure we're not meant to be.'

I could see my colleagues from ITN and Sky down in the forecourt with the rest of the pack. Although we work closely together for much of any tour, there are always moments when there's no need for a pool arrangement, and one of us might just seize an advantage. This, it seemed to me, was one of those moments. Glenn and I stayed in the shadows for as long as possible. The crowds began to ululate and cheer as their President's car came into view. Nelson Mandela walked slowly up the steps – straight towards me. Glenn and I made our move; I plucked up my courage, stuck out my microphone and addressed the great man: 'Mr Mandela, can you tell me what the Queen's visit has meant for your country?'

I expected to be pounced on by burly security men, but the President waved them away. He looked at me, smiling, and said: 'It has been one of the unforgettable moments in South Africa's history. By coming here, Her Majesty the Queen has set the seal on my country's new international standing.'

With that, he walked on towards the door. I could see the other correspondents chafing at the bit to get to my spot but they were held firmly behind the barriers. *Yes*, I thought to myself, that's brilliant – the perfect sound-bite for my final report . . . Now, *please*, go on in, Mr Mandela, so no one else can get you. I was shaking with excitement – not only to have got the sound-bite but to have talked to such a living legend. It was then that President Mandela unwittingly destroyed my short-lived hopes of an exclusive interview. Just as he reached the doorway, he turned round and, in that soft voice, said: 'Now, is there anyone else who wants to talk to me?'

My heart sank as my fellow reporters zoomed up the steps, microphones and cameras at the ready, almost weeping with relief that they could now have their own interviews with my hero. I stood and watched as my scoop evaporated into the warm night air.

It *was*, nevertheless, a magical evening as the Queen was fêted by the crowds and the Zulu dancers. She was also presented with a rather unusual gift. In keeping with Zulu custom, a pedigree bull had been carefully selected for her and put on display in a sturdy cage just outside City Hall. It had proved a source of great fascination throughout the evening. The Queen was informed that, according to tradition, she was required either to wrestle the beast to the ground or chase it until it dropped from exhaustion. *This*, I thought gleefully, was going to make stunning television. In the event, it was perhaps unsurprising that, faced with this choice, the Queen decided instead to donate the raging bull to a research centre.

She and the Duke left Durban that night, their car surrounded by cheering crowds, and the ratpack began to disband – as it must at the end of every royal tour. We had worked and lived together for the best part of ten days; we'd had many a laugh as well as the occasional fight; and now it was time for us all to go our separate ways. Some of the newspaper guys were flying straight home that night; my crew were heading back to Johannesburg early the next morning; and I was off on safari for a couple of days. It was the first, and probably the last, time that I stayed on in a country alone at the end of a tour.

When I'd first heard that I'd be going to South Africa, the chance of fulfilling a lifetime's dream of going on safari had seemed too good to miss. 'How would you feel,' I'd asked Jim one evening in London, 'if I stayed on for a day or two after the tour and went to a game park?'

'Good idea,' he answered. 'Emma and I will be fine and you may never have another chance. Do it.'

With this encouragement I'd therefore booked myself into a small safari park about four hours' drive north of Durban. Even before the taxi arrived to take me there, I had grave misgivings. As I watched my colleagues loading their luggage on to the bus for the airport – and home – I felt appallingly lonely. The pack mentality becomes instilled in you after a few days; it's comforting to be involved in all the gossip and rumours that are part and parcel of a royal tour. Like a class of rather unruly schoolchildren, we travel around the world whingeing and laughing, winding one another up and moaning – but always *sharing* our many adventures. Inevitably, when a tour is over and the pack disperses, you tend to feel alone and isolated. In the clear light of day, I was also at a loss to explain to myself how I could possibly either justify or enjoy being away from my husband and little girl for a day longer than necessary. It was in this confused and depressed state of mind that I reluctantly climbed into the taxi for the long drive north.

The game park was wonderful; my room was superb, the setting magnificent. On night drives and early morning treks both on foot and on horseback, I got close to animals I had only ever seen in zoos. Everyone was delightfully kind to me. And I was miserable. After twelve hours I could see *no* point in remaining there a minute longer and did my best to find a plane home. But everything was fully booked. I was stuck. I endured the rest of my stay with as good grace as I could muster and fled back to Durban for my flight home vowing that I would never again stay away for a minute longer than my job required. When I finally walked through the front door, I hugged Emma as tightly as if we'd been apart for a month.

The summer was dominated by the commemorations to mark the fiftieth anniversary of the end of the Second World War. Hyde Park was the hub of a weekend of VE Day ceremonies, opened by the Queen Mother and attended by hundreds of thousands of people. It was a major national event and one that I was both privileged and daunted to cover. These are occasions that the BBC cannot afford to get wrong; news editors get incredibly jumpy at the merest suggestion that there may be problems with your report. It has to be thoughtfully scripted, tastefully paced, superbly filmed and – more than anything else – ready for transmission on time. We were based in a noisy Portakabin on one side of Hyde Park which began to feel like home after several eighteen-hour days. The stress levels were high, the pressure intense but, as the final fireworks exploded, we cracked open a bottle of champagne for a job which, I hope, was well done.

In July the Palace petrified me with a sudden announce-ment that the Queen Mother was in hospital after an oper-ation. Fortunately, I was in the office when the call came through.

'What do you mean she's in hospital?' I demanded. 'Why didn't somebody tell me?'

'Because Queen Elizabeth regards it as a private matter,' came the curt Palace reply.

Panic was surging through the newsroom by this time. News editors were buzzing round my desk as I sought to establish the facts. Incredibly, the news hadn't leaked out that the Queen Mother had been admitted to hospital the day before, or that the surgery – for a cataract – had been planned for some time. She'd recovered well, I was told, and would be going home shortly. There was just enough time for us to scramble a crew down to the hospital before she came out, looking astonishingly fit for someone of her age who had just undergone an operation.

Three weeks later she celebrated her ninety-fifth birthday. As always, I arrived at Clarence House shortly after 6 in the morning. Several dozen loyal royal fans were already queuing outside the gates; some had spent two nights sleeping on the pavement in order to guarantee a front-row position. As I got out of the car, a cheer went up. Familiar faces from all the birthdays gone by were waiting to greet me and show off some of the gifts and cards they had brought for the Queen Mother. It was, though, something of a surprise to find myself the recipient of a carefully wrapped parcel. And it was one that proved that, however smart I may appear to the untutored eye, I am by nature a complete slattern.

'This is for you,' said one of the Queen Mother's most ardent followers, leaning over the barrier towards me.

'That's very kind,' I answered. 'But why on earth have you brought *me* a present?'

'Well, I do hope you won't be offended,' she said apologetically. 'But I couldn't help noticing last year that your make-up bag was a bit of a mess. So I bought you a new one. I hope you like it.'

I have never mastered the art of assessing exactly how much will fit into a handbag. Consequently, mine are forever spewing open, revealing an unappetising jumble of possessions which spill over on to the pavement while I address the camera. Suitably abashed that this thoughtful woman had seen the execrable state of my make-up bag – its battered contents oozing cosmetics, with blobs of discarded chewing gum stuck to the lipsticks – I accepted her gift with humility. It was a glamorous, gold bag, which served me well for some months before it, too, fell prey to my slovenly ways.

The more hectic my life, the worse the handbag problem becomes and, in November, it was dire. I was all set for a visit to Argentina with the Princess of Wales when one of my bosses called me into his office. His tone was serious, his expression grave.

'You need to know that Diana has recorded an interview for *Panorama*. I can't tell you what she's said because I don't know, but it's obviously going to be a major story. I think we'd better review the decision to send you to Argentina.'

The first shock was that the Princess had chosen to speak to *Panorama* at all. The second was that, after our frank and friendly meeting, she had given the interview to someone else in the BBC. What's more, it was now threatening my trip to a part of the world I'd never seen. I was horrified.

'Well, I can't agree,' I argued. 'I need to be wherever the Princess is – that's obviously where the story will be. I think I should go.'

We agreed to postpone any decision about Argentina while I handled the avalanche of interest in the revelation that the Princess had opened up her heart to Martin Bashir. Not that the newsroom was given any inkling at that stage of just how devastating the programme would be; but the very fact that it was happening at all was enough to lead every bulletin. Two days later Diana-fever was still running high, but I was enjoying a little light relief from it by presenting the news. The *One o'Clock News* had just come off air when a call from Buckingham Palace came through to my desk.

'Jennie?' It was the dulcet tones of the Queen's press secretary, Charles Anson, sounding as if he was massaging body oil into my back. 'I just thought you'd appreciate a word of warning that we'll be making an announcement of some interest in about an hour.'

'What's it about, Charles?' I asked, ruing the day I had agreed to read the news that week. 'Do I need to get myself off newsreading?'

'I can't tell you what it is but, yes, I think that would be a good idea.'

Further attempts to wheedle more information out of him met a brick wall. I thanked him and hung up. The phone went again immediately. It was one of my Fleet Street colleagues. 'Any idea what's up?' he asked anxiously. 'There's definitely something going on. Do you think it's an announcement of a divorce for Diana? Or could it be Edward and Sophie? An engagement?'

I told him I was as much in the dark as him. We promised to call one another if we found out any more. I ran over to the news organiser and told her what I knew. Then I set about trying to find someone else to read the news. Unfortunately, everyone who could help was at lunch, so it fell to one of my fellow reporters to step into the breach – in the nick of time.

The phone rang again. It was the Palace. 'Jennie, this is to let you know that the Queen Mother is in hospital.' My heart sank, once again fearing the worst. 'She's had an operation to replace her right hip. She's come through it well and is expected to stay in hospital for about two weeks.'

The Tannoy announcement that rang through Television Centre brought BBC bosses out of the woodwork and into the newsroom like a swarm of locusts. We went straight on air, with my fellow reporter sitting in the presenter's chair I had so recently vacated, while I resumed my role of a correspondent relaying the latest news. And I was only too aware of the consequences of that news: over the next fortnight I was going to be spending a great deal of time outside the King Edward VII Hospital for Officers. Any lingering hopes of going to Argentina had now comprehensively evaporated.

For the next few days I saw nothing of my family as I covered these two major stories. Between long stints outside the hospital, I had to report on the fierce speculation about the content of the Princess's *Panorama* interview. Fuel was added to the fire when the Press Complaints Commission issued a stiff warning that she would 'have to face the consequences' of her decision to speak out. The Palace admitted candidly that they'd had no idea that the Princess had recorded the interview. There was a palpable sense of shock that she'd gone off on her own tack, and they were unhappy that the BBC had not kept them informed.

There are few dilemmas worse for a correspondent than dealing with a royal story that has in-house overtones. You have the Palace breathing down your neck from one corner and your bosses from the other. Here, I had one with trumps: a cracking story with the potential to rock the monarchy to its roots in which the BBC had been the main collaborator. I was left in the middle, trying to persuade the Palace to give me their reaction to an event which the BBC had helped bring about. I rang Charles Anson: 'What's the Queen had to say about this?'

'I can't tell you anything about Her Majesty's response,' came the cool reply. 'She knows no more about the contents of the programme than what has been issued by the BBC. And she doesn't generally watch *Panorama*.'

I squirmed at the cold tones Charles was adopting. We normally got on pretty well.

'So is there any reaction from the Prince of Wales?' I ventured.

'No,' came the response. 'He wasn't informed about it at all. This was something the Princess undertook entirely on her own initiative.'

It was clear that the Palace was as much in the dark as I was. Even though I worked for the BBC, that darkness was total: I wasn't privy to anything the Princess had said. All in all, it was an extraordinary build-up to the programme, and guaranteed it headline news every day. Finally, on 20 November – three years to the day that the fire at Windsor Castle had commanded national attention – the most sensational *Panorama* ever was screened.

In various parts of Television Centre, my bosses were gathered in small groups to watch this historic transmission. The contents remained top secret; only a select few, who did not include me, had been told what to expect. I found an empty desk in the newsroom and sat, notebook poised, already feeling exhausted after a long day. But, like the 20 million people who were watching *Panorama* around the country that night, I was soon agog at the Princess's brutal candour. It was riveting stuff – even if I'd already heard much of it during our meeting at Kensington Palace. Some of the phrases were particularly familiar: 'there were three of us in this marriage; it was a bit crowded' was one that no one would forget. Her coy revelation of her adultery with James Hewitt was a sensation in itself, but her comments about the remoteness of monarchy and her questioning of her husband's fitness to be King were explosive.

My work for the next forty-eight hours was cut out – and most of it would have to be done without the luxury of sleep. I worked through the night, putting together a report for *Breakfast*; I had just enough time to refresh my make-up before dashing down to the Palace, well before dawn, to go live on air at the start of another marathon day. We'd spent hours drawing up lists of interviewees, and now we pounced on them for their reaction to the night's events. We had producers and cameras everywhere – looking for the Princess, following the Prince and talking to their friends. It was an intense and frantic day. Eventually, I crawled home some forty hours after I'd left the house, shattered and drained by all that had happened.

There's no doubt that Diana had prepared meticulously for her *Panorama* performance. I have been told since that she did her hair herself – deliberately badly – and consciously applied theatrically heavy make-up. If it was not scripted, which some close to her say it most definitely *was*, it was certainly thoroughly rehearsed. The Princess had played a stealthy game, but her decision not to tell anyone at the Palace about her interview had left her more alienated than ever. Shortly afterwards, her press secretary, Geoff Crawford, resigned – to be followed soon after by her private secretary, Patrick Jephson.

The fallout from the programme dominated the news agenda for days. The Princess flew off to Argentina with one of our reporters, Margaret Gilmore, in tow while I stayed behind to analyse the *Panorama* aftermath and report on the Queen Mother's recovery. It was a sensible division of duties, but I still longed to be in South America with the rest of the ratpack. I have to admit that when I saw Margaret doing a piece to camera off the coast of Patagonia, with whales dancing in the ocean behind her, I loudly bemoaned my fate in having been left behind to mind the shop.

But there was plenty of shop to mind. Three days after *Panorama*, Prince Charles's private secretary, Richard Aylard, told me that the atmosphere at the Palace had been electric as the programme had gone out. He said the Prince hadn't watched it; 'it would have destroyed him'. Instead, it had fallen to Richard to tell the Prince about the contents.

'There was great sadness – and deep hurt – at what was said,' he told me. 'But the most shocking part of it all was when the Princess questioned whether the Prince's character was suited to be King.'

He claimed that this had been one of Diana's constant themes over the years, and a source of great dismay. He was unusually frank about the consequences of the programme. 'There's absolutely no doubt', he told me, 'that this has hastened divorce proceedings. It's no longer a question of *if* but of *when*.'

And so it proved. Five days before Christmas, I'd taken advantage of having got home early and – with Emma already asleep – I'd just got out of the bath when the office rang.

'It looks as if the Queen has written to Charles and Diana telling them to get a divorce,' said the news organiser. *'Newsnight* want you on set in less than an hour. Can you do it?'

I sat staring at my freshly cleansed face in the mirror, groaned and told them I'd be there in forty minutes. *On* went the make-up I had so recently removed, *off* came the nightie, to be replaced by a business suit, and into the car I jumped for the race to Television Centre. It turned out to be another night with precious little sleep. As soon as Jeremy Paxman had finished interrogating me, the demands began to roll in from *Breakfast*. After another gargantuan session at work, I finally returned home feeling that the situation had at least been clarified in time for Christmas. I had every intention of enjoying the remainder of the festive season with my family undisturbed, if I could possibly help it, by royalty.

CHAPTER ELEVEN

Divorce

The aftershocks from the Princess's *Panorama* interview continued for weeks, creating a series of small earthquakes in my life. Behind the scenes, briefings against her became more frequent.

'She's clearly an unhappy woman,' I was told. 'Her malicious intent towards the Prince was obvious from the start to the finish of that interview. It's changed the whole framework.'

The Queen's letter urging Charles and Diana to divorce was tantamount to a command, and there was little question that it would be obeyed. But as the Princess had made so clear on *Panorama*, she had no intention of 'going quietly'.

'That's the problem,' she'd told the nation. 'I'll fight to the end, because I believe I have a role to fulfil and I have two children to bring up.'

Now she was battling for that role before agreeing to end her marriage.

'She doesn't really know what she wants,' the Palace voices told me. 'She thinks she's something between the Princess

Royal and Audrey Hepburn – but she just flits from thing to thing.'

In a sudden but unsurprising about-turn, the Princess announced that she wouldn't be spending Christmas with the rest of the Royal Family at Sandringham. The Prince, facing an avalanche of speculation that divorce from Diana would lead to marriage to Camilla Parker Bowles, moved swiftly to announce that he 'had no intention of remarrying'. Lawyers stepped in to tackle the messy task of unravelling the fairy-tale marriage. Ironically, divorce – which had once been such anathema in royal circles – had now become the only honourable way out. But it took two months of tough negotiation before the Princess finally complied with the Queen's recommendation. As always, it came out of the blue, and it sent my blood pressure soaring.

It was the end of February. My day had been spent covering a service at St Paul's Cathedral to honour the British troops who had died in the Gulf War. The Queen had been greeted by her troublesome son, Prince Charles, who'd planted a reverential kiss on her gloved hand. It was a fascinating moment to witness at such a difficult time in their relationship. The service had passed off uneventfully, and, after a busy morning and afternoon writing and editing, I was enjoying a moment's peace back in the newsroom. The *Six o'Clock News* had just started as I sat down to watch my report go out.

Some people imagine that I sit in an office with a secretary at my beck and call. Nothing could be further from the truth. Although I have in recent years acquired a corner I can call my own – albeit back to back with other correspondents – for many of those frantic years I worked in the newsroom itself, 'hot-desking' with the rest of the reporters. As soon as someone finished their shift, you would take over their seat and computer terminal. It worked as an incentive to get in early; otherwise you'd often find there was nowhere to sit at all. It was overcrowded and noisy, but those are the surroundings I've worked in for most of my life. I've always enjoyed the vibrant atmosphere of news breaking around you, the sense of being at the centre of the communications machine.

On the night in question the *Six o'Clock News* was running smoothly, and I was silently wondering whether I'd be required to make any changes for the 9 p.m. news or – joy of joys – be allowed to head home. Suddenly a newsflash from the Press Association made it abundantly clear that I wouldn't be going home at *all* that night: 'Princess of Wales has agreed to divorce.'

The words on my computer screen were like a drill boring through my head.

As the Tannoy announcement blasted through the newsroom, everyone was galvanised into action. The phones lit up, my pager bleeped crazily and news editors hissed around me like a plague of mosquitoes.

'Is it true? What's the Palace saying about it? Where's Diana? Has the Queen said anything?'

They volleyed questions at me as if I had a direct line to the Palace.

'I need to make some calls,' I pleaded.

'You've got five minutes – no more,' I was told. 'You have to be in the studio by then. They want you live with all the latest on this immediately after your report about the Gulf service.'

'Thanks,' I said sarcastically as I sat with two phones glued to my ears: one waiting to talk to Buckingham Palace, the other to the Princess's new press secretary, Jane Atkinson. Producers surrounded me, putting in calls to Diana's lawyers and friends.

No one was responding, and the seconds were haemorrhaging away with alarming speed.

By now the Press Association was making it clear that the statement had been authorised by the Princess herself. Of course, I was desperate to check the facts, but the news gallery was shouting for me. I decided that as long as we sourced what we said to the news agency, it was enough to go on air with. My report about the Gulf service was already being broadcast: I had one minute and forty-five seconds to get to the studio.

Clutching in my hand the few details I had, I raced down the corridor, brushed past the powder puff proffered by the waiting make-up artist and took my place next to Anna Ford. Shoving the microphone up my jacket, I had just enough time to whisper to Anna that I knew next to nothing, before the countdown began and we were on air. It was 6.25 already, and the bulletin was almost over.

There was time to say what I knew: that the Princess had agreed to a divorce, that she would be known in future as Diana, Princess of Wales – apparently without the HRH – and that she would continue to live at Kensington Palace. Sadly, there was also just time to say what I *didn't* know, in response to Anna's very reasonable question: 'There must be a great sense of relief at the Palace about this?' she asked, with a sympathetic look towards me, knowing the pressure I was under.

'Indeed,' I mused, wishing I'd been given the chance to talk to the Palace before coming into the studio. 'Everyone must be very relieved that these protracted negotiations now seem closer to some sort of resolution. I've no doubt we'll be getting more details about the settlement later tonight.'

I looked at Anna, hoping that she wouldn't ask me anything more. Sensing that the facts were thin on the ground, she invited me only to give a résumé of all that had happened before releasing me to dash back to the newsroom. There, I seized the phone to talk to the Palace.

The press office line was busy, and there were several calls holding, but eventually I got through. Far from being 'relieved', as I had just suggested, it was obvious that the Palace officials had been completely taken by surprise by the Princess's statement. The first some of them had heard about it was when I'd turned up on the *Six o'Clock News*. And they were hopping mad. Shell-shocked, they were trying to gather themselves together.

'I'm afraid we've got nothing to say about this at the moment, Jennie. We'll call you back in a while.'

'But . . .' I began in protest.

'Nothing at the moment, Jennie. We'll call you as soon as we have something to say.'

The tone of voice was final. There was no point in arguing. I hung up and dialled Jane Atkinson. She was her usual cool and efficient self – even in the midst of such a maelstrom.

'In the end, it was a very cordial meeting,' she told me. 'It was just the two of them, and the Princess agreed to a divorce. She'll lose the HRH, she imagines, from the time the divorce is absolute. It's up to the lawyers, now, to sort out the financial arrangements.'

'And what about her role in the future?' I asked.

'She'll go on working for her charities,' said Jane.

This was good information, and we needed it on camera. Jane wasn't keen but, like every other news organisation, we sent a camera to doorstep her anyway. Others were dispatched to the Palace, to Neasden – where the Prince was carrying out an evening engagement – and to Kensington Palace, in case the Princess emerged. The hunt was on, too, to find her lawyer,

Anthony Julius. The newsroom was humming. Producers raced around digging out the 'backgrounders' about the royal marriage, which had been under preparation for several weeks. The time had come for them to be broadcast.

'Jennie, it's the Palace for you,' someone yelled at me from across the room.

Grabbing my notebook, I took the call.

'We *can* now confirm that a meeting between the Prince and the Princess took place this afternoon,' I was told. 'The Queen was most interested to hear that the Princess has agreed to a divorce.'

It was a starkly curious phrase.

'Most interested?' I queried.

'Yes,' I was told, 'that's right.'

'Well, is she relieved about it?' I asked.

'As I said, she was most interested to hear about it.'

This was clearly all we were going to learn about the Queen's reaction.

'So the Princess is going to lose her HRH, is she?' I enquired.

'The details of the settlement were *not* discussed at the meeting,' came the reply, 'and neither was the Princess's role. All such matters remain to be settled, and that will take some time.'

The Palace was steering an exceptionally frosty course on this one. More worryingly, it was seriously at odds with the Princess's version of events. It was obvious that everyone, including the Queen, had been stung by Diana's decision to announce the outcome of the meeting without reference to the Palace. I was told that the Queen's original statement had said that she 'welcomed' the Princess's decision to agree to a divorce. But when she saw me on the news and realised that Diana had put out an announcement, she changed the wording to 'most interested to hear'.

Diana: head and
shoulders above them
all. At a gala evening
in Chicago. 1996
(TIM GRAHAM)

Diana's note to me:
a Christmas surprise
along with seven
pairs of tights

KENSINGTON PALACE 14·12·96.

I hope you see the amusing
side of this package —
anyway, wishing you a
happy christmas!
from. Diana.

Diana strikes up a friendship
with thirteen-year-old Sandra Tigica,
who lost her leg in a
landmine blast. Angola 1997
(TIM GRAHAM)

The Princess says farewell
to one of her dresses before
the auction in New York, 1997
(TIM GRAHAM)

The nation bids farewell to Diana, Princess of Wales. September 1997
(TIM GRAHAM)

Prince Harry meets Baby Spice and Posh Spice
in Johannesburg, 1997
(TIM GRAHAM)

Time to catch up on some gossip. In Whistler, Canada, with
Prince Charles' spin doctor, Mark Bolland. 1998

Prince Charles is shown around Sea Lion Island in the Falklands. 1999 (TIM GRAHAM)

The beach was inhabited by elephant seals – which did little other than fart and belch

The Sun's royal photographer Arthur Edwards, outside the portacabins that served as home for the hacks on the Falklands

Prince Charles at
the Kaieteur Falls in
Guyana. February 2000
(TIM GRAHAM)

Watching my report
go out on the Internet
after a particularly
hairy edit in Seoul,
South Korea. 1999

Prince William poses at Eton
for pictures to mark his
18th birthday. June 2000
(TIM GRAHAM)

William shows off his driving
skills at Highgrove the day
before passing his test
(PHOTOGRAPHERS INTERNATIONAL)

The Earl and Countess of Wessex putting on a brave face despite the row over what Sophie told the bogus sheikh. 2001
(TIM GRAHAM)

Preparing for the One o'Clock News: in the edit truck by Buckingham Palace with Duncan, my picture editor, on the Queen Mother's 100th birthday

The whole episode was symptomatic of the deep distrust that had grown up between the two sides. Each believed that the other was leaking stories to the newspapers. The Princess had left the meeting convinced that her husband's staff would immediately plant the story with their favoured journalists.

'What shall we do?' she'd demanded of her press adviser, who'd been waiting in a room near by. 'They'll be leaking it already.'

Jane had replied that they had three choices: wait for a leak, leak it themselves or make an announcement to the Press Association, which would be flashed around the world in a matter of minutes. The Princess hadn't hesitated.

'We'll announce it,' she told Jane.

Diana had written the statement herself, pausing only to phone her mother and the Queen to tell them she had agreed to a divorce. She then authorised Jane to issue it to the PA. There were reports in the subsequent days that, even as the Princess was writing the announcement, calls were coming in to her office asking for confirmation that she'd agreed to a divorce. The implication was that the Prince's side had been still quicker off the mark.

For the correspondent trapped in the middle of all this distrust, the result was profoundly confusing. The only solid facts to go on appeared to be that the Prince and Princess had indeed had a meeting, and that the Princess had agreed to a divorce. Beyond that, it was a jungle. *Had* the Princess agreed to give up her HRH? *Would* she be staying at Kensington Palace? According to Buckingham Palace – peeved that their plan to announce a neatly finished divorce package had been thwarted – *nothing* had yet been settled. And behind the scenes Prince Charles's staff went further. The question of her title, I was told, had not even been *raised* at that meeting.

The truth is ultimately known only by the two people who were there: the Prince and the Princess. But many close to them believe that in the emotion of the moment the Princess may have said: 'So it's to be Diana, Princess of Wales, then?'

To which the Prince may have meekly agreed, possibly without even thinking about the omission of the HRH. It is, though, stretching credulity to believe that the issue of the Princess's title had not been a subject of discussion between the Prince and his advisers in the weeks leading up to that meeting.

None of this, though, was particularly helpful to me on that night of a thousand conversations before I found myself again in the studio, this time being quizzed by Michael Buerk on the *Nine o'Clock News*. *Newsnight* followed, and then the requests from *Breakfast*. I worked through most of the night, but managed to snatch a couple of hours' rest in a dressing room before struggling to repair the ravages of the past twenty-four hours with dollops of blusher and mascara. It was 6 a.m. and time to head down to the Palace to appear on the early morning news: the first of another long day of bulletins.

My life, though, was not totally dominated by the machinations of the Prince and Princess of Wales. Periodically, the pre-dawn phone calls summoned me to different pastures. One, for example, was to alert me to the fact that the Queen had made it known that she would no longer subsidise the lifestyle of the Duchess of York, thought at the time to be in debt to the tune of more than a million pounds (it turned out to be considerably more). There was a scandal over a taped phone conversation involving the Duke of Edinburgh. And there were my routine early morning alarm calls to get up to read the news. Throughout all this, viewers continued to keep me amused.

'You are one of the most elegant and refined women on television,' someone kindly wrote to me. 'Why don't you do something outrageous like wear a bikini and flex your biceps while reading the news?'

It is an image I toy with from time to time as I contemplate the end of my career.

There was further respite from the war of the Waleses when, in late March, I kissed goodbye to my husband and daughter and flew off to Poland and the Czech Republic with the Queen. It was the first visit by a reigning British monarch to either of those countries, and as I set eyes on the magnificent old quarter of Warsaw I was rather glad she'd decided to go there. From the very start, though, the tour proved to be full of the usual pitfalls, both for the Palace and for me.

The Queen's programme was not to the liking of some of the Jewish community in Britain. Why, they demanded, was she not going to visit Auschwitz? The explanation given by the Foreign Office was that there wasn't enough time, but it did little to placate offended feelings. Suddenly, a new engagement was added to the schedule: a stop at the monument in Warsaw where thousands of Jews were herded into wagons for the journey to the death camps at Treblinka. We hurried there with our cameras and interviewed some of the crowds who had gathered. Many, though, did not view this hastily arranged gesture as sufficient.

There was further embarrassment when the Queen addressed the Polish parliament. The press had been given transcripts of her speech which, as always, we checked as she spoke. There was therefore some bewilderment in our ranks when she left out a key passage referring to the fate of Polish Jews in the war. It seemed an extraordinary omission. As we stood, crushed together in one of the doorways, we whispered to one another, trying to make sense of what had happened. In front of us, the formalities of the occasion were proceeding as planned, while we tried to establish whether we had a major diplomatic incident brewing. Before long, we managed to track down a rather flustered member of the Queen's staff, who told us that the omission had been the result of a 'computer cock-up'.

'It was a complete mistake,' he said, no doubt already imagining the headlines. 'A clerical error – and most unfortunate. The Queen fully intended to say those words, but they were left out of her script, and we take total responsibility.'

You could only feel sorry for them, but, of course, their error made the news. As I was soon to discover, the Queen wasn't alone in being the victim of innocent blunders.

The trickiest part of many a royal tour is when it moves on halfway through a day from one country to another. We have to decide whether to stay behind and file our reports from the first country or to fly on to the next, unload our equipment, get to the hotel and hope we can organise ourselves quickly enough to file from there. When the Queen moved on from Poland to the Czech Republic, we opted to go with her. It was, perhaps, an unwise decision. We spent the morning in Kraków, in deep snow and freezing temperatures. The crowds were huge, the organisation chaotic and the local security oppressive. At one point my producer almost came to blows with a brawny guard who was implacable in his resolve to prevent us from seeing the Queen. Like a couple of harridans, we screamed abuse at him and pushed against his burly frame until, cursing at us under his breath, he finally surrendered and let us through. At a predetermined time, we all made our escape and raced through the icy streets to the press buses for a fast and furious ride to the airport and our flight to Prague. On the plane, I wrote the opening of my report for the *Six o'Clock News*; the rest would be about the Queen's welcome in the Czech Republic.

'You head straight to the first engagement,' my producer instructed me. 'I'll go to the hotel and make sure we have all the editing equipment set up by the time you get there. We'll have to work fast – I reckon you'll have about forty minutes if we're lucky.'

Standing on the ornate Charles Bridge in the centre of Prague, watching the Queen and President Václav Havel being cheered by the crowds in the late afternoon sunshine, I resented the fact that I couldn't simply enjoy the moment. I not only had to finish my script but had to think of another of those pieces to camera. Occasionally, I try to be extra cute and record my words just as the Queen comes into frame behind me. This seemed like an ideal opportunity, even though it always adds pressure because you get only one chance, or at the most two, to get it right. The cameraman and I waited for the precise instant that I could leap into the picture and start talking. It arrived, I leaped – and promptly forgot my words. I tried again, but the setting sun suddenly blinded me. I composed myself for a third try, but by then the Queen had passed by. I cursed myself and did a straightforward piece to camera: word-perfect but with no Queen.

There was no time to lament what might have been. I snatched the tape and ran to the press bus. The doors were closing; fellow ratpackers were shouting at the uncomprehending driver to ignore any latecomers and to step on it so they could get to the hotel and send their pictures back to London. We bounced through the streets of Prague and stampeded into the hotel, forming a disorderly line at reception. Everyone was surreptitiously shoving and pushing to get their room key first. I decided to bypass the formalities and, instead, to head straight to my picture editor's room. They'd done a brilliant job in transporting all the equipment from the airport and setting it up so that everything was ready as soon as I walked in. We launched into the script I'd begun on the plane and half-finished on the bridge. It went well but, as my producer had warned me, time was extremely tight, and as we put down the final shot we were all sweating with the tension of trying to meet the deadline.

'You go without me,' I said, trying to sound calm. 'I'm useless at the satellite station. I'll see you when you get back.'

Panting slightly, my picture editor slotted the tape of the completed report into its box and ran out of the room. The producer was holding the lift, and the taxi was waiting. I watched them go and decided I'd earned a drink.

Downstairs in the hotel bar, I found that none of my colleagues had finished their work yet and there was no one I knew. There were only a few tables, so I chose one where a well-dressed woman was sitting quietly, and waited to be served. Nothing happened. I smiled at my companion. Beneath lashings of mascara, she glowered back. Feeling that my presence was decidedly unwelcome, I got up and moved to another table occupied by an equally smart young woman. She looked at me as if I was a sack of manure. I tried to attract the barman's attention. Just then, a couple of my Fleet Street colleagues arrived downstairs, having successfully wired their work to their news desks in London. They looked at me with wide grins on their faces.

'Here, Jen,' they said, laughing. 'What are you doing sitting with those hookers?'

As I hastily got up and changed tables yet again, I could feel myself blushing, though I did my best to laugh with them. While they finally secured a glass of wine for me, I wondered to myself how I could be so naïve at my advanced age. When their cackling had finally subsided, we settled down to share our horror stories of the day. We'd just launched into a second round of drinks when I saw a taxi draw up outside. It was my team, back from the TV station. As they came through the door, I could see instantly from my picture editor's crestfallen face that all had not gone well. He walked over to me, shoulders slumped and eyes full of apology.

'Oh, Jen,' he said as if the world had fallen in. 'I'm so sorry. In that rush to get out of the room I picked up the wrong tape. I took a blank one with me to the TV station. Your report's still upstairs.'

There was no point in adding to his agony. I patted him on the back, told him not to worry and bought him a drink. The news desk was pretty displeased with us. We were reminded that they'd paid for a satellite feed that we hadn't used, and that we'd left a hole in the bulletin's running order. But as I grow older I comfort myself with the thought that there are more serious catastrophes in the world than a missed TV report. I bought another round of drinks and sat back to listen to the inimitable Robert Hardman – then royal correspondent of the *Daily Telegraph* – playing his exquisite repertoire on the hotel piano.

Back in the UK, the Yorks abruptly stepped centre stage with an announcement that they were taking their separation to its natural conclusion by seeking a divorce. In the Duchess's own words, they remained 'the bestest friends' and no one seemed able to explain why they had suddenly decided to end their marriage formally. We tracked Fergie down to her holiday chalet in Verbier, where she said she was very sad but threw no light on the decision. Some of her friends, though, suggested that after her financial difficulties had become public knowledge, the pressure from the Royal Family for her to cut her ties had become intense. I was one of about twenty-five journalists who sat in court to witness the end of another royal marriage, another failure for the modern-day monarchy.

Meanwhile, the negotiations to end the marriage of the Prince and Princess of Wales had become bogged down in a mire of claim and counterclaim. In mid-May the news leaked out that the Princess had appealed directly to the Queen to try to unblock the stalemate.

'They don't understand the word "negotiate",' I was told by the Princess's camp. 'They simply want to legislate. Frankly, we may as well abandon the whole thing and wait the five years for a straightforward divorce.'

'The Princess's legal team would argue over anything,' I was told by the Prince's side. 'They'd have a dispute over which day of the week it is if they could.'

For the wretched correspondent, caught in this crossfire, there was only one avenue to pursue: stick to the few facts available and try not to be drawn down the path of speculation. I did my best.

A couple of weeks later, it was time to pack my suitcase again. Diana was leaving her divorce problems behind and flying to Chicago. For the first time in my life I was about to set foot in my husband's homeland, and I was consumed with curiosity. Jim had left the United States in 1965 because he didn't like the country or the people. He'd been true to his word: never returning to the land of his birth, despite my protestations that

I'd like to see where he'd been brought up. Now, though, my work was finally taking me to America.

I'm not a city person, even though I've lived in one for thirty years, and I'd far rather have been given the chance to explore some of the wide-open plains of the United States. Nevertheless, the sight of what appeared to be an ocean – but was in fact Lake Michigan – made me feel that this was not a bad place to be. There were boats on the water, a beach and some interesting architecture. It looked like fun.

The Princess was there as the guest of Chicago's Northwestern University, which was hosting a conference on breast cancer. The press interest was phenomenal. Five hundred journalists and cameramen had signed up to cover her brief trip, and Jane Atkinson summoned us to a convention centre to discuss the arrangements. Sitting on the edge of the stage, she looked refreshingly informal as she offered to answer our questions.

'Where are the fixed points for the Princess's walkabout? What sound facilities are there for the speech – is there a box we can plug into? What direction will the Princess arrive from? Which side of the car will she get out of? Why can't you get more than four British press in that pool?'

The queries peppered Jane like gunshot, and she had her work cut out to satisfy us all. She was learning how to deal with the Princess's complex personality, which had confused so many of her staff in the past. Diana's sharp mood swings, which led her to treat her entourage sometimes as friends, sometimes as traitors, kept everyone on their toes. There was a dichotomy, too, about whether she wanted to be regarded as 'one of the gang' or as a royal princess. On that first night in Chicago, she was showered with gifts from the city's movers and shakers. When she got back to the hotel after a cocktail party, she went to bed while her staff began logging the presents so that thank-you notes could be written. Suddenly, Diana padded back along the corridor in bare feet, knelt down with the rest of them on the floor and joined in. Some of the gifts were truly eccentric, and the Princess roared with laughter alongside her staff. After half an hour or so, she got up as abruptly as she had come in and, looking pensive, went quietly back along the corridor to bed. Her natural gregariousness always had to be tempered by perceived expectations of 'royal' behaviour.

The worldwide publicity about her divorce negotiations seemed only to have increased public interest in her. Wherever she went in Chicago, she was fêted like a Hollywood star. I was left open-mouthed as fleets of grotesquely stretched white limousines queued to disgorge their fabulously rich occupants on to the red carpet that marked the path to a gala dinner. Diana herself looked stunning in a deep purple gown that hugged her well-honed figure. It was an occasion designed to raise a million dollars for charity – and she looked every inch the part. As a lowly reporter, standing on the edge of such glittering occasions with your hair and make-up ravaged by the pressures of the day, and probably needing a pee, you feel irreversibly graceless and wish you could hide in a hole somewhere.

But Chicago *was* exciting. I was reporting for both television and radio, and my feet didn't touch the ground. Only when the Princess was safely in the air on her way home did we – the royal hacks – have time to sample the delights of the city at first hand. I recollect, though, that several of us enjoyed that final evening a little *too* enthusiastically, and the next morning was all a bit of a blur. Bizarrely enough, so was Chicago itself. As I pulled back the curtains, holding my fragile head, I gazed out at a city shrouded in a cool mist that obscured the top few storeys of all the skyscrapers. It was an eerie sight. Through this double mist of brain and buildings, I remembered that everyone had told me that Chicago was synonymous with shopping and, with a few hours to spare before my flight, I duly tottered off – swaying gently – towards one of the main malls. It proved, however, to be a short expedition. In a bargain basement I found a perfectly tailored blue dress going for a song. I have worn it dozens of times since on royal stories around the world, and it always reminds me of Chicago. But the exertion of trying it on in my condition was utterly exhausting. So when I spied a shop full of massage equipment, I was drawn to it like a magnet. Inside, there was every kind of electric gadget for soothing your aches and pains. But it was the ample, soft leather armchair with full body massage gear built in that slayed me. I collapsed into its inviting seat and pressed all the buttons at once. My legs began to vibrate, a roller passed up my spine – kneading me as if I were a lump of dough – my arms and shoulders tingled, and it felt as though someone was playing the piano on my head. I fell in love with that chair there and then. I lay back and closed my eyes.

'Excuse me, ma'am.' The strange American voice seemed to be stuck in a rut. It kept repeating itself and was becoming distinctly annoying. And there was someone snoring in the background as well.

'Ma'am,' the voice drawled on, 'may I ask if you're considering buying that chair?'

I jerked myself awake. The sales assistant was bending over me, looking half-amused and half-cross.

'Well,' I replied haughtily, 'if you're going to interrupt me when I'm assessing its efficiency, then I'll go elsewhere.'

Inwardly cringing at the excruciating embarrassment of having been found fast asleep, I stomped out of the shop – in search of a place to hide.

It was a couple of weeks later that I took a call from the Prince of Wales's private secretary, Richard Aylard. 'Jennie, we've been giving some serious thought to your request to meet the Prince again, and he'd like you to come to tea next Thursday. Is that OK?'

'That's more than OK, Richard,' I said. 'That's brilliant.'

I put the phone down, feeling chuffed. It would be my second visit to Highgrove. The first had been about a year earlier, in response to my relentless campaign of nagging the Palace to help me get to know him better. We'd sat in his drawing room on settees facing one another, with an ottoman chest between us laden with country magazines and coffee-table books. Richard had taken his place in a chair to one side of the Prince: a constant presence in case I overstepped the mark. It was made absolutely clear that I was *not* there to discuss affairs of the heart.

'I do hope you enjoyed looking around the garden,' said the Prince, as a butler stood over me, carrying an awkwardly high-lipped tray. Struggling from my deep settee to reach up and extricate the cup from its resting place, I enthused – quite genuinely – about all that I had just been shown during a guided tour by Richard. The gardens at Highgrove are indeed exquisite. From the fragrant thyme walk and pockets of woodland and wild flowers, right through to the reed-bed sewage system, the Prince has created his own very personal vision.

'I always think', he went on, 'that a brief stroll around the gardens helps people to relax. So often they seem a little overwhelmed to find themselves here, but I find that once they've had a walk and got the general feel of the place, they're far more at home.'

It was his walled kitchen garden, with its raised beds and organic vegetables, that had caught my eye. Jim and I were early fanatics of organic gardening and had our own, rather less pristine, raised beds in London. It is, perhaps, odd to think of the BBC's royal correspondent sitting with the Prince of Wales on a chilly afternoon discussing the merits of white custard marrows. But that's what we did. He'd never heard of them, and I told him how attractive they were and suggested he grew some for himself.

'Would you like to see some photos of how the house used to be?' he asked, warming to this domestic theme.

'I'd love to,' I replied.

He reached for a photo album and set it on the ottoman. I moved across and sat on the floor as he thumbed through the pictures showing all the changes he'd made at Highgrove over the years. He seemed just like anyone else who'd struggled over making improvements to somewhere they loved. All in all, it was a thoroughly pleasant afternoon and, as I left, the Prince said: 'You must come back one day and see the gardens in better weather.'

Now, it seemed, that moment had come. It was 4 July and I was driving up to Highgrove, this time with my BBC colleague Paul Reynolds, still reporting on royalty for radio. I stopped at the police box for a security check and then drove on to the parking area beside the house. We were met by Richard Aylard, our guide, once more, for the horticultural tour. The gardens did indeed look even more splendid in the sunshine and, after walking around them for half an hour or so, we sat in wicker chairs on the terrace with the Prince.

'Oh, *poor* Miss Bond,' he said, smiling. 'You've had to go round the gardens *again*. I do hope it wasn't too boring.'

He seemed a tortured soul after all that had happened in the past year. Though he was affable to us, his antipathy towards the press in general appeared to have increased, and his mood was unsettled. He talked of his growing concern about genetic engineering. It was a topic few were discussing at that time, but he was in the forefront of the debate and he was angry about food production methods. At one point he was wanted on the phone. It was brought out to him by one of his staff and he took the call where he was. He spoke quietly, in curt phrases. Paul and I made polite conversation while the Prince was occupied. It was only later that evening that I wondered whether that phone call had been the reason I suddenly found myself yanked back to work at the end of our day at Highgrove.

I'd just dropped Paul off at his home when our pagers started bleeping simultaneously: 'Phone news desk. Urgent.'

The message looked ominous. I rang from the car.

'Prince Charles has made a financial offer to Diana to settle the divorce,' the news organiser briefed me. 'We need you on the *Nine o'Clock News*.'

I was only two miles from home and we'd been planning a 4 July barbecue in the garden in recognition of my husband's American roots. I turned the car round and headed for the office. On the way, I rang Jim and Emma to tell them the bad news. They were not amused. Another dinner ruined, another promise broken.

My old friend John Humphrys put me through my paces on the evening news. I felt rather foolish that I had probably been with the Prince at the very moment that the offer to Diana had been finalised, and yet I'd known nothing about it. But that's the score in the world of royal reporting. A week later, the terms of the divorce were agreed and before I knew it I was at Somerset

House witnessing the end of one of the most public marriages of recent times.

It was a strange feeling to shuffle into the small courtroom, its desks neatly arranged rather like a classroom, knowing that this was a piece of history that would be chronicled for centuries to come. I felt a little nervous and hoped my non-existent shorthand would rise to the occasion. There were about thirty journalists in the room. Most of us had shared the turmoil of the breakdown of the marriage. It seemed as if we'd all travelled down a very long and bumpy road, and now there was at last a sense of finality. The proceedings took just two minutes. The clerk of the court read out the list of petitioners in alphabetical order. There was a brutal simplicity about the last of the thirty-two entries: 'HRH the Prince of Wales *v.* HRH the Princess of Wales.'

After a moment's pause, Judge Gerald Angel asked: 'Does any party or person wish to show cause against the decrees being pronounced?'

Only the scribbling of the assembled scribes disturbed the silence. He then pronounced the decrees nisi for all thirty-two couples. There was no special treatment for this historic divorce. It was simply one of a job lot.

I raced outside, stopping only to buy a copy of the list of petitioners so that we could film it and show it to viewers. The camera was waiting; I quickly brushed my hair, dabbed on some powder and we were on air.

'In the end,' I reported, 'it was all so ordinary. A unique moment in history, played out in Court Number One: a small room with bare, pale green walls. The only witnesses . . . some thirty journalists.'

The next morning I took Emma to school. Walking hand in hand, I was explaining to her why I had come home so very late the night before when my pager rudely interrupted me. I phoned the desk. Reports were coming in that Diana was giving up almost all her charity work. So much for the divorce signalling a more peaceful life for me. Various expletives passed my lips as I abandoned my plans for a quiet day and, having kissed Emma goodbye, rushed home to rummage through my wardrobe for a suitable jacket. My drive to work was the usual adventure, with my phone overheating and my mind buzzing with all that we now had to do. Getting the facts straight was obviously the priority; then we had to contact all the major charities and send cameras and producers to interview their chief executives. Where was the Princess? Where was Charles? What on-the-day pictures could we find?

By lunchtime we had established that the Princess had resigned as patron of nearly a hundred charities. It was big news, but the explanation seemed confused. I was told that she no longer felt she could offer them the commitment she had in the past. But, as I said on the *One o'Clock News*, this didn't wash. More convincing was the suggestion that she was so miffed about losing her HRH that she could no longer see any point in carrying out royal engagements. Whatever the reason, the upshot, it seemed to me, was that my life would now be quieter.

By September, however, she was back: on her first public engagement abroad since her divorce. We were off to Washington. The main purpose of the Princess's visit was another gala dinner to raise money for breast cancer research.

'So what do you make of the Princess meeting Hillary, then?' asked my cab driver as we motored into the city from the airport. I was feeling a bit weary after the flight, but this made me sit up.

'What do you mean? She's here for the dinner; she's not going near the White House.'

'That's not what the radio here's saying, lady,' came the surly reply. 'Breakfast together tomorrow. That's what I heard, anyhow.'

I seized my phone and rang the BBC's Washington office. They'd heard the same rumour and, a few calls later, I confirmed that it was indeed true. A late addition to the Princess's schedule meant we'd all be heading for the White House in the morning. The knock-on effect of *that* was that the desks back home wanted me on air immediately. I headed straight to the office: do not pass go, do not go to your hotel, do not unpack. But the prospect of seeing inside one of the most famous seats of power in the world struck me as rather exciting.

The next day we were interrogated and searched, signed in and verified before, finally, we were shown into the White House press room, where I have watched so many Presidents make historic statements. It seemed curiously small and shabby. I laughed at myself for being surprised; after all, I knew as well as anyone that television makes most things – including me – look quite different. We were then taken through to a vast room where Mrs Clinton welcomed the Princess as 'one of the nicest British invasions the White House has ever seen'. I looked at them and thought: there stand two of the most famous, and possibly most powerful, women in the world! It was the start of a brief but successful visit for the Princess that put her back on the world stage.

A fortnight later she took on her first official engagement in the UK since her divorce, but it was hijacked by a story in the *Sun*.

'DI SPY VIDEO SCANDAL' the front page screamed at me from

the newsagent's stand. After the inevitable early call from the office, I'd run up the road to buy the paper before driving to the Princess's engagement. The paper boasted that it had acquired a video showing Diana cavorting at Highgrove with her former lover, James Hewitt. The pictures were blurred but appeared to back up the paper's claims. The story was the only topic of conversation when I arrived at the London Lighthouse, where the Princess was due to launch a new appeal for Aids sufferers. Seasoned royal reporters stood around in huddles minutely examining the pictures and making whispered phone calls to their contacts. The air was thick with conspiracy. We all wondered how the Princess would react to this most public embarrassment. The answer was that she ignored it totally and carried on with her speech. That wasn't an option open to us; the video was big news.

Looking back on that difficult day, I can feel only gratitude that years of journalistic training led me to add caveats throughout my reports. I spoke of a video that *apparently* showed the Princess and James Hewitt, and sourced all the claims very firmly to the *Sun*. On grounds of taste, the BBC had also very wisely taken the decision not to show any of the pictures or the video. Which was just as well because, minutes after the *Six o'Clock News* came off air, a Press Association snap popped up on our computer screens saying that the video had been proved a hoax. The *Sun* was left with oodles of egg on its face, and we had a frantic evening piecing together how the hoaxers had done it.

The weeks following the royal divorce were not as tranquil as I'd imagined they might be. The Duchess of York decided to appear in a wacky television programme with the delightful and dangerous Ruby Wax. (Missed Emma's school run and parents' evening.) She also published her autobiography. (Cancelled lunch with my parents.) Prince Charles ventured perilously close to political controversy by calling for a new approach to farming in the face of the BSE crisis. (Missed dinner with husband and daughter.)

The view at the Palace was that the divorce had left Prince Charles increasingly vulnerable to criticism and even more a prisoner of his ex-wife.

'Until the Princess is seen by the public to be happy,' I was told, 'the Prince will be viewed as the man who wronged her, and Camilla as the woman who broke up the marriage. Ideally, she'd get married again . . . perhaps have a new family. But there doesn't seem much prospect of that at the moment.'

Indeed, Diana was rather too busy travelling – and it was her globetrotting, combined with a state visit to Thailand by the Queen, that led to another long absence from my family at the end of 1996. After a quick trip to Italy with the Princess, I pulled out all my summer frocks for our expedition to Bangkok. It was half-term; I was with Jim and Emma in Devon and, as usual, left my departure to the last moment. The drive up from the West Country to Heathrow was pretty arduous, but I was convinced that supermum could handle it and then pour herself on to the plane. Perhaps it was the drive, perhaps it was the two-hour delay on the tarmac, but, for whatever reason, halfway through the night I suddenly found myself lying on the aircraft floor. I'd fainted and, rather delicately, slumped to the ground. Fortunately, and curiously comically, no one had noticed me lying there in the darkness. Thoroughly embarrassed even though alone, I crawled back into my seat to continue the journey.

It was steaming hot in Thailand and, as we stood at the airport waiting for the Queen to arrive, my cameraman looked as if he, too, was about to expire. The King of Thailand is still revered as a demigod. His titles include Strength of the Land, Incomparable Power and, intriguingly, Keeper of the Twenty-Four Golden Umbrellas. We'd all been given precise instructions about showing the correct measure of respect. Unfortunately for my cameraman, *that* entailed wearing a heavy, dark suit in blazing sunshine. I fared somewhat better in a light dress with a long-sleeved jacket, which I whipped off whenever I thought no one was looking.

I loved being back in the tropics; the lushness of Southeast Asia was as compelling as ever. The Queen looked as if she was enjoying herself, too, as she was given a noisy welcome by the crowds. Some of them had become so enthused by the occasion that they'd been told off for pinching the official decorations. For me, though, the visit posed something of a dilemma because the Princess of Wales had fixed up a trip to Australia that overlapped with the Queen's stay in Thailand. Which was the bigger news story? My bosses had come up with the compromise that I'd cover half the Queen's visit and then, leaving my radio colleague to report on the remainder for television as well, I'd fly down to Australia. I certainly wasn't about to complain, and the first few days passed peacefully enough. Having filed my last report from Thailand, I said farewell to my team, wished them well with the rest of the trip and went to bed.

'What do you mean it's half-past five?' I shouted down the phone at the hotel concierge. 'You *promised* to wake me at quarter to five. I'm going to miss my plane now.'

I was throwing clothes into my suitcase as I spoke, my head throbbing with the ghastly realisation that all my carefully laid plans had gone awry. It was still dark in Bangkok, but it was exceedingly hot and sticky. Even so, there was no time now for a shower or hair-wash. No time, even, for any make-up (thank God for dark glasses!). If I went hell for leather, there was *just* a chance that I could make the flight.

'Get me a taxi, *now*,' I screamed unpleasantly. On the way to the airport I could see the sun rising and wondered what the office would say if I missed the Princess's arrival in Australia. The terminal was mercifully empty when I got there, but the check-in had just closed. I must have cut a picture of misery because, after a moment or two, an airline official took pity on me, relieved me of my suitcase and escorted me to the waiting lounge, where I saw some of my tabloid friends, who were set on the same path, happily sipping cups of tea.

''Ere, Jen, you look as if you've just got out of bed,' they quipped helpfully. I cowered behind my sunglasses and wondered how I was going to get some mascara on before I had to look anyone in the face.

Australia was as wonderful as ever, but the Princess's trip Down Under did not turn out to be one of her most successful. By now she had parted company with her media adviser, Jane Atkinson, and was effectively running her own affairs. On visits like this, however, she depended almost entirely on the public relations firms that were employed by the charities she was helping. A royal tour, with frenetic media attention, was more than most could handle. They set about marketing her like a soap powder. It was blatant commercialisation of a superstar, with exclusive rights to some of her appearances being sold to Australian TV networks. It was chaotic, and the British press were not happy about being barred from some of these 'exclusive' events. I decided that the time had come for another chat with the Princess.

At the Victor Chang Heart Research Institute, which the

Princess had come to Sydney to support, I sidled up to her lady-in-waiting.

'This *isn't* working, you know,' I whispered as, a few yards away, Diana was shown the latest technology to help heart transplant patients. 'Selling off bits of this tour to various companies and keeping out the British press really doesn't make us happy. And if the British press aren't happy, their coverage won't be the sort she'll want to see. I think the Princess and I need to talk.'

She nodded in agreement and promised to pass on my thoughts to Diana.

CHAPTER TWELVE

We meet again

Two days after our return from Australia, I found that my gamble had paid off. It had been risky to tell the Princess of Wales that her press arrangements were shambolic. I was afraid she'd bristle at any kind of criticism, but to her credit she took my comments seriously and once again asked me to Kensington Palace to discuss what should be done.

As I drove up the private road to the Palace, I wondered whether this encounter would be as friendly and open as the last. A lot had happened since our first meeting. The Princess had bared her soul on *Panorama*, gone through acrimonious divorce proceedings and was now officially a single woman again. But how much had she changed?

This time the front door was closed. It was a chill November morning. I knocked gently and waited. Before long, her butler, Paul Burrell, welcomed me in. As on my previous visit, I was struck by the sensuous smell of fresh flowers and perfumed candles.

'I'm sure you remember the way up,' said Paul, waving me

towards the staircase. As I arrived at the top, the Princess – in a crisp navy and white dress, and with perfect timing – came bursting out of the drawing room.

'Jennie, thanks for coming.' I wondered if she meant it, but she was all smiles as she ushered me in and invited me to take a seat on one of the big, squashy settees. 'Would you like a drink?' she asked.

'Yes, thanks. What are you having?'

'My usual,' she said. 'Iced water.'

I said I'd have the same, and in no time at all Paul was there with a small tray and two tall glasses of deliciously cold water. I launched into my list of complaints about how the press arrangements had been handled in Australia.

I told her she needed professional help again in her office now that she'd parted ways with Jane Atkinson. She insisted she was very happy with the set-up she now had. She had assumed control of things herself and was perfectly content with the two women now dealing with most of the press enquiries.

'But they can never answer my questions,' I complained. 'They're extremely sweet and polite, but we really do need some concrete information from time to time.'

'They do just what I want,' Diana replied, smiling. 'They give you monosyllabic answers – and that's fine.'

I decided to change tack. 'These last few months must have taken their toll,' I suggested.

'Yes,' she said, 'it's been the cruellest period of my life.' She was delighted that her divorce lawyer, Anthony Julius, had found Buckingham Palace so difficult to deal with during the negotiations. 'Now,' she said, 'someone else can see what I've been up against all these years.'

She told me that she had taken advice from two others

who'd gone through a royal divorce: Mark Phillips and Tony Snowdon.

'They both told me to make sure everything was settled before I signed anything,' she said. 'But the Palace kept trying to get it all through before the details had been decided. That's why I threatened to pull out of the negotiations altogether.' She smiled ruefully. 'That did the trick.'

'But what was it like on the day the divorce came through?' I asked. 'You faced us all – the reporters and cameras – on that visit to the English National Ballet . . . What was going through your mind?'

She answered quietly: 'I was just desperately sad. My emotions were raw all through that appearance. When I got home I even toyed with the idea of ringing Charles, but I thought I'd only end up blabbing down the phone. And then he'd think I was unstable again.'

After it was all over, she said, she'd received 'a pompous' letter from one of the Queen's senior courtiers which had appalled her. In confidence, she told me who had sent it and what was in it; she claimed she'd kept it in case she ever needed it.

This was extraordinarily frank talk from a princess. But it still wasn't a heart-to-heart conversation between two friends; she knew perfectly well that she was talking to a journalist, and I had no doubt that her answers were geared to that. Once again, she was disarmingly willing to discuss Camilla Parker Bowles. This time, she went even further.

'Let's face it,' she said. 'Camilla is the love of Charles's life, and always has been. I don't feel any animosity towards her any more. In fact, I really think she deserves some form of recognition. After all, she's been loyal to him and extremely discreet for such a long time.'

Her words astounded me. This was not the fighting talk I'd expected. If it was genuine, it was a magnanimous gesture from a woman who was finally resigned to a situation she couldn't change, and who had decided to try to move on.

I asked her what she meant by 'recognition' for Camilla. Did she mean marriage?

'No, not necessarily,' she said. 'I'm not sure what kind of recognition, but I don't really see any need for them to marry.'

She was clearly annoyed, though, that the Prince and Camilla had been pictured together – albeit surreptitiously – a week before the divorce.

'Now that was madness,' she said. 'A week *before* was just crazy. A week afterwards would have been fine.'

She told me that Prince Charles had called round to Kensington Palace in June. He'd arrived by helicopter, on his way to the Party in the Park, run by his Trust. But he was early, so he'd decided to pop in to see the boys, who were staying with her.

'I was gobsmacked,' she said. 'I was sitting at my desk here, doing some work, and he just came in. He was very friendly and we had a nice chat. I said to him: "Have you come to check over the furniture? Because you're not having any."' She laughed. 'It was a joke, and he enjoyed it. But when he left I felt very tearful. You know, we could have been such a great couple.'

That was one of the Princess's continual refrains. Whether she said it simply to try to convince herself or whether she really believed it to be true, it was clearly a comforting thought for her.

'I'm not *in* love with him any more,' she went on. 'But I do still *love* him. After all, he is the father of my children, and that makes me care about him.'

She said she was surprised that he didn't seem any happier

after the divorce. 'I thought he would, but he looks sad to me.'

I asked her about that most controversial statement in her *Panorama* interview when she had questioned whether Prince Charles would be able to adapt to the role of King. She showed no inclination to retract it. She told me that she still believed strongly that the Prince would never be King. She said she had discussed it with him many times, and in her opinion he was 'having enough problems being Prince of Wales. He really couldn't handle being King. Anyway,' she went on, 'I honestly believe he'd be far happier living in Italy painting and studying architecture.'

Diana seemed to have few qualms about discussing her ex-husband's future with me. But there was no bitterness in her tone of voice. She seemed to be genuinely concerned about his welfare. That either the Prince or his advisers would have welcomed her concern is doubtful, but she was obviously keeping a close watch on his public, as well as his private, life.

'Do you know,' she continued. 'I really think he ought at least to take some time out from his role. He needs to reassess his life. Look at his programme: it's stuck in a rut. He's doing exactly the same sort of thing he was doing ten years ago.'

As she had before, she raged against the Prince's former private secretary, Richard Aylard, a man she held responsible for many of her ills. He'd resigned suddenly a few weeks earlier, and she'd clearly been glad to see the back of him.

'He was the one behind most of the things that have happened in the last few years,' she complained. She looked angry and hurt – and then amused as she continued: 'But now he's gone, too, so somebody must have agreed with me.' She laughed, with a sense of triumph.

Not unexpectedly, perhaps, her relationship with her former in-laws appeared to have cooled somewhat in the aftermath of *Panorama* and the divorce. She said she now saw very little of the rest of the family; she talked with the Queen occasionally but kept 'right out' of the Duke of Edinburgh's way. And she said she found the Queen Mother 'intimidating'.

My thoughts turned to Christmas, just six weeks away. In view of what she had just said, it seemed unlikely that she'd be joining them at Sandringham.

'No,' she said, with a look of horror. 'I've no intention of going. I might spend Christmas abroad. But the boys will go, of course, because that's where they belong, and they love it there.'

She added that she regarded it as a major sacrifice to be separated from her children at Christmas, and she hoped that Prince Charles recognised it as such.

'Does he?' I asked.

'Well,' she smiled, 'we're getting there.'

I couldn't leave without asking why she had finally decided to go on camera with all her feelings when, at our last meeting, she had been adamant that she never would.

'Well, Jennie,' she said with a sympathetic look towards me, 'when we talked last time I really had no intention of giving an interview. But suddenly, with the divorce and a gagging clause drawing ever nearer, it just seemed right. It was then or never.'

She said she'd had masses of positive feedback about *Panorama* from both men and women, some with marital problems, some with bulimia. But she felt that her stated ambition to be an 'ambassador' for Britain had been misinterpreted.

'All I meant was that I wanted to support this country around the world in the way I'm doing now,' she insisted.

And she was even more certain that her choice of words in saying that she wanted to be the 'Queen of People's Hearts' had been a 'dreadful' mistake. She paused for a moment, and then went off on a rather telling tangent. 'Of course, I'm passionate about the heart, you know,' she said, clasping her hands together almost in prayer. 'Without a heart, we're nothing. That's why I'm so fascinated to watch heart surgery; I'm absolutely in awe of what they do.'

I wondered whether she was inviting me to discuss her much-rumoured love for the Brompton Hospital heart surgeon Hasnat Khan, but she carried on breathlessly: 'I simply adore visiting people in hospital. I've been doing a lot of it lately, and I don't mean just holding hands, but really comforting them. We talk about the meaning of life and death, about being a victim of their illness and about seeing it positively if they can. It's so fulfilling.'

She clearly felt she had a vocation for comforting, even counselling, the sick. It brought her into contact with ordinary people at a very difficult time in their lives, when concerns about royal protocol were irrelevant. That was undoubtedly part of its appeal because, as she told me, she yearned to recapture something of an ordinary life now she was no longer strictly royal.

'They've taken my HRH away, so surely I *ought* to have a bit more freedom.'

'Would you like to have kept it?' I asked her.

'Well, yes, I would have preferred to have kept it,' she answered in a resigned tone of voice. 'But I accept that after a divorce you can't expect to keep all the equipment of married life. Once it was gone, though, I thought I wouldn't be of the same value to my charities; that's why I gave most of them up.'

It seemed to me more likely that her decision to quit so much of her charity work had been taken in a fit of pique, but the explanation that she didn't feel worthy of them any longer was one that had been put about at the time.

'Anyway,' she continued, 'it doesn't matter any more. And William told me I was jolly lucky to be able to give up the HRH.'

She said her son also envied her for being able to go about without a bodyguard. She herself had loathed having them in the car with her all the time.

'But', I argued, 'you can't get away from the fact that you're probably the most famous woman in the world.'

'I know,' she replied with no pleasure. 'But I certainly don't wake up every morning thinking, Yippee! I'm famous. Surely losing the HRH should have bought me some rights to privacy? I really don't want to be in the papers every other day, and I *despise* the fact that there are always photographers wherever I go.'

Treading on eggshells, I steered the conversation gently towards some of the men in her life. Her back straightened and she threw her eyes towards the ceiling.

'Well, Jennie, I've come to the conclusion that I'm a pretty bad judge of men. Look at James Hewitt,' she said, anger flickering across her forehead. 'I was so badly let down by him. He betrayed me in the end.'

She took on the look of a victim and repeated what she'd told me at our last meeting: that any man would have to be immensely strong to put up with all that came with her. But she hinted that she *would* like to be married again, and perhaps start a new family. I wanted to know if she thought her sons would mind.

'The boys would be fine,' she answered. 'As long as they know that their papa and I are happy.'

As we sat there sipping our water and talking so openly, she struck me as a woman much more in tune with her world than before.

'This is a new life,' she said, smiling. 'A new regime, with new rules. I'm grown-up now; I just want to be treated that way.'

After about an hour or so I began to take my leave. I asked her whether she'd like to come to the BBC for lunch. She said she'd love to, and I promised to fix it up with senior management. She showed me out to the landing and, as we shook hands, I looked again at those magnificent legs.

'Look, I know this is a bit cheeky of me,' I ventured. 'But your legs always look so great – what tights do you wear? I always seem to end up with really grotty ones.'

She laughed, throwing her head back, and said: 'Just wait there a second.'

With that she disappeared deeper into her apartment. I stood alone, wondering whether I had overstepped the mark. But she reappeared a few moments later, all smiles, carrying a brand-new pair of tights which she held out to me.

'That's brilliant,' I said, memorising the make and style. 'I'll get some tomorrow.'

'Don't be silly,' said the Princess. 'These are for you; I've got dozens of them in the bedroom.'

I thanked her profusely, told her they'd be known as my 'royal tights' and said goodbye. In the car I reflected on our meeting. It was impossible not to be charmed by Diana's open manner, her girlishness and her elegant beauty. I'd heard too many accounts of her wild mood swings to doubt that there *was* another side to her personality, but I had yet to see it. I wondered what *she* had got out of our discussions, since it was fairly obvious that she wasn't going to take a jot of notice of my criticism about her office. At least she had seen fit to discuss the problems with me and, in my job, that was refreshing.

A couple of weeks later the Princess went to the charity Centrepoint to launch a campaign for young runaways. In the crush of the crowds and media, one of her ladies-in-waiting sidled up to me and whispered: 'The Princess wants to know whether you're wearing your royal tights.'

It was Diana's idea of a joke, and I sent a message back saying that I was indeed wearing the tights and they were doing just fine. Later, I thought I saw her give me a sly wink. Before long, though, catastrophe inevitably struck my treasured hosiery: I laddered them. I wrote a letter to the Princess:

Dear Ma'am,
It is with great regret that I have to inform you that I have laddered my royal tights. They were splendid while they lasted and I thank you very much for them. I have to admit, though, that even with my royal tights, my legs still never looked anything like yours!

A few days after sending this letter, I was getting ready to do some Christmas shopping when the phone rang. As always, my heart plummeted. It was bound to be the office calling me in for some unexpected story.

'Yes, what is it?' I said, sounding deliberately busy and unfriendly.

'Oh, it's Victoria here from the Princess of Wales's office,' came the somewhat shocked reply. 'Sorry to disturb you.'

'No, that's fine,' I said. 'Sorry. I was just on the way out. What can I do for you?'

'Well, it's just that the Princess asked me to ring you to say could you come to St James's Palace some time because she's got a Christmas present for you?'

Feeling even more churlish for my initial rudeness, I replied that of *course* I could find time to drop into the Palace: how would this afternoon suit? Abandoning all thoughts of Christmas shopping, I sat down with a cup of coffee racking my brains to think what Diana might have bought me.

I arrived at St James's Palace at about 3. The Princess's office was still sited there, although plans were being made to move it to Kensington. I was greeted by some of the women who ran the office, but of the Princess there was no sign.

'I'm afraid the Princess can't be here,' they said. 'But she wanted you to have this.'

I felt a stab of disappointment and then thought how stupid I had been to expect to see her. They handed me a large white box, decorated with a huge gold ribbon. I was dying to tear it open there and then but opted to play it cool.

'Well, please thank her very much indeed, and wish her a very happy Christmas from me,' I said, picking up the box. It was so light that it almost flew out of my hands. I couldn't imagine what was inside.

It wasn't until I got home that I finally opened it. With Emma's help, I untied the ribbon and carefully lifted the lid. Inside, I unearthed seven pairs of tights, identical to the ones I'd so recently ruined. With them was a note from the Princess, handwritten on a blue card. It said:

I hope you see the amusing side of this package.
Anyway, wishing you a happy Christmas.
  From Diana

I still have the note – and two pairs of my royal tights.

CHAPTER THIRTEEN

On a mission

It always felt rather special to be wearing tights given to me by the Princess of Wales, and they had their first outing or two over the Christmas period. With her divorce now finalised and her official diary comparatively empty, it seemed that, as 1997 dawned, the royal reporting waters were pretty tranquil. Not for the first time, I was to be proved sorely wrong.

The phone rang on a chilly, damp morning in Devon. We were still recovering from prolonged New Year celebrations, and the intrusion by the office was unwelcome.

'Diana's going to Angola,' I was told. 'She's campaigning against land mines. Can you go?'

'When?' I asked, trying to think of what was already lined up for the coming months.

'Next week,' came the reply.

Oh, shit! I thought. How can I possibly do all the research and make the arrangements without ruining the rest of the holiday with Emma and Jim?

'OK,' I said. 'That's fine – I'll get working on it.'

I broke the news to Emma later that day. She was upset. Now almost seven, she noticed my absence more than ever, and I'd been away longer than she'd liked the year before. I explained that this was going to be an important visit and promised to bring her back something unusual from Africa, which went some way to appeasing her. Over the next few days I found myself split in two – like so many working parents – keeping her company and playing games whenever I could, while frantically preparing for my trip in any spare moments. There was so much to learn about land mines. It wasn't a subject I'd ever considered in any depth, but, like the Princess herself, I quickly became engrossed in the shocking facts and figures.

For years, my job had been one in which I was starved of facts. Mine was all too often a world of nuance and inference. Now I had acres of detailed statistics outlining an issue which seemed unarguably to matter. They made gruesome reading, and I devoured them. At that time it was estimated that there were 110 million land mines littering the world: one for every sixteen children. In Angola the figures were even worse: one person killed or maimed by a mine every twenty minutes, and the highest number of amputees anywhere on earth. Diana was on a mission to try to draw attention to their plight, and I was only too pleased to be going with her.

A few days after returning to London from Devon, I flew out from Heathrow bound for Johannesburg. There, my picture editor and I were picking up a producer and cameraman before flying on to Luanda, the capital of Angola. We knew that this was a country ravaged by the effects of a twenty-year civil war. There would be no question of using sophisticated satellite links to send our reports back to London; instead, we took with us a new piece of technology called Toko. Essentially, it meant that we could squeeze our television pictures through a phone line; it was a slow way of working, and the quality wasn't ideal, but it was our only option.

I didn't know what to expect of Angola. I knew it was dangerous and that the war had exacted a terrible price not only on the population but on the economy too. Inflation was running so high (at more than 3,000 per cent) that money had little meaning and much of the country's basic infrastructure had broken down. We were tired by the time we got to Luanda, and the heat and dust hit us as soon as we got off the plane. We walked across the tarmac to the dark, dingy terminal, where a frustrating wait began for our luggage and equipment. A single, ancient carousel lay in front of us, obstinately refusing to move. Plump, juicy cockroaches scurried across the floor, and the air was heavy with the smell of sweat. I was fascinated, as always, by the sensations of Africa.

After twenty minutes or so, with no sign of action from the carousel, I began to wish I'd had a pee before we landed. Peering through the gloom of the terminal, I finally made out the sign for the loos and, crunching a few cockroaches underfoot as I went, ventured in. There was only one cubicle; it was painted a sickly yellow and the loo itself was cracked and without the benefit of a seat. On the wall, a piece of wire held some small sheets of torn-up newspaper. I tried to close the door, but it fell off its rusty hinges. There was no alternative but to squat – and whistle. Just then two young Angolan men, glassy-eyed and carrying guns, lurched into what I had assumed was the ladies' loo, talking loudly. Suddenly all my bodily urges evaporated and I made a hasty exit, trotting back to my crew by the carousel which, by then, had jolted into action.

It took a lot of paperwork and a good deal of cajoling to

secure our passage through Customs, but eventually we loaded our boxes and bags into a taxi and headed for the hotel. The roads were potholed and the buildings scarred, but the hotel itself turned out to be rather a pleasant surprise. The rooms were small, brown and basic, but the view over the port and the Atlantic Ocean was most acceptable. And the excellent seafood was an unexpected bonus. We settled in for our stay.

We were a day ahead of the Princess, which gave us the chance to look around and gauge the reaction to her visit. The first and obvious point of call was the local newspaper; we couldn't get through on the phone and so decided to chance it and head straight there. Wherever we went, an armed guard came with us, but I can't say that I felt Luanda was a threatening place.

'Can you take us to the *Journal d'Angola*, please?' we asked the driver we'd hired. He took us to a dilapidated building not far from the hotel. There was no bell on the door and no sign that it was the editorial headquarters of the Angolan press. In the late afternoon sunlight, we stood in the street and shouted up towards the open window on the first floor. Eventually, a young man – who turned out to be the editor – came down to let us in. Suddenly, we were back in another era. In a bare room, with paint peeling off the walls, the two or three journalists who comprised the paper's entire staff were tapping out their stories on antediluvian typewriters. The layout of the latest edition was being mapped out by a sub-editor using a pencil, rubber and ruler. For a moment I thought I'd returned to my first incarnation as a journalist, on the *Richmond Herald*. They told me that they knew next to nothing about the British Royal Family, had no idea about the Princess's marriage problems and cared even less. To them, she was simply someone very famous who was coming to try to help their country. Proudly, they showed me their headline: PRINCESS DIANA IN ANGOLA: WOW! I wish I could be allowed to show such emotion in *my* reports.

We filmed in and around Luanda. Looking stupidly smart, I did my piece to camera against a backdrop of street poverty and wished I'd thought harder about which clothes to pack. Once we'd gathered all the shots and interviews we needed, we raced back to the hotel to edit. Before very long we became painfully aware that the promised air-conditioning was more a wish than a reality and, with the heat of the editing equipment boosting the temperature still further, we sat and sweltered. The cockroaches seemed to appreciate the extra warmth and basked on our machines. A couple of sweaty hours later, the preview piece was finished. The next task was to set up our Toko machine and send the report to London using the satellite phone we'd brought with us. It was then that the heat proved almost fatal. The satellite phone took an instant dislike to the conditions; it repeatedly cut out, overheating rapidly because its internal fan had seized up. Drastic measures were required.

'It needs some kind of lubricant,' concluded Duncan, my picture editor, after a detailed examination of the fan's internal mechanism. 'Have you got any Vaseline?'

Strange as it may seem, Vaseline is not high on my list of priorities when I'm packing for a royal tour and I was unable to oblige. From what we had seen of Luanda, most of the shops were devoid even of the bare necessities of life; the chances of finding a lubricant were negligible. Duncan and I rummaged through our possessions for a substitute. It seemed a hopeless task until – almost simultaneously – our eyes alighted on the washbags given to us on the flight out from London. We emptied the contents on to the bed.

'Got it!' said Duncan, grabbing a tube of lip balm. 'That's worth a try.'

Meticulously, he massaged the fan with balm until it spluttered into action, cooling and soothing the phone, which then agreed to work without argument. We sent the report to London and stored the rest of our lip balm away as if it were gold dust.

Standing at the airport the next day, waiting for the Princess's plane to touch down, a reporter from the *Guardian* sidled up with a question that countless male colleagues have bored me with over the years: 'What do you think she'll be wearing?' he asked.

My head was still full of the appalling statistics of the legacy of the war. Frankly, I couldn't have cared less about what clothes Diana might have chosen. It is a presumption men have constantly made on royal tours: that I would have a deep interest in and intimate knowledge of the precise shade and cut of cloth of the royal wardrobe.

I gave him what I hoped was a suitably withering look.

'I have absolutely *no* idea,' I sniffed. 'It's not the sort of detail I need on television; people can see for themselves.'

He looked faintly offended by my arrogance, but I explained that I'd always refused to regard points of dress-style as part of my brief as royal correspondent. I *certainly* never described the clothes in my reports.

Ten minutes later, the Princess stepped off the plane wearing pale blue jeans, a white T-shirt and a blazer. It was a clear statement of intent. She had come to work, not to dazzle. It was also an obvious and annoyingly integral part of the story and I was about to eat my words. For the first time, my script that day began with a fashion note.

'The Princess was pointedly dressed for a working visit,' I

wrote, cursing myself for having been so cocky to my fellow reporter and feeling hopelessly overdressed myself.

Over the next two days, Diana saw some of the harsh reality of life in Angola. She visited a Red Cross field hospital where amputees were fitted with new limbs, and she went to a series of briefings about the extent of the land-mine problem. She seemed deeply involved, taking notes and asking questions. In the midst of such grim statistics, though, there were moments of perverse humour. One of her destinations was a health centre outside Luanda, in a sprawling township called Kikolo. A small fleet of press minibuses set out a good two hours ahead of the Princess, bumping and bouncing along roads that were little more than dirt tracks. We urged the drivers on, anxious to get to the health centre in time to gather our facts and sort out camera positions.

'Come on! Let's go a bit faster,' we nagged. Our entreaties had little effect. These were men who knew how easily a bus that had seen better days could lose what remained of its suspension. We chugged on through the dust for what seemed like an eternity.

'We're going to be late,' we bleated. 'We've *got* to go faster or she'll be there before us.'

Just then, in the driver's mirror, we saw headlights blazing in the far distance. Soon, the inevitable whine of a police siren penetrated our closed windows.

'For God's sake – there's the convoy. She's catching us up,' we groaned in unison. 'We *told* you this was going to happen – now step on it!'

The driver looked at us, stared into his mirror and, wrenching his steering wheel sharply to the right, pulled off the road, switched off the engine and folded his arms. The might of the British press had been silenced. We were powerless, and we knew it. The Princess was coming through, and we were going to be forced to watch her go, knowing that there wouldn't be a single British camera at the health centre to record her arrival. There was nothing to be done. As the sirens reached a crescendo, we jumped out of the van and stood at the side of the road, waving morosely to Diana as she sped by. She waved back cheerfully, giggling like a schoolgirl as she disappeared over the bumpy horizon.

It turned out to be a long day in the ramshackle suburbs of Luanda, and by the time we had laboriously sent our report back to London we were exhausted. We'd been forced to perch our satellite phone and Toko machine halfway up the concrete back staircase of the hotel because that was the best place to pick up the signal. It meant a lot of running up and down from our edit room, copious apologies as people tried to get by our bulky equipment, and a few frayed tempers. After the evening report was finished, we'd had to sit down and prepare a preview of the next day's events, when the Princess was due to see the mine-clearance programme during a visit to the former rebel stronghold of Huambo. We finally quit work at about half-past ten, but after a glass or two of imported wine and some stupendously fat and delicious prawns in the hotel restaurant I felt placated.

I'd been in bed for about an hour when the phone impaled my dreams. My eyes sprang open; it was pitch-black and, try as I might, I had absolutely *no* idea where I was. I groped for the offending instrument of torture and sought to silence it with a viciously hissed, 'Yes?'

'Hi, is that Jennie Bond?' a voice enquired tentatively.

'It is,' I replied, surrendering immediately as I recognised the tones of the news organiser.

'Oh, Jennie, sorry to wake you, but you need to know what the papers are saying about the Princess.'

I swung my legs out of bed, turned on the light and grabbed a pen. 'Tell me about it,' I said.

'It's the lead story in *The Times*,' said the news organiser. 'It quotes a government minister who calls her a "loose cannon". He's not named, but he says the Princess is straying into the political arena. He's accused her of siding with Labour. He says she's ill-advised, unrealistic and not being at all helpful. Can you check it out, please?'

How, I thought, am I to check out this highly political story, with its roots in the UK, as I sit in this cockroach-infested hotel in the middle of Angola?

'I'll make some calls,' I said. 'I'll get back to you as soon as I can.'

I sat for a moment and considered whether I had the heart to ruin someone else's night. There was no choice. I rang the ever-helpful director-general of the British Red Cross, Mike Whitlam, who was acting as Diana's right-hand man on this trip. The phone rang three times before he answered, sounding bravely upbeat. I told him what was going on. He was shocked but grateful to have been given an early warning of the impending row. Of *course* the Princess wasn't a loose cannon, he told me. She'd been thoroughly briefed about the British government's position; the Foreign Office had approved the visit; and she certainly wouldn't accept that she was going against official policy. But, as both Mike and I knew, this was clearly a story that was going to make waves, and one thing was for sure: there'd be no more sleep for either of us that night.

I'd already set my alarm for 5 a.m. because we had to be at a military airport by 6 o'clock for flights to two of the most war-torn cities in Angola: Cuito and Huambo. Now I was in a race against time to rewrite my piece for *Breakfast*, produce reports for the morning radio bulletins and prerecord interviews with the *Today* programme before the alarm went off. When it did, I had already been up all night and was feeling like death.

On the short, bouncy flight to Cuito in a ten-seater UN plane, I planned what I had to do. The Princess would have to be asked about the accusations that had been so prominently displayed in *The Times*. I'd have to pick my moment carefully and 'ambush' her with a question. I knew she'd hate it, but at least Mike Whitlam would have told her about the reports beforehand.

It was an explosive situation – in every sense. As we landed on the tiny airstrip, the impossibly delicate business of locating mines was going on in the grasslands around us. Men in luminous orange boilersuits and huge visors were scouring the scrubland inch by inch, risking their lives with every step. We jumped into a couple of Jeeps and were driven to a briefing where the law was laid down to us in no uncertain terms. If we strayed away from our guides or refused to obey their instructions, we'd be transported straight back to the airstrip – Princess or no Princess.

She arrived in a separate plane and joined us in this once-pretty city, now said to be the most mined in the world. An appalling assortment of uncovered weaponry had been put on display near the remains of what had once been the city centre, and the Princess was given a graphic account of the damage each could wreak. I felt sick at heart about the prospect of lobbing a question at her; she was quite likely to be furious, and it could ruin all the progress I'd made in getting to know her. But I knew it had to be done, both for my integrity as a journalist and because I felt she should have the right of reply.

My moment came when she was invited to walk a short distance along the crumbling pavements to see some of the pockmarked houses at closer quarters. Cursing my white stilettos as I picked my way through the rubble alongside the gang of reporters and camera crews who were recording her every step, I seized my only chance: 'Ma'am,' I said, holding out my microphone and walking alongside her, 'a government minister at home has described you as a loose cannon. What's your reaction to that?'

Even in her flat shoes, she towered above me. She stopped for a moment, squinting slightly in the sunlight and, looking resigned to the inevitable, she answered me: 'Well, Jennie, I'm only trying to highlight a problem that's going on all over the world. That's all.'

Everyone else was silent, waiting to see if I'd risk another question.

'It's been said that you're aligning yourself with Labour policy. What do you say to that?'

Now she looked annoyed. She began walking on, but wanted to know more: 'Who's saying that?' she asked. 'I don't know what you mean . . . I'm only trying to help.'

She quickened her pace; I deliberately fell behind, breathed a huge sigh of relief and tried to merge into the background. The tour of Cuito continued; I scrambled together a piece to camera and began mapping out a script in my head. Somehow this tape had to get back to Luanda in time for the *One o'Clock News*, but I was flying on to Huambo, so I'd thrown myself on the mercy of one of the UN pilots who'd agreed to fly the tape back to my picture editor. Suddenly, I found the Princess walking alongside me again. She looked down at me, plaintively. 'Jennie, please don't ever do that to me again,' she said before turning away sharply to resume her conversation with the mine-clearance expert.

I accepted her rebuke in silence and jumped into the Jeep to scribble out my script. It was a job in itself to keep my pen steady as we bounced our way back to the airstrip, but I didn't dare wait because I knew we'd have only a few minutes before we had to get on the next plane. Standing on the tarmac, sheltering from the African sun under the wing of a small aircraft, my cameraman and I struggled to get my words recorded on his tape over the roar of jet engines. Mobile phones didn't work in the bush, so I jotted down some hasty instructions for my producer back in Luanda. 'Make sure London knows about this,' I wrote. 'Diana has responded to the criticism. There are some great shots of her in Cuito and then my questions to her. Tell them it's really good material.'

My script was virtually illegible to anyone except me, but I tore it out from my notebook and put it in the tape box to help with the edit before handing the whole lot to the pilot. I thanked him profusely and impressed on him that my future career depended on his making contact with my producer.

Sitting on the next plane, bound for Huambo, my thoughts turned to the Princess, who was in a separate plane. I saw no reason for her to be angry with me, but I knew she disliked being 'doorstepped'. I decided to write her a note:

Dear Ma'am,
I'm sorry if you were taken by surprise when I asked you those questions, but you must realise that this criticism has come from a government minister and it's front-page news back home. Surely you can see that it was vital to get a quick response from you so that people can judge for themselves?

I know you hate talking off the cuff like that but, believe

me, what you said was fine – and it will be on the news in
a couple of hours.

I didn't have an envelope, but I folded it as neatly as possible and stored it inside my notebook. It was hot and airless inside the cramped plane; I was feeling the effects of being up for thirty hours with almost no sleep; and we still had a long day ahead. The land below us looked strangely barren; the long war and the land mines had taken a savage toll on the wildlife as well as on the human population. On the horizon I could see our next destination, Huambo, which, I'd read, was once called 'The City of Flowers'. Now, though, it was more like a ghost town, with remnants of elegant houses half-demolished by war. From the airport, we were taken straight to a minefield to witness what turned out to be the Princess's most publicised exploit of the entire tour. In front of the cameras she donned full protective gear for a walk through a 'safe corridor' to view the mine-clearance work close up. There was, of course, no danger that anything would be allowed to happen to her, but it was nevertheless a brave and highly effective stunt.

While she was getting ready, I did my best to attract the attention of my friend, Mike Whitlam. 'Could you give this note to the Princess, please?' I pleaded. 'It's really important that she reads it.' He promised to do what he could.

An hour later, after Diana had provided some dramatic pictures for us, the media party were invited to join her at a buffet lunch at the Red Cross office in Huambo. It was a stand-up affair and extremely informal; we were only too delighted to be given such good access to her. In a white shirt and trousers, she moved around the room, discussing all she'd seen and learned that day. I wondered if she would deliberately avoid me, but she was smiling as she came across.

I spoke first. 'I hope you read my note because I wanted you to understand why I pounced on you like that.'

'Yes,' she said, 'thanks for that. I was just so surprised when you came up to me, and I didn't want to say the wrong thing. But I understand now – and it's OK.'

I felt relieved that I hadn't blown my relationship with her – such as it was – and asked her what she made of all she'd seen.

'It's been so very humbling,' she told me. 'I've seen some horrifying things, but I've been so impressed by the work that's going on.'

We chatted for a few minutes, but her schedule was pressing and we all had to move on. Before she left, though, she tapped me on the shoulder and said: 'You know, you really ought to wear more red. It suits you. I keep seeing you in yellow, but that just drains all the colour from your face. So stick to red!'

It reminded me of when I'd heard that advice for the first time: when I'd been washing the kitchen floor. To hear it again, this time directly from the Princess and in the middle of Angola, struck me as even more bizarre. I considered myself forgiven.

A month later she surprised us all by revealing that she'd made a video diary of her visit to Angola. In it, she acted as reporter, narrator and campaigner for this new cause in her life: the drive to ban anti-personnel land mines.

'I'd read all the statistics,' she said in a film showing highlights of her trip. 'But nothing could have prepared me for the reality of what I found. For people like this, the only thing to hang on to is your own dignity. No one can take that away from you.'

Inevitably, her account included the moment when I'd sprung

my question on her in Cuito. 'I felt ready to burst into tears,' she confessed on the soundtrack. 'I wanted to know who'd called me a loose cannon. I'm a humanitarian figure. I always have been, and I always will be.'

I sat in the preview theatre watching her film and feeling faintly guilty that I had all but reduced the Princess to tears. But both she and I knew that her visit had boosted her image. She'd been seen around the world spearheading a campaign that had global impact and to which she was now firmly committed.

At the BBC, we soon found ourselves committed to another campaign: the general election had been called for 1 May and it looked as though the Tories were in trouble. This time, I followed the proceedings from the comfort of the studio, presenting *Breakfast* and daily bulletins during any pauses in royal business. But on the morning after Labour's landslide, I was once again perched outside the Palace to watch the outgoing Prime Minister go in and the incoming Prime Minister come out. Tony Blair was taking over the reins of power. My part in our live broadcast that day was minimal, but it was a thrill just to be there, along with thousands of other people, and to join in a moment of history.

Two weeks later I was packing my bags for another adventure with Diana – this time to Washington – when a call came through that Camilla Parker Bowles had been involved in a road accident. She'd been driving to Highgrove when it happened; she'd escaped without serious injury but the other car ended up in a ditch. I rushed to the office. Gradually, Camilla's business was becoming mine, too.

The business in hand, however, was the land-mine campaign that was now taking the Princess to Washington. She'd accepted an invitation to join forces with the head of the American Red

Cross, Elizabeth Dole, wife of Bob Dole, the former presidential candidate. As we waited for the two women to address the waiting media, it became clear that there was some kind of problem. The Princess had certainly arrived at the Red Cross headquarters on time, but she had yet to emerge with Mrs Dole. American security men strutted around bristling with wires and looking self-important.

'You all just stay right where you are,' they drawled as the press ranks became agitated by the delay. 'Those two ladies will be out when they're good an' ready.'

The truth was finally given to us by one of the British officials. Mrs Dole's worst nightmare had come true: her royal guest had turned up in a smart suit almost *exactly* the same shade of lilac as hers. It had been too much for her to bear. To Diana's huge amusement, Mrs Dole had made her excuses and scuttled off to scramble into a substitute canary-yellow outfit before daring to face the cameras.

Whatever they were wearing, it was certainly the Princess with her first-hand experience of the land-mine problem in Angola who came over better. She spoke fluently and powerfully, using both her brains and, at a gala dinner, her beauty to raise the profile of the whole issue and half a million dollars for the campaign. It was a short, sharp working visit. I enjoyed being back in the States and admired the wide-open spaces of Washington, but within three days it was time to head home. Unusually, I found myself travelling on the same plane as the Princess, and I was toying with the idea of sending a note up to First Class to say hello when Mike Whitlam of the Red Cross came back to see me.

'The Princess wants to know whether you'd like to join her for a chat,' he whispered in my ear.

I felt unashamedly chuffed. 'I'd be delighted,' I replied quietly.

'Come through in five minutes or so,' said Mike.

The cabin crew had been told to expect me and ushered me through discreetly. Diana was standing up, looking comfortable in airline socks and a baggy jumper, talking to an elderly couple she'd clearly just met. The conversation seemed earnest, and I did my best to stay in the background. They were discussing the woman's fight against cancer, and the Princess was in her element, offering comfort and advice. After a few minutes she patted their hands gently and moved away.

'Hello, Jennie,' she said, smiling. 'Come and sit down.'

She stretched out, snuggling under one of the white duvets that are a perk of first-class travel. 'I'm *exhausted*,' she said. 'Was it very hard work for you?'

We talked for a while about how the trip had gone, giggled about Elizabeth Dole and compared notes on the gala dinner. She looked tired and was obviously planning to sleep for the rest of the flight; I didn't want to outstay my welcome.

'Well, I'd better get back to my seat now,' I said. 'What will you do when you get home?'

'Oh, I'll sit down and write all my thank-you letters to everyone who helped with the trip,' she said. 'I always like to get that done straight away.' She smiled and looked a little wistful. 'I suppose you'll have your family waiting for you?'

I nodded and said goodbye, thinking how different our homecomings would be. With any luck, I'd get back in time for Emma to fling her arms around me and tear open my suitcase to find her gift. The dog would go wild, my parents would probably ring, Jim would moan about all the noise and I'd end up taking Emma to school. It seemed to be a far preferable scenario to the solitary picture the Princess had painted.

Our conversation had been no more than a friendly chat, and it had lasted a mere quarter of an hour. As fate decreed, it turned out to be our final meeting.

I *did*, though, go on one more trip with the Princess, one on which I saw her not as the rather vulnerable young woman I knew but as the extraordinarily glamorous superstar she had become. It was just a week later, and once again I was crossing the Atlantic, this time bound for New York.

'You'll *hate* it,' my husband had warned me. 'It's a hideous place – noisy, dirty and claustrophobic.'

'You'll *love* it,' my colleagues told me. 'It's got a buzz like no other city on earth.'

I was curious to find out who was right. My first impressions were not favourable. The Big Apple was sweltering in late June sunshine, the traffic was gridlocked and my hotel room appeared to have been designed for a pygmy. Squeezing past the wardrobe, I lay down on the bed and spread out my notes about the auction of Diana's dresses that I was there to cover. The phone made me jump.

'Hello, Jennie – it's the foreign desk here. Did you have a good flight?'

My suspicions were aroused immediately by this kindly enquiry.

'Yes, fine,' I said. 'But I'm a bit tired now.' It seemed prudent to add this note of disgruntlement.

'It's just that the bulletins are wondering if you could do us a piece about this row over the Princess taking her sons to a film about the IRA.'

'*What* film?' I asked. 'I've been travelling for goodness knows how many hours. I don't know anything about a film.'

The Princess, it transpired, had taken William and Harry to a controversial film in London the night before and had paid the price with some harsh headlines. She'd fallen on her sword immediately and apologised for an error of judgement – which made it even more of a story. I threw on some fresh clothes, jumped into a yellow cab and found my way to the New York office, where I introduced myself to the resident team and begged them to show me the ropes. With minutes to spare, I managed to file a rather makeshift report to London.

Diana arrived in New York the following day. She'd decided not to attend the auction itself, but she was there to publicise it and to say a final farewell to the eighty or so dresses she was selling for charity. The crush of media outside Christie's left little room for the crowds who'd sweated their way across town to see the Princess. I guarded my spot on Park Avenue jealously. The sticky evening heat was exacerbated by the steam that belched erratically from the drains, just as it does in old American movies. As the crowds grew bigger and the cops got more and more frazzled, I felt as if were in a scene from *NYPD Blue*.

'You can't stand there, lady,' growled a bloated bluebottle in uniform. 'Lady Di's coming through.'

'I am *perfectly* well aware that the Princess is about to arrive,' I snapped back in my most clipped and pompous tones. 'And she would *certainly* want the BBC to witness it, thank you.'

'Well, you *and* the BBC can witness it somewhere else, lady,' he barked – and shoved me to one side.

Fortunately, just at that moment, the wailing of police sirens signalled that the Princess was, indeed, about to make an appearance. Awkwardly straddling one of the geyser-like drains, and hoping that it would resist the temptation to gush forth, I stood on tiptoe and was rewarded with a glimpse of the Princess's hair as she passed by. Luckily, my cameraman had a better view and, as his pictures showed, Diana was looking her most dazzling in a Catherine Walker creation that hugged her strong, meticulously toned figure.

The auction itself, a day or two later, seemed a little sad without her. Nevertheless, I had to admit that it was a night when the Big Apple was truly buzzing. I was one of more than a thousand people packed into the salesrooms to watch the dresses that had acquired such fame through their owner appear now as stars in their own right: one by one on a revolving stage. The bids rolled in to a steady crescendo of gasps as the prices spiralled; the first million dollars came within forty minutes. By the end of the evening, my head was buzzing, too, as I struggled to feed the bi-medial beast that is continuous news: filing constantly for *World News* and Five Live between grabbing interviews with successful bidders and preparing reports for the main bulletins. I left New York unconvinced that it was a city I'd ever wish to revisit, but glad that I'd been there.

Back in London, I was soon embroiled in the renewed debate about whether Prince Charles could ever marry Camilla Parker Bowles. It had been given a fresh lease of life by his decision to throw a fiftieth birthday party for her at Highgrove. It was a bold move by the Prince which sent dozens of reporters, including myself, careering around the country to assess opinion. The upshot was the usual mixed bag, with some people vehemently against the relationship, others quite indifferent to it and the Church unsure which way to turn. The day of the party itself was one of those on which you wonder whether this really is a grown-up job as, alongside colleagues from around the world,

I spent twelve hours perched on the wall outside Highgrove watching catering vans and luxury portaloos come and go. Eventually, in late evening sunshine, the guests began to arrive, and we worked ourselves into a ferment of excitement as word spread that Camilla was on her way. After a few false alarms that had our hearts racing, her car swept into the drive to an explosion of flashbulbs. It was so quick that we had to show it on TV in slow motion, but it was the shot we'd waited for so patiently all day.

As the summer drifted on, I watched with interest as the papers charted the progress of the relationship between Diana and her new boyfriend, Dodi Al Fayed. As far as the BBC was concerned, the holidays she shared with him were private and we did not intrude. My own holiday was due to start in the last week of August. Jim and Emma had been in Devon since July, and I'd promised that *nothing* would stop me from joining them for the final fortnight of the school vacation. I arrived late at night; the smell of the sea was bewitching and the stars were startlingly bright. Curled up in an armchair, ready for bed, Emma was stoically fighting off sleep. She ran over and hugged me as I whispered in her ear: 'Now you've got your mummy all to yourself for two whole weeks!'

A few days later we were invited to a drinks party by our neighbours, who were moving house. It was a lovely evening with all our friends, and the wine flowed freely. Unusually, though, by about 11 o'clock I felt a powerful urge to go home. Jim and Emma were still thoroughly enjoying themselves, so I left quietly and walked back up our little valley. I'd been in bed for about an hour when I heard them come in; Emma snuggled up beside me and was asleep in seconds. She didn't hear the shrill ring of the phone. It sent a shudder of alarm through my body: a call so late at night was almost certainly bad news. I heard Jim answer it, sounding rather the worse for wear.

'Who the hell's ringing so late?' he demanded gruffly. There was silence as he listened. 'I see,' he said. 'OK, I'll tell her.'

He walked through to the bedroom.

'Diana's had some kind of car crash – they want to talk to you.'

CHAPTER FOURTEEN

The death of Diana

'How bad is it?' I asked the news organiser as I stood in my nightie looking out at the pitch-black hillside.

'Well, all we've got so far is that she's been injured in a crash in Paris. At the moment it looks as if she's not as bad as some of the others in the car. Can you make some calls?'

'Yes, of course,' I said.

But the Palace knew no more than us – or, if they did, they weren't saying. The Queen and the Duke were at Balmoral; so were Prince Charles and the boys.

Each time I put down the phone, it immediately rang again. The office was desperate for news. By now, some of the bosses were heading into TV Centre. But still, all the indications were that the Princess had escaped with relatively minor injuries. There was even a report from an alleged eyewitness who claimed he'd seen a blonde woman walk away from the accident. Briefly, I clung to the hope that it would turn out to be a storm in a teacup, that someone else could handle it and I would be saved from breaking my reckless promise to

Emma. Even as I thought it, I knew in my heart that it was a forlorn hope.

'I *know* you're on leave, but *can* you possibly get back to London tonight?' The bosses had arrived in the office. 'We still don't know what's happened to Diana, but an Arabic-looking man who was with her is dead. We think it's Dodi.'

I realised I had no choice.

'I've got to go,' I whispered to Jim, who was in bed by now. 'I'm taking the car – tell Emma I'm sorry.'

He looked at me and growled: 'If you get in that car, I'll call the police. You're over the limit.'

He was right, of course, even though I felt as sober as the day I was born.

'Tell them to get you a taxi,' he slurred helpfully.

Oh, Christ! I thought. Here I am, stuck in the boondocks of Devon in the middle of the night with a major crisis on my hands and no car. How on *earth* am I going to get a taxi all the way to London? I reached for Yellow Pages.

'You want to go *where*?' the cab controller asked in an astonished Devon lilt. 'You mean all the way to *London* at this hour of the night? No, we couldn't *possibly* do that.'

I stood barefoot in my chilly kitchen and felt desperate. Between phone calls I was glued to the radio, following the latest developments. The situation in Paris was still very confused.

Eventually, one of the taxi firms took pity on me and, at about 2.30 a.m., a cab gingerly made its way down our bumpy track. There were two drivers so that they could take shifts; by now they, too, knew the urgency of the journey, and they unscrewed the name banner on top of the car to reduce the wind resistance. We simply flew up the motorways; I lay in the back with my ear pressed to my radio. Every few minutes my pager or mobile phone summoned me and, halfway to London, it was one of those calls that struck horror into my heart.

'Jennie, you need to be aware of what we're hearing from the Philippines.' It was one of my bosses. 'The reporters travelling with the Foreign Secretary have been told that the Princess is dead. We can't get confirmation, but it sounds pretty definite.'

I felt numbed by the enormity of what was happening. *How* could those early reports have been so catastrophically wrong? *How* could Diana – so young, so complex and so much a part of my life – be dead? I asked the driver to go still faster and listened intently as the tone of our radio coverage abruptly changed from guarded optimism to uncertain despondency. The confirmation came through at 4 a.m. In a state of shock, I listened as the national anthem was played. The death of a major national figure was a scenario the newsroom had rehearsed many times. We'd even rehearsed the death of the Princess of Wales a year or so earlier. But the realisation that, this time, there was nothing fake about it was overpowering.

The taxi swept into the BBC at 6.22 a.m. The newsroom was crowded and feverish; the atmosphere urgent and sombre. Martyn Lewis was going on air at 6.30, and they wanted me in there, too. While I quickly skimmed through the latest agency reports, a make-up artist did her best to make me presentable and a producer ran to the wardrobe to fetch the black jacket I always keep there. I put it on, hoping the cameras wouldn't pick up the fact that I was still wearing a pair of casual trousers and beach shoes. With a deep breath, I went into the studio.

It was the start of a momentous week's broadcasting for us all. I had no doubt that this was the biggest news story I was ever likely to handle, and I did my best to stay calm, reasoned and, more than anything, to get the tone right. We broadcast non-stop throughout that Sunday. First with Martyn and then with Peter Sissons, I helped chart the events in Paris and the UK as they unfolded. We deployed reporters to France, to Balmoral, to Kensington, St James's and Buckingham Palaces and to Althorp; we sent crews to track down Earl Spencer in South Africa and outside broadcast units to RAF Northolt to record the tragic, final homecoming of our fairy-tale Princess. I sat in the studio and talked for hours about the woman I had known, the life she had lived and the legacy she had left us. But it was only when, in the middle of that live broadcast, we saw the first pictures of her coffin being carried from the hospital in Paris that the appalling reality of what I was reporting truly hit home.

People have often asked whether I was choking back the tears during those long days of broadcasting. I have to say that I wasn't. At times like that, your professional instincts take over and you find yourself entirely focused on the job: the sole issue is to get it right and to do it with coherence and dignity.

After fifteen hours in the studio and more than thirty-six without sleep, I was driven home to our empty house in London. I was still high on adrenalin and poured myself a large drink. Sitting on the bed watching all the rival channels, I remembered that I hadn't had time to ring Emma to explain why I'd broken my solemn promise and disappeared from her life again in the middle of the night. I felt bereft. Gradually, guilt, exhaustion and grief merged to send me fitfully to sleep.

The alarm startled me at 6 a.m. For a split second, my mind refused to acknowledge what had happened, but I felt overwhelmed by an oppressive, dark cloud. Then I remembered. I struggled out of bed to get ready for work. My eyes were like two slits with black hammocks hanging beneath them;

the make-up girls would have their work cut out today, I thought.

The national sense of grief at the loss of Diana was taking hold. I spent another day in the studio analysing the mood and reporting on the latest developments. As yet, there was no indication of when the Royal Family would return to London, but the presumption was that it would be soon. We were all taken aback by the depth of emotion that was becoming apparent on the streets, and by early evening I felt I could no longer go on talking about it without some first-hand experience. I was sure it had been exaggerated.

'You've *got* to let me out of the studio,' I begged my bosses. 'I need to see and feel what's going on out there.'

Reluctantly, they agreed to send me to St James's Palace for the *Nine o'Clock News*. The first books of condolence had been opened, and the queues were already so long that people were preparing to stay all night. As I got out of the car, I was struck by the near silence of such a mass of humanity. Many stood in solitary reflection; others shared whispered memories as they awaited their turn to pay tribute to Diana. The first person I approached was a middle-aged man with a beard, who looked utterly rational.

'Hello,' I said quietly. 'How long have you been waiting?'

He looked at me and burst into tears. Nothing could have driven home the point more powerfully; for whatever reason, the grief that people were feeling was genuine.

My live spot for the news that night was almost a disaster. We had last-minute technical problems and Peter Sissons couldn't hear me; the crowds who'd gathered around the camera watched with interest as the panic levels rose. I began to wish I'd stayed in the comfort of the studio. With seconds to spare, we managed to establish communication and I was on. I looked tense and haggard; at one point my mind went completely blank, my eyes stared wildly and I had to rely on my mouth to keep talking on autopilot. I felt a wreck and, when it was over, went home with a sense of emptiness.

Matters were not made any easier by the word from Devon that Emma had found my sudden disappearance very unsettling. She, too, was upset by the Princess's death and confused by her mother's absence. My guilt was overpowering. After a third eighteen-hour day, I took the extraordinary decision to ask whether I could go home to Devon for twenty-four hours. My bosses agreed; the story seemed to have gone quieter and they understood my dilemma. I took the train to the West Country, feeling excited to be on my way to Emma, but hideously guilty about leaving London. It was the classic working mother's nightmare, and it didn't get any better. I spent an uneasy few hours with my husband and daughter desperately trying to be an untroubled wife and mother, while my mind was in turmoil at having abandoned the only news story that anyone was talking about. I got up well before dawn and raced back to the BBC.

Far from quietening down, the drama that followed the Princess's death was becoming more gripping with every hour. The clamour for the Queen to return to London to lead the nation's mourning had spawned blunt headlines: 'WHERE IS OUR QUEEN?' the papers screamed. The answer, of course, was that she was at Balmoral trying to comfort and protect her grandsons in their hour of greatest need. But she, too, was caught in a dilemma. She wasn't simply a grandmother; she was the Queen – and the country demanded her presence. The public mood was turning nasty, and there was a whiff of revolution in the air. At the eleventh hour, the Palace grasped that this was serious. The Queen's press secretary, who had inexplicably taken several days to get back from a holiday in Australia, went on camera to say that the Queen and the Royal Family were hurt by the suggestions that they were indifferent to the country's sorrow. They would leave Balmoral earlier than planned, the Queen would broadcast to the nation and the Union Flag would fly at half-mast over Buckingham Palace. Meanwhile, the Duke of York and Prince Edward were deployed to St James's Palace to view the books of condolence and to walk among the crowds. In the nick of time, the Palace was fighting back.

As a journalist caught in the middle of something like this, you have to set your sights on one bulletin at a time. As soon as one is over, the next comes hurtling towards you like a tidal wave. You sink or swim with each. By Friday, the day before the funeral, we were into 'rolling news' mode again, broadcasting through much of the afternoon as first Prince Charles and his sons, and then the Queen and the Duke arrived in London. Thousands of people were milling around the Palace, where a sea of flowers for Diana stretched out into the Mall. There was a feeling in the air that the people had spoken; they had demanded concessions – a flag at half-mast, a longer funeral route and the presence of their Queen. Now that they had secured them, they were ready to sympathise with, and be comforted by, their monarch.

At 6 o'clock I was poised in the studio ready to comment on the Queen's live broadcast from the Palace. It was a moment of history which would require instant analysis; there would be no time to prepare. In the event, my job was made easy by the Queen. She struck precisely the right note, speaking in unusually personal terms not only 'as your Queen but as a grandmother'. She paid tribute to the Princess, describing her as an 'exceptional and gifted human being . . . who had made many, many people happy'. Crucially, she made one more concession, saying: 'I, for one, believe that there are lessons to be drawn from Diana's life and from the extraordinary and moving reaction to her death.'

The institution of monarchy, she implied, was not impervious to emotion or to the need for change. It was a masterly performance.

That evening the Princess's coffin was moved, in darkness, from St James's Palace to her home at Kensington Palace in preparation for the funeral. My final task of the day was to report on that sad journey as the hearse motored slowly past the largely silent crowds. As it reached Buckingham Palace, a spontaneous round of applause broke out. It was as if they believed Diana could still hear them.

After so many days of talking about the Princess, I found myself almost lost for words as I struggled to meet a tight deadline. Quite frankly, the pictures spoke for themselves, and anything I said seemed superfluous. I'd run out of energy to panic, and surrendered to my word block by leaving long gaps in my commentary. In the end, they seemed appropriate. At 11 o'clock I crawled home, flung myself on the bed with a glass of wine and stared at the mounds of newspapers I'd brought back during the week. From every front page, Diana stared back at me. I felt her loss acutely.

It was still dark when I arrived at Buckingham Palace the next morning, some six hours before the funeral was due to begin. The scene was unearthly; hundreds of people were spending the night in the open, huddled around candles, singing softly or saying prayers. Camera crews and reporters from around the world moved quietly among them, filming and interviewing; TV presenters stood in rows beneath bright lights relaying the news to every corner of the globe. St John Ambulance staff dispensed tea, coffee and foil blankets to stave off the early autumn chill. There was something chimerical about it all, as if I'd walked on to the set of a movie that was being shot in slow motion.

In the specially constructed BBC studio just across from the Palace, Jill Dando and a team of producers were getting ready to go on air. I joined them, glad to be on more familiar territory. We broadcast through those early hours as London prepared for one of its saddest days. By the time my part in the programme was finished, the crowds were ten deep along the funeral route. The air was heavy with emotion and, without prompting, people came up to me to share their thoughts and their memories of the Princess as I walked slowly towards Westminster Abbey. There, in a temporary studio overlooking the Great West Door, I joined David Dimbleby for our live broadcast of the funeral. It was not where I wanted to be. My preference had been to do the main news package on the day's events; to report on Diana's final laying to rest as I had reported on so much of her life. But my bosses had insisted that I was needed for the live programme. As I had predicted, I wasn't required at all and simply sat in the studio feeling angry.

The position changed rapidly, though, when Earl Spencer astonished the world with his hard-hitting oration from the pulpit. His pointed remarks about the way the Princess had been treated by the Royal Family and the media, and his pledge to watch over the way in which her sons were brought up, constituted a separate news story in their own right. I was quickly summoned back to TV Centre.

It had been a harrowing day at the end of a devastating week. It finally drew to a close for me with my report on Earl Spencer's speech and a live spot on our evening news in which I attempted to sum up an historic seven days. I was so tired by this time that I'd lost control of my body temperature; one minute I was shivering, the next sweltering. When we came out of the studio after that final broadcast, there was a sense of satisfaction that we had all acquitted ourselves well. There was also a sense of anticlimax and sorrow. I sat in the newsroom and watched John Simpson's half-hour special about the day I had just witnessed. Freed at last from the tyranny of worrying about the next bulletin, it was the first time I'd felt able to see the events from a personal – rather than professional – perspective. I found it profoundly moving.

Eventually, I rang home. It had been a lovely day in Devon. Jim and Emma had seen nothing of the funeral; instead, they'd gone fishing.

CHAPTER FIFTEEN

Picking up
the pieces

It was over. The Princess had been buried, and my job would never be quite the same again. On the day after her funeral I felt as if I'd been run over by a lorry, both physically and emotionally. I tried to sleep late, but woke early; I tried not to think about the past week but found my mind going over every detail. My little family was coming back from Devon that day, but not until late, so I got up and went 'home' to my parents. The talk everywhere was still about Diana. Everyone had an opinion, a view of her life and legacy, a theory about her death. I was happy to listen, for I, too, was still struggling to make sense of what had happened.

It had been a cataclysmic seven days for the Royal Family. Just as she had shocked and shaken them so often in life, Diana had rocked them to their roots in death. The country had been dragged through a gamut of emotions from shock and grief to anger and reconciliation. At one point there had been near panic among the Queen's advisers that the public mood was swinging irreversibly against the monarchy. In the family itself there'd been conflict over what form of funeral the Princess should be given. It had been an ugly week in every way. But the Queen's acknowledgement that there were lessons to be learned reinforced the feeling that the Princess's influence over the style of monarchy in this country would continue long after her death.

There is, however, a healing quality about the routine of life and, with Jim and Emma home and the new school year under way, things began to get back to normal. For the Queen, the business of monarchy marched on regardless of personal turmoil. She was about to embark on a particularly sensitive tour: her first visit to Pakistan for thirty-six years and then on to India. Royal tours are long in the planning and rarely cancelled. Diana's death had made this one even more newsworthy, and a large press contingent was preparing to fly out with the Queen. It was a Friday morning early in October when I packed my bags for what promised to be two hectic weeks. I took Emma to school, kissed her goodbye and, trying not to cry, headed for the airport. There I met up with my crew and found our ITN colleagues were travelling on the same plane, which augured well for a convivial few hours. After the usual paranoia and jealousy about who, if anyone, would get upgraded, we discovered that we *all* had seats in Business Class and settled back for a good gossip. Four hours later, we'd just about exhausted our store of the latest mishaps and misdemeanours perpetrated by our respective newsrooms – and we were *still* on the tarmac. I'd been delayed many times before, but this was by far the longest wait on board a plane and we were getting fed up.

'Ladies and gentlemen,' the captain announced ominously, 'I'm very sorry to say that we've been unable to overcome our technical difficulties. We have no choice but to ask you to return home or to go to a hotel for the night while the aircraft is repaired.'

We felt like a bunch of pricked balloons. Most of the gang decided to go straight to a hotel for a few drinks and a meal. I plumped for racing home to spend one last night with Emma and Jim. I pictured how full of joy their faces would be when I came through the front door so unexpectedly; it was almost worth the tedium of the delay. An hour or so later, I put my key in the lock as quietly as possible and peeped in. The house was strangely silent; the dog didn't bark, the TV was switched off; it looked deserted. With a stab of pain I guessed instantly what had happened: on the spur of the moment they'd decided to head to Devon for the weekend. I was right. Too miserable to care for myself properly, I opened a can of tuna, sat on the stairs and ate it out of the tin, quietly weeping.

In many ways that episode turned out to be symbolic of the tour itself. Despite the best intentions of the Queen and the Duke, matters went seriously awry almost from the start – and the visit became headline news day after day. It was the thorny issue of Kashmir that sent it into a tailspin. Though the name of that hotly disputed territory never passed her lips, the Queen was judged to have alluded to it during her speech to Pakistan's National Assembly when, on the advice of her ministers, she urged India and Pakistan to work towards a better relationship. The Foreign Secretary, Robin Cook, was accused of going further during private talks with Pakistani ministers. As the Queen padded around the Faisal Mosque in a pair of socks, a diplomatic row was brewing.

We had to keep pace not only with the political sensitivities of the region but with the tour itself. In temperatures of forty degrees or more, we trotted from engagement to engagement. In Islamabad, the Queen held her usual reception for the media and we all downed tools to meet her. With two of my colleagues I stood on the shady veranda of the British Embassy, watching her work her way around the crowd of journalists.

'You know, we *really* must say something worthwhile when she comes over,' I said. 'Something about Diana – we can't just pretend it hasn't happened.'

My two male companions nodded in agreement. It was less than six weeks since the Princess had died, and emotions were still raw. We discussed the sort of remarks we might make, looking nervously over our shoulders in case she suddenly approached our little gathering. It's surprising how tongue-tied even hard-nosed reporters can become when the Royal Family are about to descend on them. As the Queen came towards us, we braced ourselves to say something meaningful. A diminutive figure in cool cucumber green she stood before us smiling. A rather strident female voice pierced the silence.

'It's good to see you again, Ma'am,' it shrieked, 'but it's *frightfully* hot here, isn't it?'

As we all cheerfully conversed about the weather conditions, I realised with horror that the shrill tones had been none other than my own. I kicked myself inwardly for such an inane opening gambit. Four minutes later, after an illuminating discourse on the effects of too much sunshine, the Queen was gone – and we had lost our chance to engage her in a sensible discussion. I vowed never to be so stupid again.

From Islamabad, we flew to Karachi, where we bustled around in pursuit of the Queen for just four hours before loading all our equipment back on to the plane to fly on to Lahore. It was dark by the time the press bus rolled up at the hotel, and our deadline was only a couple of hours away. I'd been scribbling my script on board the plane; the urgency now was to set up our editing equipment. It was on a separate bus and, in the warm evening air, the editors and producers from the three British TV channels waited anxiously for it to arrive. As the bus pulled in, they set on it like children with a bag of sweets, tugging at the big silver boxes that were piled precariously high. Everyone scampered off with their treasures to begin the race to complete our reports. Everyone, that is, except the BBC. With a shudder of impending disaster, we searched the empty bus for our most essential piece of equipment – our Toko machine, the only link for sending my report back to London. It was nowhere to be seen.

As vital minutes seeped away, we turned the hotel upside down, looking for our missing box. We rang the airport and implored them to search the hold of the plane; they assured us that there was nothing left on board. We returned to the bus and took it apart seat by seat. We had British and Pakistani officials hurtling around on our behalf, but all to no avail. I rang London.

'We're in big trouble here,' I told them. 'Our Toko is lost somewhere between Karachi and Lahore. You may not get a report tonight.'

They were sympathetic, but annoyed.

'Maybe one of you should go to the airport to take a look,' the foreign duty editor suggested.

It seemed as good an idea as any, so my producer set off across town. But it would take him at least an hour, and in the meantime I could see only one solution: to beg. One of our rival networks owed us a favour and this seemed the perfect moment to call it in.

'If you let us borrow your Toko when you've finished, we

might *just* get a short report back to London – and I *promise* I'll make it up to you,' I pleaded.

To my surprise, they agreed – on condition that we kept it a secret. No one wanted a turf war breaking out, and the other lot had thought it very amusing that we'd lost our equipment. The remainder of that sweaty evening was spent frantically editing, though if anyone knocked we pretended simply to be whiling away the hours until our machine was located. When the tape was finished, we wandered nonchalantly through the hotel lobby, hiding the borrowed machine between us before scooting up the back stairway to the roof. There, after threading our path through the air-conditioning drums and vents, we set up the Toko machine and pointed the satellite phone skywards. In conspiratorial tones, we congratulated one another as the report winged its way to London. Half an hour later, my producer arrived back from the airport triumphant. He'd forced his way on to the plane in the dead of night and searched the hold himself. There, lost and alone, was our Toko machine, which he had duly retrieved.

The following day, half a dozen of us were invited to join the Duke of Edinburgh on board a small plane to fly into Pakistan's hinterland: the Hindu Kush. It was one of those occasions when you know that you're incredibly lucky to be paid to go on such adventures. The Duke sat in a comfortable front cabin, which gave him privacy from our prying eyes as we flew over the spectacular terrain of the foothills of the Himalayas. Our destination was just twenty miles from the border with Afghanistan, and we approached it through an alarmingly narrow corridor with towering grey mountains on either side. It was one of the most remote and barren regions I've ever seen and, as the pilot took a run at the tiny landing strip, I wondered if it would be the *last* place I'd see. Safely on the ground, however, we jumped into a fleet of Jeeps to take us in convoy along the twisting dirt tracks. As we bounced over the potholes, I looked out at the arid hillside and wished – once again – that I had forsaken my stilettos.

Motorised transport seemed something of a novelty: everyone else got about by donkey. Blazing a trail of dust, we arrived at a water-treatment project where the local village folk were sitting in neat rows on the ground. The women were almost completely covered by their colourful robes, but I could see them sneaking glances at me and giggling to one another. I wondered if they thought I was the Queen. As the Duke was given a briefing about the project, I stood quietly in the background trying to make eye contact with these shy but deeply curious women. I was equally curious about them and longed to find out about their lives and thoughts but, whenever our eyes fleetingly met, they turned away. Before I could seek out the services of an interpreter, we were shepherded into our Jeeps again.

Flying back to Lahore, life seemed strangely surreal as I looked down on that stark but dramatic landscape, imagining what life there must be like. My shoes were still covered with the grit of the Hindu Kush, but here I was sitting in a private jet thousands of feet above the dust and donkeys, being served English tea from a silver pot with warm scones and jam.

The outing was a pleasant interlude in a tour that was becoming ever more troubled. It had always been a high-risk strategy to combine a visit to Pakistan with one to India, and by the time we arrived in Delhi things were getting decidedly sticky.

'This visit has the status of a social call,' declared *The Times of India*. 'It is a photo-call for a monarchy that has been under attack after the death of Diana.' For good measure it added a reference to the Queen as 'frumpish and banal'.

This was not the kind of press generally associated with the start of a royal tour. Worse was to come: India's Prime Minister was reported to have called Britain a 'third-rate power' that had presumed to say it had a historical responsibility to solve the Kashmir issue. The report was eventually denied, but not before it had thoroughly muddied the waters.

Standing in the early morning sunshine at the presidential residence in Delhi, I watched the monkeys romp around the colonnades while the dignitaries lined up to await the Queen. Just *how*, I wondered, was she going to walk the diplomatic tightrope that stretched out before her? And how were *we* going to feed the voracious appetite of our news desk? There was still a week to go, and we were exhausted.

In the ensuing days, I felt quite sorry for the Queen as she dutifully went about the business of the tour, always smiling, constantly showing interest and unfailingly polite. There were demonstrations against her in Delhi, a delicate visit to the Sikh city of Amritsar was marred when the Duke questioned the official death toll of the 1919 massacre, and a speech the Queen had been due to make at a banquet in Madras was mysteriously cancelled. Buckingham Palace had to move swiftly to counter reports that the Queen was unhappy with the advice she'd been given by her Foreign Secretary. Untrue, it cried; she was entirely satisfied with his advice and was 'enjoying the tour very much'. But, as I reported towards the end of the week, it had all become so sensitive that almost anything anyone said on any subject was problematic.

For the travelling media, the logistics of the tour were becoming increasingly difficult. When we flew south to the scorching port of Kochin, we were packed like sardines into a cramped plane. It disgorged us on to a steaming landing strip where we unloaded our equipment and sat down on the boiling tarmac, frantically updating our reports by satellite phone. We then set off for a draining day in the sun chasing the Queen around the cultural attractions of Kochin. Eventually, we staggered back to the airport, weighed down by cameras, phones and ladders. Foolishly, I was weighed down even further by a small carved table I'd been unable to resist buying as we waited for the Queen to emerge from the spice market.

'We'll have to dub the pictures during the flight,' said my producer. 'It's our only chance of getting a piece on air tonight.'

The three camerapeople (some of our best are women) looked at one another in horror. Dripping with sweat, they climbed on board the poky plane and, as soon as we'd taken off, they scrambled together enough equipment, powered by batteries, to start copying the tapes. To their credit, no one lost their temper, despite the near-impossible conditions in which they were working. While they dubbed, crouched over one another in the narrow aisle, the reporters wrote. Every now and again, one of them would shout out: 'Come and look at this. It's a *great* shot. We've got to use this one.'

Dutifully, we would squeeze past to peer through the camera viewfinder and take note of the shot, around which we could then construct our scripts. By the time we touched down in Madras, we were ready to race back to the hotel and begin the next challenge: to get our pieces edited and sent to London in time for our bulletins.

As usual, we ended up eating dinner at about 11 o'clock at night. We were all so tired we could hardly keep a conversation going, but we were buoyed up by the thought that the next day was the last of the tour. It had been a testing time for everybody, not least the press officials from Buckingham Palace – who angrily accused the BBC of 'leading the charge' on all that had gone wrong in India. As they well knew, there had been no reason for anyone to lead a charge; it had all happened quite independently.

'We'd better send a camera to see her off from the airport,' said my producer. 'Just a precaution. I'm sure we won't use the shot.'

He was lying on the bed, bleary-eyed, talking on the phone to ITN's producer in another room. I was sitting with Louise, our picture editor, battling to put together our final report of this long and arduous tour. Lou was so weary she could barely press the right buttons; I was so numbed that my brain refused to cooperate. All three of us were almost nodding off as we waited for me to produce a script. It was like pulling teeth, but an hour or so later we laboriously came to my payoff. I said it with obvious relief: 'Jennie Bond, BBC News, Madras.'

Just then the phone rang.

'You're joking!' I heard my producer moan. 'I can't bear any more – we thought we'd finished.'

'What's happened?' I asked.

'There's been a bit of a fight at the airport,' he said. 'The Indians tried to stop Geoff Crawford [the Queen's press secretary] from getting on the plane, and there was a scuffle between all the officials. The Queen saw it all.'

Even to the bitter end, the tour had continued to produce stories. As we waited for the pictures of this final drama to be brought back to the hotel, we cheered wearily as we heard the Queen's plane fly overhead, bound for Britain. It had been a fantastic news story – but thank God it was over.

Home at last, I put down my suitcase, waved the taxi farewell and rang the doorbell. There was no reply. With feelings of *déjà vu*, I put my key in the lock and peeped in. The house was strangely silent; the dog didn't bark, the TV was switched off; it looked deserted. They'd done it again! With a stab of pain, I guessed instantly that they'd decided to head to Devon for the weekend. This time, though, I didn't cry or comfort myself with tuna. It was Sunday afternoon, and I knew it would only be a matter of hours before they were home. I unpacked my Kochin table and settled down to wait for them.

It was good to be the mother and wife for once, on hand to welcome the family home, rather than the other way round. But there was no point in getting used to it; a week later I was off again, this time with Prince Charles. We were heading to southern Africa. It was the Prince's first trip abroad since Diana's death, and Prince Harry would be with him for much of the time. It promised to be important in shaping public opinion about Charles in those difficult post-Diana days.

'This is your room, ma'am.' The porter at our hotel in Swaziland ushered me in. I stepped into a huge lounge, with cocktail cabinets, a luxurious suite and an enormous television. Walking on, I discovered an equally spacious bedroom with another TV and, leading off from that, a bathroom to die for. I'd often wondered what Swaziland was like, but this was certainly *not* what I'd expected.

As a royal correspondent you sometimes end up in the strangest places reporting on obscure aspects of life. The next day we found ourselves transported from our splendid hotel to a sweet factory, where I discovered the hitherto little-known fact that chocolate éclairs are the most popular sweet in southern Africa; and here they produced 4 million of them a day. As

Prince Charles donned a white coat and hat to look around, the scene offered me a gift of a script line: 'Charlie', I wrote, 'was at last in the chocolate factory.' There were other fascinating facts to disseminate as well: for example, I learned that in Swaziland's polygamous society, King Mswati III had six wives and ruled in conjunction with the Queen Mother, otherwise known as 'The Great She Elephant'. These were splashes of colour that were food and drink to a hungry reporter.

If Swaziland was oddly beguiling, our next destination was positively bizarre. Whoever would have thought that I would one day attend the coronation of the King of Lesotho? But that's where the Prince of Wales and his band of intrepid reporters found themselves on a Friday morning in late October. The new King, Letsie III, larger than life and dressed in a leopardskin cloak, arrived twenty minutes late to raucous cheers from twenty thousand of his people crowded into Maseru Sports Stadium. It was like a scene from a blockbuster movie as he paraded around the arena in the back of a white Land-Rover, flanked by a motorcycle escort that wouldn't have been out of place in *Easy Rider*. Horsemen in tribal dress followed behind, though one of them came to grief when his charge bucked him off. Topless maidens danced for the King, who at the age of thirty-four was known to be urgently seeking a wife.

Beneath the scorching sun, I stood in the middle of this cacophony, as kings and presidents – including Nelson Mandela – looked on. The ceremony was set to continue for five hours or more, but, thankfully, after about three the British press were given the signal to make our escape. We were flying on with the Prince to Johannesburg, and the plane was waiting.

On board, he came back to see us and promised that his own coronation would be a little more restrained – and a great deal shorter. It was the second time during the trip that he'd openly courted the media, deliberately making the effort to chat to us. This was a sharp contrast to a tour of central Asia a year or so earlier, during which he had omitted even to say good morning to the half-dozen journalists who'd accompanied him on a small plane over ten days. Now, even the Prince realised that he needed to win favour with the media if his public image was to recover after Diana's death. His exchanges with us were strictly light-hearted; there was no mention of the Princess, and you could feel his anxiety about walking into the lion's den. But his advisers were slowly impressing on him the fact that, in this post-Diana climate, he would ignore the press at his peril. In Johannesburg he played to the cameras as he and Prince Harry met the Spice Girls. There was delight that he had taken his son to their concert but dismay that Harry had been dressed in a suit for such a distinctly unstuffy occasion.

From there we flew to Durban, and then north again to a small Zulu settlement called Dukuduku. The name alone was enticing enough, and as I settled back into the soft beige leather of a six-seater plane I felt the old familiar thrill of an adventure coming on. We were bouncing through the turbulence above a clear blue ocean, with the allure of Africa mapped out beneath us, heading for a destination that would never have entered into my life if I hadn't become a reporter. I felt lucky.

Dukuduku did not live up to its name. It turned out to be a rather dull group of prefabricated buildings in the middle of nowhere. But on a square of flattened earth young Zulu dancers stamped out a rhythmic welcome for the two princes; the wild beat of the drum surged through my body and made me long to jump out and join them. But *that* would have been the *real* me – not the BBC correspondent I am expected to be. Demurely,

I studied the princes, Charles looking protectively towards his small and vulnerable son, who had lost his mother only two months earlier. The truth is that Prince Charles has always been close to his sons but, in public at least, it was the Princess who was tactile and demonstrative with them. Now, the Prince was taking over that role as well, and he was no longer embarrassed to show his concern for them. His speeches, too, took on a more personal note, frequently peppered with references to his boys.

'It's been a great pleasure to bring Harry along,' he told his audience back in Durban. 'It's been a real voyage of discovery for him. My only disappointment is that my elder son couldn't be here, too. Like many other parents, I have the problem of my children having different half-terms, and so William had to stay behind studying.'

He added that there'd be trouble when he got back because he and Harry had collected so many gifts – including several Zulu warrior fighting sticks – that he'd have his work cut out preventing a war at home. This was a new and more human persona than the Prince had been used to revealing. It was one that would prove effective in the gradual rehabilitation of his image – a word he hates, but one that his public relations team were beginning to force him to cultivate.

There were other signs that the Royal Family as a whole had taken to heart the concept that lessons had to be drawn from Diana's death. At their golden wedding celebrations a couple of weeks after we returned from southern Africa, the Queen and the Duke paid public tribute to one another in a way that was uncharacteristic of this normally buttoned-up family. While he praised her tolerance during their long years of marriage, she was even more personal: 'Philip has quite simply been my strength and stay all these years, and I and the whole family owe him a debt of gratitude greater than he would ever claim or we shall ever know.'

There was a sense of fallibility and frailty about them after the trauma of tragedy. In that same speech, the Queen acknowledged the need for the Royal Family to read public opinion. But she also gave an insight into how difficult that can be for someone in her position. 'Governments', she said, as Tony Blair sat beside her, 'can gauge support through the ballot box. For us, though, it is not always easy. The message can be obscured by deference or rhetoric. But read it we must. With Philip's love and support I have done my best to read it correctly over the years. And, as a family, we will try to do so in future.'

There was, it seemed to me, a new humility about the monarchy, and I wondered how long it would last. It was symbolised a few days later by the solemn decommissioning of the royal yacht, *Britannia*.

It was a damp day in early December, and I staggered sleepily downstairs to the hotel lobby at 6.15 a.m. We'd stayed overnight in Portsmouth, and *Breakfast* wanted me live on air at 7 o'clock. As my producer, Sally, and I stepped reluctantly out into the wind and rain, my phone played its merry little tune.

'Yes?' I whimpered.

'Oh, Jennie, it's *Breakfast* here, just to say we don't need you at 7 now. Can you be at the dockside for 8?'

Thoughts of what an extra hour in bed would have been like flashed through my head and I felt ready to commit murder.

'Right,' I said curtly. 'Eight o'clock it is. Thank you *so* much for leaving it until now to tell us.'

Sally and I cowered in a corner of the hotel while they rustled up a cup of coffee. Coveting the warmth, we left it until the last moment to jump into the car – and to our horror immediately ran smack bang into the Portsmouth rush hour. What's more, we got lost.

A little humility on *my* part would not have gone amiss when we finally rolled up next to *Britannia*, having comprehensively missed our only live spot of the morning. My punishment was to stand on that gale-lashed dockside for thirteen hours, watching the end of an era unfold as *Britannia* gave up her credentials as a royal yacht. The Queen, the Duke and their children all came to say farewell to the ship that had been a floating home for them for forty years. It was noted that the Queen had to fight back tears for the loss of this old friend – though she had not wept publicly at Diana's funeral. They accepted this new bereavement with silent dignity, and there was an impression that, willingly or not, the Royal Family was being dragged into a less ostentatious way of life.

There was certainly nothing ostentatious about my way of life that day as I stood in the shadow of *Britannia* slowly freezing, despite five layers of clothes. I was so cold by the time it came to the *Nine o'Clock News* that it took all my willpower to stop shaking on air. My hair was plastered to one side of my head by the hurricane blowing off the sea, and I was in the direst need of a pee.

This, I reminded myself as I stood shivering – tired, miserable and hungry – waiting for Michael Buerk to talk to me through my earpiece, is the glamorous world of television!

CHAPTER SIXTEEN

Stepping off the roller-coaster

W henever the glamour fades from the job, which is frequently, there is usually a foreign tour to brighten the horizon. As we turned the corner into 1998, I had the bonus of a family holiday in the Caribbean in prospect as well as an early winter outing to Sri Lanka, Nepal and Bhutan with the Prince of Wales. I'd spent my honeymoon in Sri Lanka and was enthralled with the idea of returning.

A couple of weeks before we were due to fly out to Colombo, the phone woke me from a deep sleep. It was almost midnight, and I stumbled downstairs to take the call.

'Jennie, we've just been told that the Queen Mother's broken her hip. She fell over at Sandringham, and she's been brought to London. She's in the King Edward VII again.'

The news organiser's voice sounded urgent and worried; it is a recurrent nightmare of all news editors that 'the big one' will happen on their shift. I didn't feel much better, as I saw my night's sleep whisked away with one ring of the phone. I made my calls to the Palace, established the facts and, way before dawn broke, took up my post outside the hospital. It was the start of a long and painfully chilly stint on the pavement. Apart from the Queen Mother's health, the main talking point seemed to be whether or not I should wear my fake fur hat on television. I was so cold that I was determined to keep it on; my bosses tactfully tried to persuade me to relinquish it; the newsroom egged me on to stand firm. In the end we had an Internet opinion poll on the suitability of the hat, the outcome of which – astutely – expressed astonishment that managers had time to waste on such trivialities.

I was also in dispute with the bosses over going on tour with Prince Charles. With the Queen Mother making romping pro-gress, I could see no reason to keep me in this country. But they disagreed, and I was grounded. It was a huge disappointment and, in the months that followed, I had to listen jealously as my colleagues regaled me with tales of how they'd played elephant polo in Nepal and gone trekking with the Prince in the remote and extraordinary hills of Bhutan. There was, however, some consolation to be had from the rapid approach of our first big holiday since buying our house in Devon. We were jetting off to Tobago to celebrate Emma's eighth birthday.

It's only when you finally stop that you realise just how fast your normal pace has become. Emma and Jim acclimatised themselves almost instantly to a slothful life centred on the swimming pool at our beachside hotel. I felt fidgety and wanted to explore the island; they protested that we had two whole weeks for that. Gradually, I quietened down and learned to enjoy the non-eventful, gentle drift of Caribbean life. It was in this mood that, just before lunch one day, I sauntered vacantly back to our room – and espied a fax underneath our door. By this stage of the holiday, faxes were not part of my universe and it took me a moment or two to focus on it.

'ATTENTION JENNIE BOND' it read, rather alarmingly. I sat on the bed and turned to the next page. It was from the BBC. 'Princess Margaret has had a stroke on Mustique. She's being treated in Barbados. Can you get there in time to file for the *Nine o'Clock News*?'

I sat there in my bikini, my holiday heart valiantly trying to work itself up to a respectable pounding, and felt utterly bemused. *How* would I ever be able to explain to Emma that I had to abandon her on her birthday holiday in the Caribbean? I knew, though, that this was serious, and dutifully made a series of calls to airlines and charter companies. Fortunately, it proved impossible to get to Barbados in time and, with undisguised relief, I phoned the news desk to tell them. I was thanked and dismissed from duty. But the panic had reactivated my usual frenetic pace of life and I felt unsettled about missing a big story. I'm a firm believer that the day a reporter doesn't care about someone else trespassing on his or her patch is the day he or she should give up. Of course, I was immensely relieved to be able to stay with Emma, but I never quite recaptured full holiday mode again, especially when fellow tourists sidled up to me and said: 'Oh! We thought *you'd* have been called back to London by now. Don't you know Margaret's in hospital?'

With Diana gone, life was undoubtedly quieter. In a funny way I missed the roller-coaster existence that she'd created for the ratpack, and for a time we all wondered whether our jobs had died with her. But the Fund set up in her name soon began to produce a steady trickle of news stories, and in early March it was preparing to announce its first tranche of grants. There was considerable news interest, but a strict embargo had been put on any details.

'Can you do a piece for the morning?' I was asked by my news desk.

'Only if I can persuade the Fund to tell me today who's getting the money. Then I can call up the charities and get some reaction,' I replied.

It took a good deal of whispered negotiation. In exchange for a list of where the money was going, the Fund's spokeswoman extracted a solemn pledge from me not to broadcast any details before the morning. I worked flat out all day, gathering reaction from the chosen charities and putting together a piece for *Breakfast*. It was just before 10 p.m. when I finished and, as I wearily swung my bag over my shoulder to go home, I caught the ITN headlines.

'And tonight ITN can reveal exclusively who will benefit from the Diana Memorial Fund.'

My jaw dropped as I watched the lead story unfold. All the details – and more – that I'd faithfully promised to keep secret until the morning were being broadcast to millions of people. My whole day's work was now out of date and redundant. I was livid: initially with ITN for apparently breaking the embargo, and then with the Fund as it transpired that they had deliberately given the story to ITN first. I seized the phone to scream at the Fund's spokeswoman but got only her voicemail. I stomped around the newsroom, swearing loudly. Eventually, I drove home in a mire of misery; a single light had been left on for me – everyone was in bed. Still muttering to myself, I grabbed a bottle of wine from the fridge and skulked through to the conservatory, where my eyes alighted on a large bowl of burned roast parsnips, now cold and coagulated, that had understandably been rejected both by the cook (my husband) and my daughter. Wallowing in my unhappiness, I sat at the table with only my wine for company and munched my way through the entire contents of the bowl, quietly weeping at the injustice of the world. Half an hour later, swollen with parsnips and fairly inebriated, I swayed upstairs and peered at Emma's sleeping form. Gently stroking her hair, I pondered on how preposterously I was behaving. Surely, I told myself, all that *truly* mattered was whether life had treated *her* fairly that day. It was a thought that put everything in perspective. And the next day I was rewarded with trumps when the Fund not only rang to apologise but offered me an exclusive interview with the Princess's former butler, Paul Burrell. It was more than a fair bargain, for this was a man we had all been trying to talk to since Diana's death. A couple of days later, he spoke to me at length at Kensington Palace and my report led all the bulletins. I felt vindicated.

If Diana was no longer with us, she'd left a legacy that was shaping up to keep us quite as busy as she had: her sons.

'Charles is taking William and Harry to Canada: a couple of official engagements in Vancouver and then skiing in Whistler. Can you go?' It was the news desk, and they needed an immediate answer.

'Sure I can,' I answered. 'When?'

'End of March – just for a few days.'

'Fine,' I said, thinking how ill-equipped I was for a skiing trip. I'd been only once before and had found the whole experience so deeply humiliating that I'd eschewed it ever since. But who could resist going to a place called Whistler?

We arrived in the resort late at night and could see nothing but the dark silhouette of the mountains around us. With the rest of the pack, I'd already spent a busy couple of days in

Vancouver, where Prince William had been mobbed like a rock star. Hundreds of screaming girls had waited in the rain to see him, tears rolling down their cheeks if he so much as glanced in their direction. The teenage William had looked flushed and rather embarrassed to find himself a pin-up, but Harry had thoroughly enjoyed it and, behind the scenes, had repeatedly nudged his big brother, whispering: 'Go on, give them another wave.' Now, though, they were looking for a quieter time in the mountains.

After we'd hauled all the equipment up to our rooms, there was barely time for a nightcap before we turned in. A few hours later, as the morning light seeped through my window, I lay in bed with my eyes closed and, as so often on my travels, played the mind game of trying to remember where I was. When the answer slowly dawned, it pleased me: somewhere new; somewhere very different. I jumped out of bed and drew back the curtains. A magnificent larger-than-life picture postcard met my eyes. The mountains were monstrous and piled high with gleaming white snow; the chair-lifts were already clanking up the slopes; and early birds were taking advantage of the sunshine. You could ski straight out from the hotel, stopping only to admire the oval swimming pool and jacuzzi that were steaming five floors below me in the crisp morning air. *This*, I thought, looks like fun.

Our photo-call with the three princes was high up the mountain and lasted only seven or eight minutes. Unsafe at any speed on skis, I shivered quietly in my borrowed boots and mountain fleece as the princes performed for us. It's a part of the holiday they always dislike, but it's a deal that buys them a large measure of privacy for the remainder of their stay. For me, the dreaded piece to camera was a real problem as the camera kept freezing and my mouth was so cold I could hardly talk. One way or another, though, we got the shots we wanted and jumped in the cable car to return to earth. The warmth of the edit suite in our hotel room gave me new life, and we put the piece together in record time. Cheered by the thought that my main task in Whistler was completed (for this was the only photo-call they were giving), I ambled off for lunch with one of Charles's non-skiing advisers. My producer and editor, meanwhile, set off for the feed point to send the report to London.

I was in the middle of lunch when the phone call came.

'Jennie.' The voice was that of my producer, and it sounded contrite. 'I'm afraid there was a bit of a cock-up at the feed point. No one seemed to have booked a line. We did everything we could but the piece didn't get through in time. Sorry.'

Well, *that*, I groaned, is just brilliant! I've been sent halfway across the world and up a huge mountain for this one story, and we've buggered it up. The bosses are going to be *delighted* about that.

We held an inquest that evening into how it could all have gone so wrong, but it didn't help. The only solace I could find was in the jacuzzi under the stars, with sensuously warm water whipping my body as snowflakes the size of saucers floated down on to my hair. In that context, a lost report suddenly seemed altogether inconsequential.

It was, though, a matter for regret because photo-calls are among the rare occasions when journalists are more or less invited to throw a question. In general, the Royal Family have a horror of being seen to act like politicians; they therefore consistently resist pressure to give sound-bites. It's a legitimate point of view, but a brief comment can give a tremendous lift to a television report. It could make the crucial difference between a piece getting on air or being dropped; and surely they would prefer that their work is publicised? For years, I've waged a battle to persuade them not to shy away from my microphone, but it has proved an uphill struggle. I learned that lesson again when, not long after the trip to Canada, I drove down to Poundbury, the Dorset town built on ecological principles set out by Prince Charles. The Queen was going to see the results of her son's work, and it struck me as the perfect opportunity for her to say a few words about it. I bided my time until the visit was all but over and positioned myself so that she would have to walk within two yards of me as she made her way to her car. As she passed by, I plucked up courage and said: 'Ma'am, may I ask what you think of Poundbury now that you've seen it?'

The Queen looked straight at me and then, it seemed, straight *through* me before walking on as if I didn't exist. I considered it a shame that we were never to know whether she thought her son had done well. But Diana had ignored me in similar fashion.

Even in death, the Princess continued to make news. On 1 July, the day she would have been thirty-seven, Earl Spencer opened his museum commemorating her life. There were some poignant mementos of her childhood: a toy car, her school uniform and exam results (17 per cent for maths, 22 per cent for French). I was fascinated by some of her teachers' comments, which I felt could have applied to her in adulthood: 'Diana must try to be less emotional . . . she has a tendency to be quarrelsome.' There were memories, too, of the woman the world had known: her wedding gown and a selection of her designer dresses were displayed behind glass screens, a poignant reminder of our adventures as we'd followed her around the world.

We were at Althorp from early morning, broadcasting to *Breakfast* and gathering shots and interviews for the later bulletins. My production team had formed an advance party and set up a studio in a tent about a quarter of a mile from the main gate of the house. The road was closed to traffic, and the only means of transport between the two was a bicycle that the BBC had thoughtfully provided. It had been a few years since I'd ventured out on two wheels but, after interviewing some of the grieving men and women who'd come to pay tribute to the Princess, I had no choice but to strap my enormous handbag on to the back of the bike and pedal up the hill to the studio. Halfway there, the straps that had pluckily strained to hold my bag in place gave way; the entire contents – lipsticks, mascara, powder, phone, pager, Filofax, tissues, pens, passport, chewing gum, assorted earrings, hairbrush and lacquer – crashed to the ground. Puffing from the unaccustomed exertion, I dismounted and scrabbled around in the dirt to retrieve my possessions. I am *not*, I reflected, paid enough for this sort of thing, and I'm certainly too old for it! Eventually, windswept and somewhat disgruntled, I arrived at the tent-cum-studio. There was an air of panic among the team; time was tight, conditions were difficult and we would have to work fast.

Forty minutes later, I was putting the finishing touches to the voice track when my producer poked his head through the tent flap, looking aghast.

'They want a live two-way at the end of your report,' he said. 'You'll have to race down to the gates again. The camera's waiting; here's the bike.'

'Oh, *terrific*,' I said. 'I'm going to look just wonderful after flying down that hill again. Never mind. OK, I'm off.'

As I whistled down the slope, my wax jacket flapping in the wind, I saw the lenses of my snapper colleagues target me for one of the more unusual shots of the day. Worse still, I heard the raucous tones of one of my tabloid friends shout to the assembled public: 'Look out! Here comes the office bike.'

Giggling like a schoolgirl, I flung the contraption to the ground, wrestled my hairbrush from my pocket, threw off my jacket and – frantically making good the damage to my coiffure – faced the camera to go live on the *One o'Clock News*. It was a rare moment of humour in the course of a sombre day.

Almost a year had gone by since the Princess's death, and the approaching anniversary produced a flood of analysis about whether the Royal Family had indeed drawn lessons from all that had happened. The Palace had certainly sharpened its PR act: for example, by engineering photo-opportunities to make the Queen seem more in touch. We had filmed her outside McDonald's, inside a pub and with a host of showbiz stars at Windsor Castle. Prince Charles had shown himself to be a caring father, sensitive to his sons' immense loss. Most, though, agreed that there was still a way to go if the damage wreaked a year earlier was to be recouped.

The residual hostility to the Royal Family was palpable on the day of the anniversary itself. Along with most of the world's press, I was sent to Kensington Palace to assess the mood of the thousands of people who'd gathered to remember Diana. Even a year on, the grief of many of them seemed overwhelming. Nothing could match the ocean of flowers that had been placed outside the Palace after her death, but as the day wore on the floral carpet of anniversary tributes stretched far out from the gates. As always, my lunchtime report was a desperately close shave with my deadline, but I finished it with seconds to spare and, heart in mouth, raced to my spot near the Palace gates for a live interview. The crowds were circling like vultures, moving from reporter to reporter, watching the business of television being made. As I took my place, they gathered in a vast semicircle ready to devour every word I uttered. They stared and pointed. Some were friendly; others were simply curious.

The cameraman thrust a microphone into my hand. Realising that this was no time for modesty, I threaded it up my dress in full view of the crowds, snatched my earpiece from my bag and plugged myself in.

'This is studio N1 to Jennie Bond – can you hear us?' It was the studio manager talking in my ear.

'Yes,' I gasped, trying to calm my hair and powder my nose at the same time. 'You're a bit mushy, but I can manage.'

'Great! We're on air in thirty seconds – coming to you straight after your package, OK?'

'Fine,' I said. 'Is it Martyn?'

'Yes . . . Three, two, one . . . on air.'

The crowds, unable to hear anything except my side of the conversation, looked at me as if I were mad. The sound reception in my ear was poor, but I heard my report being broadcast and prepared myself for Martyn Lewis's questions. The sun was beating down and the crowds were inching ever closer, watching me expectantly. Urgently, the cameraman asked them to give me some space, but no one moved.

'And Jennie Bond joins us now from outside Kensington Palace.' Through my earpiece, I could just make out Martyn's words.

'Jennie, one of the Princess's friends has suggested that today should mark the end of the public grieving for Diana . . . that she should be allowed to rest in peace now. Is that the sense you're getting from people there?'

'Well, Martyn, I think there *is* a feeling in some quarters that this anniversary should mark a watershed in the mourning process . . .'

'*No, no. She's wrong!*' My words were almost drowned out as the crowd loudly voiced their opinions, waving their arms and trying to shout me down. I did my best to continue.

'Certainly, some of those who were close to the Princess *do* believe that it would be best for all concerned . . .'

'*She doesn't know what she's talking about . . . We'll never forget Diana . . .*'

Mass hysteria was breaking out around me, and though I continued with the interview, I couldn't hear a single word of Martyn's next question. Mercifully, after a minute or two, I vaguely made out his voice saying, 'Thank you, Jennie', and realised I was off air.

There was something unsavoury about the atmosphere outside the Palace that day. Several other reporters experienced the same treatment and, when one commentator was asked a question about Camilla Parker Bowles, a lynch-mob mentality surfaced – and the police had to be called. I've worked in a few dangerous places in my time, but I never expected to feel threatened in Kensington Palace Gardens. That afternoon, on the orders of the news desk, we retreated to the safety of a hotel roof overlooking the crowds below.

Two days later, on Prince Harry's first day at Eton, he and his brother issued a statement appealing for an end to the public mourning for their mother. It was time, they said, for people to move on. I hoped the crowds who'd protested so vociferously at the Palace were listening.

There was, however, still one princess travelling the world, and as autumn approached I got a call from our foreign desk.

'Do you want to go to Africa with the Princess Royal?'

This was an unusual proposal from the bosses. For all the good work that the Princess does – and she is beyond reproach in her dedication and professionalism – she is rarely regarded as newsworthy.

'Well, only if you think it'll get on the bulletins,' I answered. 'But I'd love to go, and I think it would be useful to remind people that we still have a truly hard-working princess.'

'Let's do it then,' came the reply.

Three new countries – Uganda, Tanzania and Kenya – on one trip. It sounded entertaining.

Sitting in the late September sunshine by the hotel pool in Kampala, I pored over the facts and figures about the issues we'd come to cover: Aids, street children and refugees. As with Diana in Angola, it was a real indulgence for me to have hard-hitting statistics about life-and-death subjects. These were facts that mattered.

At the Princess's first engagement, a support group for women who were HIV-positive, I asked her private secretary whether he thought she'd answer a question about the work that was being done there.

'Have a go,' he replied. 'There's no harm in asking.'

We filmed her as she toured the centre and chatted with the women. As she was about to leave, I seized my chance.

'Ma'am, could you tell me what you think of the support these women are getting?'

The Princess looked at me as if I was something she had trodden in and swept on towards her car.

'Ah, well. Bad luck,' mouthed her private secretary.

I had always imagined that the Princess and I might get along quite well. We're almost exactly the same age – just four days between us – and share a no-nonsense approach to our work. Sadly, I was wrong. Through Uganda, where we saw so many people dying of Aids, to Tanzania, where my crew and I befriended Kasim – one of Dar es Salaam's five thousand street children – and Kenya, where we saw the efforts to get aid to refugees from Sudan, the Princess remained frosty towards me. Her temper spilled over during an interview she grudgingly gave me in Nairobi; she took offence at the mention of Diana's work for Aids sufferers. Although she went on to answer several more questions about Africa, she said nothing when I thanked her for the interview and left the room without so much as a glance in my direction. It was a disappointing end to a worthwhile trip.

Travelling to three countries on one visit is as exhausting as it is invigorating, but a few weeks later we were off on a similar jaunt. This time it was to *four* countries; the Prince of Wales was flying the flag in Slovenia, Romania, Bulgaria and Macedonia. Our first stop was one of Slovenia's prime tourist attractions: Lake Bled. In a flotilla of brightly painted boats we were rowed out to its tiny island church; our progress was comically chaotic as the Prince's oarsman – full of Baltic pride – insisted on leading the way. This was not the plan that had been mapped out by the Prince's advisers. Photo-opportunities are everything on a royal tour, and it was essential that the media got to the island first so that we could film his arrival. His Slovenian boatman, though, clearly saw it as a point of honour to establish supremacy. Suddenly, the calm voyage across gentle waters became something akin to an extended university boat race.

'Oi! Get back where you belong, my son,' the cry went up from the press boats. But the Prince's oarsman pulled still harder, his muscles bulging.

'Sandy, *do* something – we're going to miss the shot!' This appeal was directed at the Prince's press secretary, Sandy

Henney, who was in one of the media boats. Seeing that there was little she could do, attention turned to our own oarsman. Somehow we'd have to overtake the Prince.

'Go on – in, out, in, out . . . you can do it, my boy!' This helpful instruction fell on deaf ears. *Still* the Prince was ahead of us in glorious, unrecorded isolation. He looked faintly amused. At the last moment, the day was saved by frantic waving, backed up by mobile phone calls between Sandy and the Prince's private secretary, who was in the royal boat. The proud oarsman was persuaded to take his royal charge on a brief detour, while we clambered ashore on the island with a meagre thirty seconds to set up our cameras. Worse, though, was to come.

After filming the Prince tugging at the church's quaint wishing bell (and *no*, he wouldn't tell us what he'd wished!), we were herded back to our boats to be taken to the next venue.

'*Now* . . . *go now*,' Sandy barked at us. 'If you don't go this minute, you'll miss the rest of the programme,' she warned.

I hastily finished my piece to camera (no wonder I looked worried), grabbed the tripod and trotted down the path back to the media boats. We were taken to the far side of the lake in double-quick time and had formed an orderly row of cameras by the time the Prince got there. It soon became apparent, however, that some of our party were missing – among them the Prince's press secretary.

'Where's Sandy?' we asked some of his security staff.

'Isn't she with you?' they replied.

We looked out over the lake and there, in the distance, was a tiny rowing boat slowly coming towards us. In the rush to get off the island, the rest of us had commandeered all the media boats, leaving Sandy and a couple of broadsheet stragglers stranded. Undaunted, the reporters had used their improvisational skills and 'liberated' a small boat that had looked particularly friendless. It was a gallant act to rescue Sandy and return her to us, but I sometimes wonder how long the owners of that boat were left on the island.

You can never afford to relax on a royal tour. Time and again, unforeseen events blow it off course or something unusual happens precisely when you think things have gone quiet. The visit to the Balkans became dominated by a row over claims that the Prince wanted his mother to abdicate. He issued a ferocious denial which kept us exceptionally busy with demands from every bulletin. But it was in the old town of Plovdiv in Bulgaria that I was caught napping. Like the Pied Piper of Hamelin, the Prince had led his merry troupe of media over cobbled streets through a maze of picturesque buildings. His guide was no less than Bulgaria's President, Petar Stoyanov, about whom most of us knew nothing except that he was an ardent Beatles fan. We filmed them going in and out of house after house, and our interest was beginning to wane. By the time we arrived at the final venue, only a few hardy souls were still following and we put up barely a token protest when we were asked to stay downstairs because of the cramped conditions on the first floor. Thankfully putting down our cameras, we leaned against the wall and gossiped while the Prince and his entourage went upstairs.

Ten minutes later, we heard the unmistakable sound of the Beatles' song 'All You Need Is Love' wafting down. It was a crude and amateur version, with a single pianist accompanying the voices of what – we realised with growing horror – could only be President Stoyanov himself *and* his royal guest. Snatching our cameras and equipment, we stampeded up the stairs, but security guards blocked our way. By the time we persuaded them to let us through, the music was over. Even though it wasn't of earth-shattering significance, there was no getting away from the fact that a prince and a president singing the Beatles was a good Saturday story. Soon, my news desk would be reading reports about it on the agency wires, and they'd be looking to me for the pictures. I had to use all my ingenuity to get them.

'Who was in there? Anyone?' I begged the Prince's staff as they swept out of the house.

'There *was* a camera in there, a Bulgarian I think,' was all they had time to tell me. The Prince was on the final leg of his walkabout; I had maybe ten minutes to track down the pictures and get to the press bus.

Suddenly, I saw a man with a TV camera. Stilettos clattering on the cobblestones, I launched myself at him: 'Hello, I'm from the BBC. Were you filming when your President sang just now?'

He looked at me apologetically; he didn't understand.

'Does anyone here speak English?' I implored the street at large.

With the help of a volunteer interpreter, I established that my quarry had indeed been filming when the duo had burst into song. He worked for the Mayoress of Plovdiv and was recording this momentous visit to her town. Unfortunately, he was filming on a completely different format from the one we use; there was no way to copy his tape where we were, and he was deeply unwilling to part with it. I got out my purse.

'Tell him I'll pay him a hundred dollars for it,' I instructed the interpreter. I was getting desperate: I could hear the press bus revving its engine.

Cash has a way of opening doors, and suddenly everything became possible. Unhappily for the cameraman, it was at this point that the Mayoress passed by. She enquired what was going on and, when we told her, she insisted that he should make a copy of the tape. Moreover, she promised to have it delivered to my hotel within two hours. Deftly extracting the hundred-dollar bill from her luckless cameraman's hand, she handed it back to me, saying: 'We wouldn't dream of asking our guests to pay for this. It is our pleasure.'

I thanked them both profusely and raced for the bus. On the way home to the UK, the Prince came back to see us on the plane, as has become his custom. We laughed about his attempt to emulate the Beatles and exchanged opinions about all we'd seen. We all agreed, though, that four countries in one trip was rather mind-boggling. As he turned to go back to his cabin I said: 'Have a good birthday.'

'Don't remind me,' he groaned.

For the Prince was about to hit fifty: a landmark in anyone's book, but one, for him, that inevitably generated acres of newsprint and analyses of his 'image'. There was nothing he hated more. But his team of advisers were sharply aware that this was a golden opportunity to improve their man's standing.

'You must come to Sheffield, Jennie. It's going to be great television. I can't tell you what, but if things go to plan it'll be worth your while.'

So spoke the Prince's team in advance of a day of celebrations to mark his half-centenary. And they were right. The pictures of Prince Charles in the Sheffield community centre where the movie *The Full Monty* was filmed will go down in history as classics. Volunteers from the Prince's Trust conspired with the Palace and a handful of newspaper photographers to entice him into taking part in a spoof of the film's famous dole queue sequence. To the raunchy strains of the song 'Hot Stuff', he gingerly took his place in the queue and, encouraged by one of the film's stars, Hugo Speer, clenched his fists, pumped his elbows and tapped his foot in true *Full Monty* style. It was brilliant television, and I used every frame.

With PR stunts such as this, combined with solid hard work and the inevitable softening of his image through being seen as a loving parent, the Prince had regained a fair measure of the ground lost since his divorce and Diana's death. The waters ahead, though, were not yet calm, as was made plain the next day when Camilla Parker Bowles organised a party for him at Highgrove. Kings and queens from all over Europe mingled with the Prince's friends and family. Standing outside the gates, huddled together in the winter cold, the media watched them all arrive. There was one notable absentee: our own Queen. Caught in the dilemma of whether she should be seen to condone her son's relationship with Camilla Parker Bowles, she chose to stay away from his fiftieth birthday party. It wounded the Prince deeply, but to all of us it was now clear that this was a relationship in which he would brook no compromise. The Charles and Camilla story was big – and getting bigger.

CHAPTER SEVENTEEN

Checkmate?

Camilla wasn't the only player taking up her position on the front line of the royal chessboard, as we were to find out just six days into 1999. Jim, Emma and I were sound asleep after a late-night drive back from Devon when the phone rang.

'Jennie, sorry to trouble you so early, but the *Sun* says Edward and Sophie are announcing their engagement today.'

Here we go again, I thought. By torchlight I fumbled through my wardrobe to find an appropriately cheerful suit for a 'good news' story before performing my 'manic mother' disappearing act. As I sped towards the office, my phone calls to the Palace elicited the usual coded replies: 'I'm afraid we can't confirm or deny anything, Jennie. You'll just have to wait and see.'

'Well, should we put our outside-broadcast vehicles outside the Palace, just in case?' I enquired.

'That's really up to you and your news desk.'

'But you *know* how short of resources we are,' I complained.

333

'Do you think it would be a complete waste of time to put the trucks there?'

'Well, I can only say it might be prudent, but I really can't give you any more guidance than that.'

I rang the office and told them to get the trucks down to the Palace as fast as possible.

It turned out to be the usual fraught morning, pleading with the Palace for details of the announcement and finally securing them thirty seconds before I had to go live on air. In my designer suit, I squatted on the pavement scribbling frantically as a Palace press officer dictated the statement over the phone. My cameraman looked worried: 'They're coming to us in fifteen seconds,' he warned me. I jumped up, smoothed my hair, took a deep breath and, trying to look calm, regurgitated the information I had so recently acquired.

An hour later we were summoned to a photo-call and brief news conference with the happy couple in the gardens of St James's Palace. Sophie Rhys-Jones struck us all as a far more worldly wise woman than either Diana or even Fergie had been. She was trained in public relations, intended to continue her career and had been given a firmer grounding in royal life than any bride before her. All of which augured well for the Royal Family because, as I remarked in my report that day, the House of Windsor could ill afford another failed marriage.

Prince Charles's team, meanwhile, had been working hard behind the scenes to position *their* chess pieces favourably. The aim was to win enough goodwill to allow Charles and Camilla to have something approaching a normal private life. They were tired of the skulduggery – always having to hide from the press and public – and, in the last week of January, piquant rumours began to circulate. There was to be a birthday party at the Ritz for Camilla's sister, and the word was that Charles and Camilla would face the cameras together for the first time. My calls to the Palace were excruciating.

'No, we can't confirm anything,' they insisted. 'It's a private engagement – nothing to do with us.'

I knew it would be vital to stake a place outside the Ritz at least twenty-four hours in advance if the rumours were true. I *had* to get a decent steer.

'Well, I was planning to go down to Devon for a few days,' I parried. 'Does that strike you as a good idea, or would I be wiser to hang around in London?'

There was a long pause, followed by a sotto voce reply. 'I'd stay in London if I were you.'

'Thanks,' I whispered back. 'I will.'

I ran down the corridor to the news desk.

'Get someone down to the Ritz *now* with a ladder,' I yapped. 'Charles and Camilla are coming out at the party tomorrow . . . there'll be hundreds of cameras there. We've *got* to strap a ladder in place as fast as we can.'

We were far from being the first on site; a couple of dozen ladders were already tied to the railings, but we managed to secure two good positions. They were guarded by some of our dispatch riders on a shift system until a few hours before the party itself, when the cameramen took over. I arrived an hour or so before the first guests were due. The atmosphere outside the hotel was electric; dozens of camera crews had erected a small city of ladders and lights. I took my place among them. It was a colossal news story and when, eventually, Charles and Camilla stepped out to face the media, two hundred flashbulbs lit up the night sky, almost blinding the couple as they walked warily to their car. I broadcast live on *News 24* as it happened, and the sense of drama was breathtaking; the instant that they were gone, photographers clattered to the ground and crouched over their digital cameras to send the best shots to their newspapers from right there on the pavement. The whole event had taken less than a minute, but in that maelstrom of flashguns Charles and Camilla had successfully devalued any snatched paparazzi shots of them together – and earned themselves a new way of conducting their life as a couple. The demand for the story was endless; I eventually crawled into bed at 3.30 in the morning and was up again at 6.20 for *Breakfast* and another busy day.

Just as I had never expected to attend the coronation of the King of Lesotho, so I hadn't bargained on visiting the Falkland Islands. It was therefore a thrill to discover that, in early March, we were heading to those far-flung shores with Prince Charles. The first leg of the trip was to Argentina, and it was one of the few occasions when Jim has been envious of my travels. The truth, though, is that I can remember virtually nothing of Buenos Aires, the city he would so much like to see.

We arrived on a warm summer's afternoon, and the Prince got straight down to business. But, rather like the Queen's ill-fated visit to Pakistan and India, there was an inevitability about the diplomatic row that blew up when he mentioned the Falklands during his first speech. Argentina's Vice-President took offence at the Prince's seemingly innocuous remarks; suddenly the royal trip was headline news at home; and we were working our socks off. My only clear memory is of a polo field near Buenos Aires where the game was subsumed by the political nuances of the criticism being levelled at the Prince. As darkness fell, we worked on – long after ponies, players and Prince had gone home. Perched on a black plastic box at the edge of the polo ground on a night that was equally black, I remember feeling somewhat pathetic as a giant South American toad sat beside me, my sole companion. He watched, apparently sympathetically, as I tried to write my script with only the dull glow of my mobile phone for light.

After a brief stopover in Uruguay (where the women in the BBC team stripped to our underwear and swam in the River Plate), the royal bandwagon moved on to the Falklands. It seemed so very far from the UK and yet, as I stepped off the plane, an RAF officer said: 'Hello, there. You're Jennie Bond, aren't you? I saw you on telly last night. You were hitting that chap Angus Deayton over the head with a frying pan.'

Extraordinarily, a comedy routine I'd filmed for the *End of the Year Show* had just made it to the Falklands – in March.

The islands were wild and wonderful even in the rain, and the Prince was given a hearty welcome. Port Stanley, a quaint town overlooking the water, boasts two hotels. Unfortunately for the hacks of the royal ratpack, both were full. But the Palace had foreseen this problem and thoughtfully arranged for us to be put up in a couple of Portakabins on the outskirts of the town. We're not a proud bunch and, with much ribald comment, we unloaded our gear into this rather basic accommodation. Each of us had a tiny cubicle with a cot-like bed; there were urinals in the ladies' loo as well as in the gents', and we were awoken in the morning by the shrill blast of a whistle. The only real drawback was that the walls between the cubicles were so thin that you could hear every noise that emanated from your neighbour throughout the night. After the chaps had enjoyed a few beers, it was not the most peaceful place to be.

The next day, feeling that we all knew one another rather more intimately than any of us had wished, we climbed aboard a Chinook helicopter and flew out to Sea Lion Island. It was a real perk of the job to be taken somewhere so remote and untouched. A motley assembly of cameramen, reporters and photographers, we walked across the rough grassland observed only by the island's chief inhabitants – thousands of penguins – until we came to a rugged beach. It was the home of another of the Falklands' prize exhibits: elephant seals. There before us were some forty gigantic creatures lazing on the foreshore. We had half an hour to spare before the Prince's helicopter arrived, and we spent it photographing one another with these magnificent animals. As we walked among them, it quickly became apparent that they have little to do in life except exude prodigious quantities of putrid gas from either end. It was on to this beach, resonating with the sounds of seal farts and belches, that the Prince of Wales arrived.

It was the devil's own job for us to keep a straight face as he perused these flatulent beasts, stopping to pose for us every now and then while they let rip behind him. And it was a scene that clearly tickled the Prince as well. On the flight home to the UK the next day, he came back to mull over the trip with us.

'Wasn't it great to see those elephant seals?' I said as we gathered around him.

'Yes,' he replied. 'Aren't they *wonderful* creatures? Such a privilege to see them . . . but they certainly had a bit of a problem with flatulence, didn't they?' He laughed loudly.

Quick as a flash, one of the photographers piped up: 'Cor, sir! If you thought *that* was bad, you should have been in the Portakabin last night.'

At which the Prince roared with laughter, and it seemed for a moment that he almost liked the press.

CHECKMATE?

A month later, I found myself with many of the same characters at a media reception given by the Queen at the start of a tour of South Korea. Buoyed with the success of our good-humoured encounter with the Prince, I was determined to tell the Queen about a horse I'd come across in Devon. It had once formed part of the Household Cavalry, and its new owner had assured me that if I reminded her of its name and added that it had a curious habit of blowing raspberries, she'd be sure to remember it. I broke off from editing my report to dash to the reception and, as I mingled politely with the other guests, I shamelessly looked over their shoulder to see whether the Queen was heading our way. Infuriatingly, each time I made my excuses and moved on to a more promising group, the Queen went to the one I had just left. Finally, in despair, I rather rudely inserted myself into a circle of journalists she was chatting with. As so often on these occasions, I discovered that a combination of nerves and unaccustomed good manners had rendered my colleagues' conversation anodyne at best. They were discussing which way round the world we would go on a future tour of Australia.

'I think we *might* go via Singapore,' said the Queen. 'But there again, we might go via Los Angeles.'

This provoked nods of approval and worthy discussion about which route might prove most favourable. The boredom level was almost tangible. I seized my chance.

'Ma'am, I want to pass on some good wishes from an old friend of yours,' I declared to the hushed assembly. They all stared at me. Reddening slightly, I went on: 'He's called Jupiter and he's a horse. He used to be in the Household Cavalry, and his owner tells me that you'll be sure to remember him if I tell you that he always blows raspberries.'

I waited for a glint of recognition from the Queen or the hoots of laughter from my fellow reporters. Neither was forthcoming. The silence was deafening. The Queen continued to look in my direction for a moment or two, and then turned away to the others, saying: 'I think we *will* go via Singapore, you know.'

Mortified, I slunk out of the room and back to my edit suite, vowing never to try to brighten up the conversation at such events again.

Five months after their engagement, Edward and Sophie got married. Neatly for them, but inconveniently for me, the wedding was on the Saturday after Royal Ascot. As a result, I had a feverish few days careering between the racecourse, where I was commentating on the royal procession, and Windsor, where the preparations for the wedding were going on. With hats on for the racing and off for the news, it was extremely complicated, and the day itself was a long, gruelling slog. More people than predicted turned out to see the couple, and the town was in party mood, which was fun to witness. But, as with so many of these great events, I spent almost the whole day in a scruffy truck behind the Castle logging the shots from various cameras, writing my script and flying by the seat of my pants to get a polished piece of work on air.

As the newly created Earl and Countess of Wessex moved centre stage the Royal Family's most promising young star was gradually emerging into the spotlight. Prince William was learning to drive, and the media were invited to record his progress. We all converged on Highgrove, where we were told exactly what would happen: the Prince would drive a hundred yards or so towards our cameras and then get out to greet his father and brother. There were to be no questions.

'But surely I can at least ask Prince Charles how William's doing,' I moaned.

'Well, OK,' said his press secretary. 'The boss can look after himself. But William is *absolutely* off limits.'

Reluctantly, I gave my word. After all that William and Harry have been through, I don't push the boundaries where they are concerned. In front of the princes' house, we lined up in a semicircle and William swept confidently past the cameras before posing for pictures with his father. I did as I'd been told.

'Prince Charles, sir,' I yelled across the forecourt. 'Can you tell us how William's doing at driving?'

'Well, he's doing very well,' he replied. 'But I'm not really the one to judge – you'd better ask William.'

I looked at the young Prince, who was blushing, then at the press secretary, who mouthed *no* very firmly, so I shrugged my shoulders and kept quiet. It was a coward's way out, perhaps, but an honourable one. The following day, William passed his driving test and soon motored off back to Eton – and out of our sight.

The royal chessboard was certainly quieter without Diana, but the new millennium brought the prospect of two busy tours – and a prolonged spell of winter sunshine. My destiny was to spend ten days in the Caribbean with Prince Charles and almost three weeks in Australia with the Queen. It was not, I had to concede, a bad way to pass some of the coldest months of the year, and I felt faintly guilty as I packed my sundresses and swimsuit while Emma, wrapped in winter woollies, looked on. But at least neither of the trips would clash with her tenth birthday.

We were flying out to the Caribbean from RAF Lyneham, and I spent the night in a nearby hotel. Just before going to bed, I pulled out a bottle of fake tan that one of my favourite ladies in our local bakery in Devon had acquired for me. I felt wan after the long months without sunshine and decided that a splash of facial bronze would do wonders. Quite *why*, after spraying my face, I impetuously decided to douse the rest of my body I shall never know. But I climbed into bed confident that my summer dresses would look far better on my soon-to-be-tanned physique. The alarm woke me at seven and I jumped out of bed. One glance in the mirror was enough. I looked as if someone had emptied a tub of Marmite over me; the tanning spray had evidently dribbled down my legs – in a most uneven pattern – leaving the impression that I was suffering from a chronic skin disease. I reached for the nearest pair of trousers. There is, though, no way of escaping the inquisitive powers of thirty or so Fleet Street reporters and photographers, and at RAF Lyneham I owned up immediately to my stupidity and, to the undisguised amusement of all, showed my stripy legs to anyone who showed an interest.

It was in Trinidad that I began to wonder whether the fake tan had comprehensively changed my looks. At the University of the West Indies, the Prince was giving a speech. Outside, the crowds were growing larger by the minute, and my cameraman was in trouble. He had forgotten to bring a ladder, and his view was hopelessly obscured. Annoyed that he hadn't brought one of the most essential pieces of equipment on any royal story, I burst into the university and begged to borrow a chair. 'I'm so sorry,' I explained. 'We can't see over the crowds. I'll bring it back as soon as the Prince has left.'

I marched outside, carrying the chair, and ran straight into a young West Indian man who looked dumbfounded to see me. His eyes were as wide as his smile as he leaned towards me and, in a lyrical Trinidadian croon, declared: 'Oh! You must be de Prince of Wales's mudder.'

I was so taken aback to be mistaken for the Queen – evidently carrying a chair outside for 'her boy' – that it took a moment or two to realise that he must also think I was at least seventy. So much for my glamorous image!

Sometimes, though, it seems that a little bit of fame goes a very long way. The next leg of the tour took us to Guyana, a country on the shoulder of South America that few of us, the Prince included, had visited. We knew so little about it that one of my television colleagues announced in her voice track that the Prince was 'moving on from Trinidad to the next Caribbean *island* on his programme'. As we flew over the ocean and onwards to the mainland she realised her mistake. 'Oh, shit!' she shouted as we came in to land. 'I thought it was a bloody island. The news desk are going to think I'm a complete idiot.'

Such is the pace of royal tours. Often you forget where you are, and I've frequently reached the end of a piece to camera with a sense of triumph, only to be flummoxed by the payoff. 'Jennie Bond, BBC News . . . damn it! Where the hell am I?' is a familiar cry to the cameramen I have worked with.

I was astonished that my modicum of fame could travel deep into Guyana, a country I found bewitching from the moment I looked out of my hotel window and saw cows strolling along the seashore. We were lucky enough to be flown in a fleet of small planes deep into the Iwokrama rainforest, which stretches over a million acres. There we walked with the Prince as he was shown one of Guyana's finest sights: the Kaieteur Falls, five times bigger than Niagara. Few people venture there because it's so inaccessible, but a handful of Amerindians had come to see him. Some had travelled for days by boat to get there. They were fascinated by our equipment and watched curiously as I did my piece to camera. I used the waterfalls as a stunning backdrop and recited my words without too much trouble, ending with the exotic payoff 'Jennie Bond, BBC News, at the Kaieteur Falls in Guyana.'

As I stepped away from the camera, one of the Amerindians touched my arm. 'I *thought* it was you,' he said, smiling. 'As soon as we saw you I said to my wife, "That's Jennie Bond". But she didn't believe me.'

Now it was *my* turn to be dumbfounded. I knew that my reports were often carried on the BBC's World Service, but even so it struck me as miraculous that anyone should recognise me in the middle of a rainforest. They turned out to be a most delightful couple who lived in a village miles upriver and accessible only by boat. But they'd watched World Service Television on their trips to the capital, Georgetown, and remembered seeing some of my reports on the death of the Princess of Wales.

A fortnight after returning from the Caribbean, I had to pile my summer clothes back into a suitcase for the long flight to Australia. It was the Queen's first visit since Australians had unexpectedly voted to retain the monarchy – largely because they couldn't agree on what type of republic they wanted. I revelled in being back in the land of Oz. The Opera House at night and the buzz of the waterfront were as exciting as ever, but my love affair with Sydney began to fade almost as fast as my fake tan when monsoon rain lashed the city for days on end. The Queen, a small figure in green beneath a transparent umbrella, valiantly soldiered on through the ceremonial welcome while her supporters sloshed through the puddles. Apart from the weather, it was all going like clockwork when, in unison, a chorus of mobile phones sounded throughout the press pen. We took our calls and discovered that there'd been a security alert a short distance away: a man with an eight-inch knife strapped to his leg had been overpowered by police.

For a moment it seemed like a rerun of the incident in Tumbalong Park when a student had fired a starting pistol at Prince Charles. Abandoning the welcoming ceremony, I ran through the rain to the convention centre, where the man had just been arrested. It was crawling with security officers and journalists in a spin; everyone was on the phone to their news desks. The imperative with twenty-four-hour news is to get an accurate version of events on air as rapidly as possible, which we did, initially, on the phone. But television is meant to be about pictures.

'Can you record a straight minute to camera setting out what happened?' the news desk demanded.

The details were still far from clear, but with my cameraman I stepped outside into the deluge to ad-lib a report. It was so wet underfoot that my white stilettos immediately filled with water, giving my bare feet a most unwelcome cold bath. Although I waited until the last possible moment to put down my umbrella, I was instantly transformed into a drowned rat as I addressed the camera. I'd had no time to prepare, and each time I went wrong I had to start again; the longer I stood there, the flatter my hair became and the more soaked my jacket. I felt utterly miserable.

The rest of the day was spent chasing around after both the 'knife-man story' and the Queen. By the middle of the afternoon, *Breakfast* back home had decided to lead with the story, and they wanted me live from the waterfront. I got a taxi to the outside-broadcast point overlooking the Harbour Bridge and braced myself for more misery. A gale was now blowing and the rain was horizontal. Squelching over the grass, I put up my umbrella to try to get some protection. The wind instantly whipped it inside out and almost wrenched it out of my grasp. For a moment I thought I was going to cry. At times like this there's no point in even trying to look glamorous. As I faced the camera and heard the countdown to the 7 a.m. news, three gallant men stood around me with umbrellas at every angle. But nothing could keep out the wind and rain. I could imagine the glee of my friends in Britain; here was I on their TV screens in 'sunny' Australia, soaked to the skin, freezing cold and thoroughly fed up.

The next evening I met the Queen at a media reception at Admiralty House and was amazed to find that she seemed positively to be enjoying the weather. She laughed about the downpour during the welcoming ceremony, saying she'd had to spend most of the time looking at her feet to make sure she didn't slip, and she recalled a similar monsoon on a previous visit to Sydney. Certainly, she preferred the cool air to Australia's summer heat, and seemed genuinely pleased to be back there.

With the Queen and the Duke often going in different directions, a recurring dilemma for reporters is which of them to follow. Where will the best story lie? On the day after the knife-man scare, the place to be was clearly with the Queen – assessing the strength of the security arrangements. In any case, the Duke's visit to a cheese factory in Wagga Wagga didn't look newsworthy, so just one reporter went with him, on a pool basis. As so often on these tours, we were all proved wrong.

I was just finishing my report for *Breakfast* about the Queen's visit to Sydney Children's Hospital when one of my colleagues rang.

'Have you heard about the Duke?'

'No,' I said, praying that what followed wouldn't mean a total recut of the piece I was working on.

'He didn't wear a hairnet at the cheese factory; they've got to throw away a whole vat of the stuff now.'

I turned on the TV; it was already headline news on the Australian networks. Suddenly the security worries that had seemed such a strong newspoint were jettisoned in favour of 'Duke breaks hygiene regulations row'. Any prospect of a quiet evening vanished instantly.

'We'd better track down the factory manager,' said my producer.

Frantically, from our hotel room we began making calls to Wagga Wagga. The factory was not keen to talk. We rang the Palace spokesman, who insisted that the Duke hadn't been *asked* to wear any special clothing. Time was horribly short, but we threw together the piece for the early bulletins and then began the recut for the later ones. There was no supper that night and, as so often in Australia, the time difference meant that we worked way into the small hours.

From Sydney we moved on to Tasmania. My hotel room was above a casino, but I rejoiced in the magnificent picture-window view of Hobart harbour, gleaming under blue skies and warm sunshine. There is a unique quality about Tasmania; it feels almost as remote as you could be anywhere in the world and yet there is a familiarity about its lush green hillsides and crisp, island air.

It was in the northern city of Launceston that another of those unpredictable moments that make a royal tour such a curious creature occurred. The Queen and the Duke were walking among the crowds; it was a gentle Wednesday morning and the whole event had the atmosphere of a sedate garden party.

I was standing on the edge of the park, recording a piece to camera without any real hope of the day producing a story. A buffet lunch was offered to the press and, with alacrity, we all observed the old journalists' adage: eat whenever food is available, because you never know when the next meal will be.

'Do you know, I found a tomato on the path just behind the Duke,' said one of my colleagues, tucking into his sandwich. 'Someone said it could have been thrown at him, but no one saw anything.'

We all chatted about it, jokingly interrogated him about the type of tomato, and then got on with the more serious business of eating. Half an hour later, as we waited for the press bus, another of our number said: 'You know, the Ozzie TV crew have interviewed someone who saw the tomato being thrown.'

· A few chuckles and snorts of derision went up from the press pack; one or two of us groaned at the prospect of the 'Great Tomato Scandal' becoming news. We'd all seen the walkabout, and there'd certainly been no indication that anything untoward had happened. But as we piled on to the bus, we became more and more edgy. Sometimes royal stories take on a life of their own; they can happen right beneath your nose and you don't notice. As we motored off on the long journey back to Hobart, our mobiles started singing.

'Jennie?' It was my news desk in London. 'The wires are saying the Duke was hit by a flying tomato. Have we got any pictures?'

The story was by now unstoppable. Before I knew it, I was broadcasting live by phone from the bus to *Breakfast*. To my great discomfort, I was cross-examined about who had thrown the tomato, the possible motive and where it had hit the Duke. I waffled as best I could. As soon as we got back to the hotel, we joined forces with ITN and Sky for a painstaking examination of every frame we'd shot in Launceston. We'd just about given up hope when, with a triumphant whoop, someone pinpointed a streak of red flashing across the screen and clipping the very tip of the Duke's hat. It was barely visible, but we played it back again and again in slow motion.

'That's it!' we declared. 'It's the tomato!'

Without more ado, we rushed off to file reports to our hungry news desks, wondering how an incident so seemingly insignificant that none of us had noticed it could suddenly become headline news.

After crisscrossing Australia for more than two weeks, I finally boarded a flight home from Perth. Wonderful as the winter travels had been, it was time to get back to reality, and two events that would *definitely* be headline news were looming: the eighteenth birthday of Prince William and the hundredth of the Queen Mother. Both were to keep me on my toes.

William's birthday was full of unexpected drama when a row blew up over the copyright of special photographs taken to mark the event. It cost Prince Charles's press secretary, Sandy Henney, her job. She left her desk after a fast-moving and brutal day. I was on the phone to the communications secretary at Buckingham Palace when the news came through of Sandy's resignation, but events had moved so swiftly that he clearly knew nothing about it. Feeling shocked that such a loyal and effective member of the Prince's staff had left so suddenly, I raced down to the Palace to go live on the *Six o'Clock News*.

'What do you mean we can't get a signal?' I demanded breathlessly. I'd made it to the Palace with five minutes to spare and now, quite unjustifiably, I was getting furious with the technical crew because they couldn't get a satellite signal. I was left pulling my hair out while the story of Sandy's resignation was told in the studio instead of by me. Eventually, with a minute left of the bulletin, we established a signal and I was given forty-five seconds to deliver my thoughts on air. It was a depressing afternoon.

The Queen Mother's birthday, by contrast, was a joyous affair. The celebrations began some five weeks before the day itself with a lunch given by the City of London at Guildhall. It provided a classic moment of television when the Archbishop of Canterbury mistakenly picked up the Queen Mother's glass of wine. Proving that her reflexes were as sharp as ever, she wrested it adroitly from his hand, declaring: 'That's mine!'

Over the next few weeks her stamina continued to astonish us all. Although I'm almost exactly half her age, by the time we staggered to 4 August I was beginning to wonder which of us was the younger woman. In pursuit of insights and anecdotes for features to mark her birthday, I interviewed many of Queen Elizabeth's friends and family. I learned that she loves to read cookery books, even though she has probably never boiled an egg. She thoroughly enjoyed the television series *Two Fat Ladies* and always wants her chef to try new recipes. Her own favourites, though, tend to be simple: her preference is for dishes such as cottage pie and bread-and-butter pudding.

Everyone I talked to told me about her sense of fun and her love of meeting people. Once, in Scotland, the Royal Family arrived at a favourite outdoor cabin for a picnic. To their dismay, they saw two strangers sitting at the wooden table eating lunch. The general consensus was to drive on, but the Queen Mother told the chauffeur to stop. She got out and invited the two interlopers to join her family for drinks and sandwiches, which they happily did – no doubt dining out on the story for years to come. On another occasion she met a couple of hikers walking on a hillside path. They struck up a conversation, and from that time on she's received a Christmas card signed 'from the two hikers'. I gathered so much information that it was hard to squeeze it into three short features about the Queen Mother's life, and I fought long battles with news editors to give me more time. It's the eternal moan of every correspondent that we can't do justice to our story in the space allotted. In the end, though, you have to accept that there are other news events going on and settle for a compromise.

By August I felt I had lived and breathed nothing but the Queen Mother for weeks, and it was something of a relief that the birthday itself had finally arrived. My alarm went off just after 5 a.m; Jim and Emma were already in Devon for the summer, which gave me the freedom to make as much noise as I wanted. I washed my hair, put on a bright pink frock with some marginally subtler make-up and set off for the Palace. It was cloudy and rather cool for August, and the few dozen people who'd slept out on the Mall looked chilled. In front of the Palace the TV networks had set up their stalls cheek by jowl: the BBC, *GMTV*, Sky and *The Big Breakfast* were all going live from the festivities. I'd been instructed to introduce the news on *Breakfast* from my spot and, as the minutes ticked by towards 7 o'clock, I stood rehearsing my words and shivering slightly. The countdown began in my ear, and I faced the camera.

'Good morning from Buckingham Palace on 4 August, the Queen Mother's one hundredth birthday . . .'

As I continued, I could see a strange reflection in the camera lens. I refused to let it put me off, but there was no doubt about it: a giant rabbit was hopping around behind me. Fortunately, my mouth went on working while out of the corner of my eye

I saw my producer sternly escorting the Bunny from *The Big Breakfast* – for that's who it was – out of our camera shot. It was one of those moments on television when you don't know whether simply to join in the fun or soldier on regardless. I chose the latter, which in retrospect I think was wrong. As I made my way up to Clarence House a few minutes later, I told *The Big Breakfast* crowd that I thought it had been a cheap joke – which did me no good at all because they immediately repeated my remarks, expletives and all, on their programme.

Outside Clarence House, the crowds were getting bigger. They watched me with amusement as I inelegantly clambered up a vertical twenty-foot ladder to a platform perched in the trees. This was my new position for the news at 8 o'clock. When I reached the top, my skirt billowing in the breeze, I wished fervently that I'd heeded my producer's advance warning – and remembered to wear knickers.

As the morning wore on, the tension grew. My producer and I knew that the biggest challenge of the day would be the *One o'Clock News*, because events were happening right up to our deadline. The atmosphere among the crowds – now 40,000 strong – was jubilant; the sun was now shining and there was street theatre all around. For us, though, the reality was a hot edit truck across the road from the Palace, where we did our best to keep track of all that was happening and to ensure that we logged the best shots while I scribbled away at my script. On occasions like this, there is a heightened sense of purpose – and fear – in the team; we all knew that this was another of those stories that we simply *couldn't* allow to go wrong. As the crowds cheered and the Queen Mother drove by in a flower-festooned carriage, we worked at a furious pace.

'Where's the best close-up of her face?' I demanded of a

producer whose sole function was to log each shot. 'Get us a cutaway of the crowds . . . no, not that one . . . we need them cheering . . .'

Every so often the news desk would ring: 'You *will* be finished in time, won't you? And we want you live at the top of the programme. This has *got* to work,' they threatened.

'Well, get off the line then and let me write,' I'd shout back.

At 12.58 I jumped out of the truck, powdering my nose as I ducked under the railings, and took my place in front of the camera. The crowds closed in around me; my heart was pounding and my head was aching as I manoeuvred the microphone up my dress, muttering my hastily written introduction in an effort to memorise it. I'd left the picture editor putting the final touches to my report; now my job was to look calm, collected and in control. I took a deep breath and prayed that I would remember my lines.

Ten minutes later it was over; everything had gone to plan, and we'd survived another bulletin. My producer and I, sapped for a moment of all energy, hugged one another as the crowds looked on, no doubt wondering what all the fuss was about.

When, late that night, I got back to my empty house I found I was still living the experiences of the day and scoured the TV channels for yet more news about the birthday. Finally, I collapsed into bed. Another piece of history was over; the Queen Mother had reached an extraordinary milestone and had done it with characteristic gusto. I had played my part in recording it for posterity, and now the rush of activity had stopped.

The next day, singing raucously to rock tapes as I went, I drove to Devon for a long break, hoping against hope that my pager would stay silent.

CHAPTER EIGHTEEN

What next?

I enjoyed three unbroken weeks of holiday with my family in Devon and celebrated my fiftieth birthday with a disco in our village hall. It was sure proof that the job has become less demanding and more predictable in the years since Diana's death. There are even times when I'm tempted to break my word and make a promise to Emma. But that would be rash, because there's still plenty of scope for events to sneak up and surprise me.

One such jolt came at the end of 2000, when the Queen Mother fell and reportedly broke her collarbone, causing major ructions through every newsroom in the land. Luckily, I was at my desk and able to scoot straight down to Clarence House. It was a worrying time for everyone, but her seemingly ageless constitution stood her in good stead. The collarbone was not broken but bruised, and by Christmas Eve we were all at Sandringham to see her waving to the crowds.

When the phone rang a week later – just as I was pulling on my leather trousers for a New Year's Eve party – I feared the worst. But it wasn't the Queen Mother the office had called about; it was Princess Margaret.

'The Palace won't say what's wrong with her, but doctors are carrying out tests at Sandringham,' they told me. 'Can you do *News 24* straight away?'

Sitting in the kitchen of our Devon home, half-in and half-out of my party gear, I broadcast by phone to *News 24*. A couple of hours later, after filing a track for the main television bulletin and the morning programmes, I finished getting dressed and, with my pager firmly strapped to my belt, I nervously escaped to the pub to join our friends to see in the New Year.

With the festivities over, I set off to interview Princess Margaret's former private secretary in Wiltshire. It was while I was there that news came through that she'd been taken to hospital. It was now clear that she'd had a second stroke and, even more worryingly, she hadn't eaten for days. Livid to find myself 120 miles from London when I should be doing the lead story, I drove furiously up the motorway in time to stand guard outside the hospital for the *Ten o'Clock News*. That's where I stayed for much of the next ten freezing days, swaddled in four layers of clothing, fur boots and gloves.

While the health of the older members of the family continues to give me sleepless nights, it turned out to be one of the younger royals who unexpectedly gave me the toughest week since the death of Diana.

'My Edward is *not* gay.' So trumpeted the *News of the World* on 1 April. But this was no April Fools' Day joke. The Countess of Wessex had indeed given a candid interview to the newspaper, and this was its headline. At the same time the *Mail on Sunday* published what it claimed were details of remarks the Countess had made to an undercover *News of the World* reporter posing as a sheikh. 'Sophiegate' had broken. The Countess had been the victim of a 'sting' operation and, believing the fake sheikh to be a potential client for her public relations company, she'd chatted rather too freely about her royal connections. In a disastrous effort to stop the paper publishing her remarks, the Palace had agreed to give the *News of the World* an exclusive interview with Sophie. But the details of her conversation with the 'sheikh' had leaked out anyway; it was the worst of both worlds for the Countess, and a right royal mess.

The full extent of that mess only became apparent over the next few days, and my life was put on hold as the story became the lead item on every bulletin. The issues it raised went far beyond the Countess and her unguarded remarks: a new debate was beginning about whether members of the Royal Family should work in the commercial arena at all. Despite its deal with the Palace, the *News of the World* decided to publish the full transcript of its undercover conversation with the Countess in its next edition.

Even for experienced journalists, there are moments when you think the task before you is impossible, and mine that Saturday night was to get hold of the earliest editions of the paper and turn round the story for the *Ten o'Clock News*. It was a tall order. The newspaper promised to fax us ten pages of the interview by 8 p.m. The whole newsroom was coiled, waiting by the fax machines. Nothing happened. Eventually, they spluttered into action just after 9 p.m. This was desperately late, and my head was spinning as the blurred copies of the encounter between the Countess and the bogus sheikh were churned out. Several of us got down on our hands and knees to put together the jigsaw puzzle of pages and half-pages, laying them out on the carpet. By now it was 9.10. We had only minutes in which to choose the best quotes and race them to our graphics department, while I began bashing out my script. By 9.45 the edit suite was electric with tension; I knew we were in real trouble, and there was every danger that we wouldn't be finished in time.

'Get me another edit suite going,' I screamed. 'I'll do the piece in two halves – and we can stitch it together.'

By this time the bulletin editor and several producers were rushing around trying to help. As the last ten minutes whizzed by, I bolted up and down the corridor, recording a few words in one suite and then running back to the other to complete a sentence there. It was utterly manic, and it seemed almost miraculous when, at one and a half minutes to ten, the report was finished. Like everything in television, it had been a true team effort.

Sophiegate continued with a vengeance for another forty-eight hours; the Countess stood down as chairman of her company and her partner resigned. The affair proved a catalyst for a major review of the Royal Family's business interests. At the end of it all, I collapsed into my car and, like a crumpled old woman, drove home hardly daring to believe that there was at last some respite from the relentless flow of bulletins. The next morning I woke up annoyingly early, feeling as if I'd been caught in a hurricane and then trampled underfoot by a herd of elephants. I lobbed a few possessions into the car and, with Roy Orbison belting out 'It's Over' at full volume, drove west to Devon.

It is, though, weeks like that which make this job so absorbing. When I began all those years ago, I certainly never imagined that I would be delving into such personal topics and tragedies. I didn't expect to be party to some of Prince Charles's most intimate thoughts – as revealed in 'Camillagate'; I didn't contemplate reporting on toe-sucking incidents in the South of France or bearing witness to so many marriage failures. I certainly didn't envisage having to tell the story of the death of the Princess of Wales or the drama and heartbreak of Sophie Wessex being rushed to hospital with an ectopic pregnancy.

We live in an age when, as the Queen herself has admitted, the monarchy, like other great institutions, must be open to scrutiny. Like it or not, that scrutiny extends into every area of their lives because, by definition, we expect our Royal Family to be something other than ordinary. It is an impossible aspiration. They may live a life of luxury, but they are prey to the same human frailties as the rest of us and they fall foul of those frailties in the full glare of publicity. Nevertheless, if this country is to retain a monarchy (and the polls consistently indicate that to be the majority wish), the activities and conduct of the Royal Family *do* matter, and it is the duty of the media to continue their scrutiny.

Life in that royal goldfish bowl is a prospect that has always filled Prince William with horror. But he's caught up in a destiny that makes it inevitable, and gradually, with his father's guidance, he's becoming inured to facing the cameras. It's been a carefully controlled exercise, masterminded by St James's Palace: the press leave William largely alone in exchange for occasional photo-opportunities. But this line will be increasingly difficult to hold as he grows older. With his good looks and easygoing nature, he's the sort of box-office material that will be hard to resist. Royal correspondents of the future will have to judge how closely the young Prince is pursued as he moves into manhood.

Another fish now firmly in the bowl is Camilla Parker Bowles. Her emergence as a permanent fixture in Prince Charles's life has been skilfully handled by his advisers. Public opinion has been turned around; their relationship is now generally accepted, though the polls suggest there's still strong resistance to her becoming Queen. Neither Charles nor Camilla has any urge to rock the boat further by contemplating marriage; but the passage of time could change both *their* feelings *and* public attitudes. In the meantime the Prince has found a peace of mind and middle-aged happiness that had long eluded him. He feels comfortable with Camilla. She shares his love of the great outdoors; they have the same circle of friends; and she makes him laugh. She has been accepted by his sons as the woman their father loves. Briefly, but significantly, she has met the Queen at Highgrove, and her presence both there and in every royal palace is now tolerated. Charles and Camilla have every intention of growing old together, but the precise status of their relationship in the years to come is certain to make periodic leaps to the top of the news agenda. When he is King – which he firmly intends to be – will the Church of England be content for its Supreme Governor to have a live-in lover? Or will it prefer to condone divorce by allowing him to marry Camilla? Will society judge that he will be a better King with the woman he loves at his side? Or will his public role forever be kept apart from his private life? There will be much for my successors to tackle. Not that I'm planning on hanging up my royal tights quite yet.

When I was given the job, I was told that it was 'a bit of a grave-yard'; sadly, it took me to the graveside of a young princess. The death of Diana will always be a vivid and disturbing memory. She made my life unbearably unpredictable and enticingly exciting. For all her faults, I've concluded that she was a force for good in this world and, at least for a time after she died, I believe many of us had a little more compassion in our souls. Her influence lives on in the efforts, however slight, of the Royal Family to become less remote. And her chief legacy – her two sons – will forever remind us of her.

There were, inevitably, many comparisons between the death of Diana and the death of Princess Margaret, just two months into the Queen's Golden Jubilee Year. It was, though, a very different event which drew to a close a life that had become insupportable for a woman who had once been so full of vitality.

For once I was well placed when her struggle against crippling ill-health finally came to an end. The call came when I was in bed, gently dozing and enjoying the prospect of a weekend off in London. It sounded exactly like one of our rehearsals: 'Buckingham Palace have just phoned to say they are making an important statement at half past eight about the health of a member of the Royal Family'.

I looked at the clock; it was 8.16 a.m. Bolting out of bed, I grabbed the first black suit available, smudged on some make-up and raced out of the door. I was in the studio and on air 45 minutes later – reporting on the death of the Queen's only sister. It was a tragic start to a year that should have been one of her happiest.

For myself, reporting on royalty has been far from a graveyard. It has given me a fascinating life and a job that quite a few people seem to envy. It's sometimes lampooned as the shallow end of journalism, but – as I hope I've illustrated – it can be a tricky brief in which the reporter has to use all her skills to establish the truth. It's also a brief which appears to have an infinite ability to astonish me. After my trip to Scotland to witness Prince William begin his university life at St Andrews, I was only mildly surprised when the phone rang to tell me that a television crew had been spotted in the town. Even though all the national network teams had agreed to pull out of St Andrews as soon as William was safely ensconced, there had always been a strong likelihood of someone doing the dirty on Will. So who was it?

'It's Ardent,' said the news organiser.

'It's who?' I said incredulously. 'You're having me on, surely?' What a tangled tale we had to tell that day: Prince Edward's TV company, Ardent, apparently spying on his princely nephew for a film about royalty! It was almost as riveting as the call, some months later, alerting me to the news that Prince Harry had owned up to smoking dope and getting drunk.

If only someone had explained to me when I took the job that the real agenda was sex, drugs and rock'n'roll – how much more alluring it would have seemed than the deathly title of 'Court Reporter'.

After the adventures of the past decade or so, it's hard to imagine what further surprises could possibly lie ahead. But they're certain to be lurking, ready to spring out when I am least expecting them, causing chaos all around. Only the other day, a phone call from the office ruined a weekend that Emma and I had planned to spend together.

'Mum,' she complained censoriously, 'why don't you just accept that you're a *dog*?'

'What do you mean, darling?' I asked, guiltily cramming my notebook and phone into my bag as I reached for my car keys.

'Well, they just whistle – and you *go*!' she retorted.

She's right, of course. The choke chain is still very much in place. But that's the price you pay for a job that can send your blood pressure soaring and drive you to distraction – but which can rarely, if ever, stand accused of being dull.

Jennie Bond, BBC News.

Awaiting the next episode.

INDEX

Adelaide 10–11
Aids 326
Al Fayed, Dodi 285, 288
Alder Hey Children's Hospital 47–8
Althorp 320–1
Amritsar 304
Andrew, Prince 110–11, 192, 293
    breakdown of marriage 78–83,
        97–8, 237–8
Angel, Gerald 245
Angola 265–79
Anne, Princess *see* Princess Royal
anorexia 144–5
Anson, Charles 79–83, 108–9,
    116–21, 149, 172, 218–20
Archer, Jeffrey 92
Armstrong-Jones, Lady Sarah 171
Atkinson, Jane 227–31, 239, 251, 254
Auckland 164
Australia 6–12, 163–5, 250, 254,
    341, 344–9
autocues 57–8, 94–5
Aylard, Richard 121, 195, 222,
    242–3, 257

Bacconi, Gina 60
Bakari, Ade 60
Ball, Jonathan 141

Bangkok 249–50
Barbados 315
Bartholomew, Carolyn 196
Bashir, Martin 217
BBC Radio newsroom 4–5
BBC Television newsroom 13–14,
    226–7
Beach of Passionate Love 25
Beatrice, Princess 80
Bhutan 313
The Big Breakfast 352
Birmingham 17–18
Blair, Tony 279, 311
Bondi Beach 154
Botham, Ian 92
Breakfast with Frost 88–9
briefings for royal reporters 9, 41–2,
    68, 110–11, 120–1, 134
Bristol 77
Britannia 30, 204, 311–12
Brooke, Peter 113
Brunei, Sultan of 9
Bryan, John 95–6, 99
Buckingham Palace
    opening to the public 147–8
    press office 22–4, 31, 73, 87–9,
        108, 172, 229, 306
Budapest 142–3

Buenos Aires 336
Buerk, Michael 232, 312
Bulgaria 326
bulimia 143–5, 258
Burrell, Paul 188–90, 253–4, 317

Caernarfon 170–1
Caine, Michael 92
Calcutta 74–5
cameramen 15, 29–30, 134
Camillagate 128–9, 358
Canterbury, Archbishop of 350
Cape Town 202–5
Cartland, Barbara 61
Catherine Palace, Pushkin 179–80
Centrepoint (charity) 262
Chalker, Lady 136–7
Changing of the Guard 22
Charles, Prince of Wales
  admission of adultery 168–9,
    172–3
  attacked with an aerosol 164–5
  breakdown of marriage 72–4,
    87–9, 93–5, 107–8, 114–15,
    119–22, 170–1, 192–7, 225–6,
    238–40
  and Diana's death 287, 293
  Dimbleby biography of 173–7,
    184–5, 195
  Dublin Castle speech 126–8
  fiftieth birthday 30–2, 284–5,
    330–1
  fortieth birthday 4, 17–18
  negotiations over divorce 228–31,
    244–5
  and *Panorama* programme 220–1
  polo accident 48–9
  pressure to marry Diana 174
  and Prince William 341, 359
  prospects of second

    marriage 226, 256,
    284, 360
  public image 249, 322, 331
  relationship with Camilla Parker
    Bowles 129–30, 334–5, 360
  rendition of Beatles songs 329–30
  supposed assassination attempt
    156–8, 172–3
  with survivors of Warrington
    bombing 138–9
  talking to plants 18
  talks at Highgrove with 242–4
  tapped telephone conversation
    129–30
  television documentaries on life
    and work of 66, 168–70, 195
  twenty-fifth anniversary of
    installation as Prince of
    Wales 170–1
  views on abdication 328
  views on farming and ecology
    249, 320
  visit to Canada 317
  visit to the Caribbean 341–4
  visit to the Falkland Islands 336–8
  visit to India 66–76
  visit to New Zealand 153, 164–5
  visit to Russia 167–8
  visit to Slovenia, Romania,
    Bulgaria and Macedonia 326–30
  visit to South Korea 108
  visit to southern Africa 307–10
  visit to Sri Lanka, Nepal and
    Bhutan 313–14
  visits to Australia 6–10, 153–64
Chatto, Daniel 171
Chicago 238–41
Clarence House 48, 216
Cleese, John 92
Clinton, Bill 94

INDEX

Clinton, Hillary 246–7
clothing allowances 60
Cole, Michael 4, 19
Cook, Robin 299, 304
Cowdray Park 89
Crawford, Geoff 221, 306
Cuito 274–9
Cyprus 63
Czech Republic 233–7

Daily Express 39
Daily Mail 78, 81–2, 171
Daily Telegraph 174
Dando, Jill 295
Darwin 11–12
Deayton, Angus 337
Delhi 303–4
Diana – Her True Story 87–93,
    188, 195–6
Diana, Princess of Wales
  accused of involvement in
      politics 273–8
  admission of adultery 220–1
  affair with James Hewitt 172
  auction of dresses 282
  breakdown of marriage 72–4,
      87–9, 93–5, 107–8, 114–15,
      119–22, 170–1, 192–7, 225–6,
      238–40
  chats with 184–99, 220, 251–61,
      280–2
  commemorative museum 320
  death 287–96, 360
  divorce settlement 227–32,
      238–40, 244–5, 253–5, 258
  first anniversary of death 322–4
  hoax video of 248
  lack of preparation for public
      life 191
  Memorial Fund 315–16

nuisance phone calls allegedly
    made by 171–3
phone conversation with James
    Gilbey 98–100
prospects of becoming Queen 193
relationship with Prince Charles
    49, 189–91, 255–6
relationship with Prince Philip
    191–2, 258
relationship with the Queen
    191, 258
relationship with the Queen
    Mother 258
relationships with her own staff
    239–40
removal of wisdom teeth 24–5
reports of attempted suicide 87,
    90–1, 191
return to world scene 181
secret pictures from the gym 148
sense of humour 1–2, 261–4
speech about bulimia 143–5
taking sons to film about the
    IRA 282–3
title of HRH 228–32, 246, 259–60
views on Prince Charles' suitability
    as King 221–2, 257
visit to Angola 265–79
visit to Argentina 217–21
visit to Chicago 238–40
visit to India 66–76
visit to Japan 183–4
visit to Moscow 198–9
visit to Nepal 132–8
visit to South Korea 108
visits to Australia 6–10, 250–4
visits to Washington 246–7,
    279–81
withdrawal from charity work 246,
    259–60

withdrawal from public
    engagements 149–51, 196
work for Aids sufferers 326
Dimbleby, David 295
Dimbleby, Jonathan 153, 168–9,
    173–7, 184–5, 195
divorce in the Royal Family 42–3,
    85–6, 97–8, 107–8, 118–19, 193,
    225–32, 237–49 passim, 253–8
Dole, Elizabeth 279–80
'dreaded word' syndrome 58–9
Dublin Castle 126–8
Dukuduku 309
Durban 211–15, 309–10

Edinburgh, Duke of see Philip,
    Prince
Edward, Prince 293, 333–4, 340, 356
Elizabeth, Queen see Queen, HM;
    Queen Mother
Elizabeth R (television documentary)
    65–6
embarrassing moments 51–4, 57
The End of the Year Show 337
engagements of the Royal Family,
    listing of 23
English National Ballet 255
equipment used while on tour
    9–10, 34–6, 67–8; see also Toko
    machines
Ethiopia 27

'fake sheikh' incident 356–8
Falkland Islands 336–8
Fellowes, Sir Robert 90
Feraud, Louis 60
Ferguson, Sarah see York, Duchess
    of
Ford, Anna 228–9
France 103–6

Fraser Island 163–4
Frost, David 174; see also Breakfast
    with Frost

general election coverage 76–7,
    83–4, 279
genetic engineering 244
George VI, King 21
Gilbey, James 90–1, 99, 133
Gilmore, Margaret 221
Göncz, President 141–2
Gower, David 92
'The Great She Elephant' 308
Guardian 60, 270
Guildhall 113–16
Gulf War 50, 62–3, 226–8
Guyana 343–4

Hardman, Robert 237
Harry, Prince 190–5, 256–61, 283,
    287, 292–5, 307–10, 317–18,
    322–4, 341, 360–1
Hável, Vaclav 235
Headway (charity) 151
Hendrix, Jimi 104
Henney, Sandy 326–8, 349–50
Herald of Free Enterprise 33
Hewitt, James 172, 220–1, 248, 260
Highgrove 242–4, 248, 284, 331,
    340, 360
Hindu Kush 302–3
Hoare, Oliver 171
Honours List 91–2
Huambo 272–7
Humphrys, John 38–9, 146, 244
Hungary 141–3
Hungerford shooting 33

Independent Television News

(ITN) 31–2, 67, 121, 160, 298, 316, 348–9
India 66–76, 85, 298, 303–6
interviews 15, 92–3
Islamabad 300

Jackson, Michael 141
Jaipur 73
Janvrin, Robin 21, 23
Jephson, Patrick 107–8, 121, 221
Johannesburg 205, 211–14, 266, 308–9
Juan-les-Pins 103
Julius, Anthony 229–30, 254

Kaiteur Falls 343–4
Kampala 325
Karachi 300–1
Kashmir 299, 304
Kathmandu 132
Kay, Richard 171
Keating, Paul 154
Kensington Palace 322–4
Kenya 325
Khan, Hasnat 259
Khayelitsha 204–5
Kikolo 271
King Edward VII Hospital for Officers 24–5, 128, 219, 313
Kinnock, Neil 76–7, 84
knife-man scare in Australia 345–6
Kochin 304–5
Kraków 234–5

Labour Party 84
Lahore 300–1, 303
Lake Bled 326
Lam, Willy Wo-Lap 58
land mines campaign 265–6, 271, 274–80

Launceston (Tasmania) 347–9
Laurence, Tim 40, 86, 117–18
LBC 46–7, 64
Lech 193
Letsie, King 308
letters from viewers 130–1, 233
Lewis, Martyn 289–90, 323
live broadcasting 42, 51, 57
Liverpool 140
Lockerbie disaster 33
London Lighthouse 248
Luanda 266–72, 275

Macedonia 326
MacGregor, Sue 39
Madras 304–6
Mail on Sunday 356–7
Major, John 84, 119–22
make-up facilities 55, 60–1
Malaysia 13, 25–6
Mandela, Nelson 202–4, 211–13, 308
Marchioness disaster 32–9
Margaret, Princess 43, 128
  death 361
  strokes 315, 356
media receptions 137–8, 184, 300, 339, 346
MI5 100
Mirzoeff, Edward 65–6
'missed kiss' incident 73–4
Morton, Andrew 72, 87–93, 188, 195–6
Moscow 174–51, 198–9
Mswati, King 308
multi-skilling in television crews 66–7
Mustique 315

Neil, Andrew 87–8
Nepal 132–8, 313

New Brighton (South Africa)
206–7, 211
New York 282–4
New Zealand 153, 164–5
News of the World 171, 356–7
news reporting 4–6, 33–4, 42, 47–9,
88–9, 103; *see also* general election
coverage
Newsnight 112, 222, 232
newsreading 50–60, 94–5, 130,
165–6, 218
Nippon TV 185–6

Obasanjo, Olusegun 58
organic gardening 243
Owen, Nick 31–2, 160–1

Pakistan 298–303
Panorama 172, 190, 217–22, 225,
253, 257–8
Parker Bowles, Camilla 93, 129–30,
168, 188, 190, 226, 249, 255–6,
279, 284, 324, 331, 359–60
Parry, Colin 140
Parry, Timothy 140
Pasternak, Anna 172
Paxman, Jeremy 222–3
Penang 6, 12, 25
Peterborough (columnist) 174
Philip, Prince 174–7, 191–2, 213,
232, 258, 287, 293, 299–304,
310–11
in Australia 346–9
unguarded remarks by 142–3
Phillips, Mark 40–2, 85–6, 254–5
photo-calls and photo-opportunities
318–22, 326–7, 359
pieces to camera 14–17, 25, 36–7,
69, 74, 206–9, 235, 269, 318–19,
327, 344–8

Plovdiv 328–9
'pool' arrangements 9, 134, 137, 212
Port Elizabeth 205–6, 210
Port Stanley 337
Portillo, Michael 34
Poundbury 320
Prague 235–6
'presentation' department 57
Press Association 121, 227, 231, 248
Press Complaints Commission
129, 219
Prince's Trust 17, 256, 330
Princess in Love 172
Princess Royal
breakdown of first marriage
40–5, 85–6
number of engagements 23
second wedding 117–18, 123
visit to Ethiopia 27
visit to Uganda, Tanzania and
Kenya 324–5

Queen, HM
absence from Prince Charles'
fiftieth birthday party 331
'annus horribilis' speech 114–15
attitude to Charles and Diana's
divorce 222, 225
Christmas message 124
conversations with 32, 42–3
and Diana's death 287, 292–4,
297–8
Diana's opinion of 191
golden wedding celebrations
310–11
meeting with Camilla Parker
Bowles 360
plans to pay income tax 116
sense of humour 66
television documentary on 65–6

visit to Australia 341, 344–9
visit to Hungary 141–3
visit to Pakistan and India 298–306
visit to Poland and the Czech
    Republic 233–7
visit to Poundbury 320
visit to Russia 173–81
visit to South Africa 202–15
visit to South Korea 339–40
visit to Thailand 249–50
and the Windsor Castle fire
    110–11, 113
Queen Mother
  birthdays
    eighty-ninth 29–30
    ninetieth 48–50
    ninety-fourth 171
    ninety-fifth 216
    hundredth 349–50
  bruising of collarbone 355
  choked on fish bone 145
  favourite foods 350
  hip operations 218–21, 313–14
  meeting with 30–2
  relationship with the public 350–1
  relationships with other members
    of the Royal Family 66,
    118–19, 258
Queenstown (Australia) 162–3

radio work compared with television
    14–15, 37–8, 76–7
RAF Lyneham 341
Red Cross 181, 271, 273, 277,
    279–80
Reynolds, Paul 81–2, 145–6, 243–4
Rhys-Jones, Sophie 333–4,
    340, 356–8
Richmond Herald 268
Ritz, the 335–6

Romania 326
royal reporters 7–12, 18–19, 25; see
    also briefings
royal tours 7–8, 66–7, 132–4, 328; see
    also under individual members of
    Royal Family
Russia 173–81
Ryan, Michael 33

safari 214–15
St Petersburg 167, 177–9
Save the Children 27
Scott, Rory 90
Sea Lion Island 338
Serpentine Gallery 170
Sheffield 83–4, 330–1
Simpson, John 296
Singleton, Valerie 114
Sissons, Peter 127, 290–1
Sky News 67, 121, 348–9
Slovenia 326
Slovo, Jo 59
Smith, John 165–6
Snowdon, Lord 254–5
Somerset House 244–5
Sophiegate 358
South Africa 202–15
South Korea 108, 339–40
speculation in news reports 15
Speer, Hugo 330–1
Spencer, Earl 290, 295, 320
Spice Girls 309
Springfield, Dusty 61
Squidgygate 98–100
Sri Lanka 313
Stoyanov, Petar 328
Strahan 161–2
Sun 172, 247, 333
Sunday Times 88, 173
Swaziland 307–8

Sydney 154–60, 164, 251–2, 344–6

Taj Mahal 71–4
Talbot, Godfrey 21
Tanzania 325
Tasmania 347
Taylor, Tim 95
television documentaries about the
    Royal Family 65–6, 168–70, 195
television work compared with radio
    14–15, 37–8, 76–7
Thailand 26, 249–50
Thatcher, Margaret 35–6
tights, royal 261–5
Times 273–4
Times of India 303–4
Tobago 314
Today programme 37–9, 76, 145–6,
    157, 274
Toko machines 266–9, 272, 301–2
Tokyo 185–7
Trimming, Colin 156
Trinidad 342–3
Twangawaewae 165
Two Fat Ladies 350

Uganda 325
University of the West Indies 342

Vancouver 317–18
V-E Day anniversary 215
Verbier 238
Victor Chang Heart Research
    Institute 251–2

Wagga Wagga 346–7

Wales, Prince of *see* Charles, Prince
    of Wales
Wales, Princess of *see* Diana,
    Princess of Wales
Walker, Catherine 284
Walton Hospital, Liverpool 140
Warrington bombing 138–41
Warsaw 233
Washington 279–81
Wax, Ruby 248
Wednesday List 23
Wessex, Countess of *see* Rhys-Jones,
    Sophie
Wessex, Earl of *see* Edward, Prince
Whitbread Round the World Yacht
    Race 164
Whitlam, Mike 273–4, 277, 280–1
William, Prince 190–5, 256–61, 283,
    287, 292–5, 310, 317–18, 322–4,
    340–1, 349, 359–61
Windsor, Lady Helen 95
Windsor Castle 322, 340
    fire at 110–13, 117, 147
writer's block 123–4

Yeltsin, Boris 176
York, Duchess of 45, 192, 334
    autobiography 248
    breakdown of marriage 78–83,
        97–8, 237–8
    Queen's withdrawal of financial
        support for 232
    topless photographs of 95–9, 358
York, Duke of *see* Andrew, Prince

Zeebrugge 33

CANE RIVER

LALITA TADEMY

'A compelling and unsentimental account' *The Times*

Set among the lush, swampy plantations of deepest Louisiana, *Cane River* follows the lives of the four generations of women from the time of slavery in the early 1800s, sweeping through the American Civil War and into the pre-civil rights South.

From down-trodden, philosophical Suzette, who came into womanhood as a slave, to educated, pale-skinned Emily, whose high ambitions born in freedom became her downfall, these remarkable women's struggles reflect the tragedy of slavery and, ultimately, the triumph of the human spirit.

This deeply personal saga is the result of many years of exhaustive research into the author's own family story. Evocative, powerful and absolutely unforgettable, *Cane River* introduces a brilliant new voice into the ranks of bestselling American literature.

NON-FICTION / GENERAL 0 7472 6649 2

More Non-fiction from Headline

DAWN FRENCH
The Biography

ALISON BOWYER

Having worked herself up from the early days of £7-a-night comedy clubs, Dawn French is today the doyenne of British comedy. One half of one of the funniest and most successful comedy double acts of all time, French and Saunders, her brilliantly observed performances have won the hearts of millions and established her as a formidable comic talent in her own right.

This fully updated biography tells the remarkable story of her rise to fame, from childhood and her often unhappy boarding school days, the terrible trauma of her father's death, her meeting with Jennifer Saunders and the early days of the 'alternative comedy' circuit, her 19-year marriage to Lenny Henry and beyond. It is an entertaining and often moving story and is an essential read for her millions of fans.

NON-FICTION / BIOGRAPHY 0 7472 6622 0

Now you can buy any of these other bestselling non-fiction titles from your bookshop or *direct from the publisher*.